D0936244

ANCIENT TEXANS

ANCIENT TEXANS
Rock Art and Lifeways Along the Lower Pecos

by Harry J. Shafer
Photographs by Jim Zintgraff

General Editor: Georg Zappler

Illustrations: George Strickland

WE WOULD LIKE TO EXTEND A SPECIAL THANKS TO
H. Rugeley and Kittie N. Ferguson
for their very generous support of this publication.

PUBLISHED FOR THE WITTE MUSEUM OF THE
SAN ANTONIO MUSEUM ASSOCIATION, SAN ANTONIO, TEXAS
BY

TexasMonthlyPress

Special contributions to this volume were made by:
Megan Biesele
Vaughn M. Bryant, Jr.
Peter T. Furst
Richard A. Gould
Terence Grieder
Thomas R. Hester
Mark L. Parsons
Solveig A. Turpin

Texas Monthly Press, Inc.
P.O. Box 1569
Austin, Texas 78767

A B C D E F G H

Library of Congress Cataloging-in-Publication Data

Shafer, Harry J.
  Ancient Texans.

  Bibliography: p.
  Includes index.
  1. Indians of North America—Texas—Antiquities.
2. Rock paintings—Texas.   3. Petroglyphs—Texas.
4. Indians of North America—Pecos River Valley
(N.M. and Tex.)—Antiquities.   5. Pecos River Valley
(N.M. and Tex.)—Antiquities.   6. Texas—Antiquities.
I. San Antonio Museum Association.   II. Title.
E78.T4S43   1986   976.4'901   86-14412
ISBN 0-87719-058-5

Book design by Martha Durke
Production Assistants: Eva Smith, Karen Thurman

Consulting Editor: Megan Biesele

To Joe, Julie, and Molly

To the ancient people of the lower canyons
who left us the legacy of their existence

ACKNOWLEDGMENTS

THE WITTE MUSEUM, AFTER FIFTY YEARS, is fulfilling a project started by its founder, Mrs. Ellen Quillen, to interpret the material culture and discover the lifestyle of the now extinct Lower Pecos Indians. This book is part of that project, along with a major exhibition on the 9,000-year cultural history of this unique people, which includes rock art unusual in its preservation and complexity. We hope this publication initiates a new level of awareness of a long overlooked corner of New World prehistory.

The Board of Trustees of the San Antonio Museum Association thanks the contributors to this manuscript for their hard work and diligent efforts. The contributors' enthusiasm and support have kept this project going and helped draw national attention to this important scientific investigation. They went far beyond what was asked to bring new insight and knowledge to our picture of this little-known society. All of us owe them a debt of gratitude.

Dozens of people have contributed to this project, but these deserve special mention. Roberta McGregor, with the help of Fred Valdez, handled the brunt of the coordination of this publication with intelligence and grace. Jim Zintgraff's professional photographs were the impetus for this book. His good nature and determination to do anything to make it a success were exceptional. Ganahl Walker deserves credit for the energy that started the publication; without him there would be no book. Georg Zappler's skillful touch helped the entire manuscript flow visually and verbally. The author, Harry Shafer, impressed everyone with the speed, depth, and detail of his work, done in an enthusiastic, flexible manner. George Strickland's concern for authenticity in the illustrations and his skill have strongly supported the professionalism throughout the book. Thanks also to Martha Durke, who designed the book, coordinated the photographs with the text, and brought the whole project together with skill and dedication; and to Kathy Lewis, for her meticulous copy editing and sensitivity to the content.

H. Rugeley and Kittie N. Ferguson deserve the greatest appreciation, because without their generosity, patience, interest, and support we could not share our knowledge and understanding of this extinct society with thousands of people for generations to come. Through the Fergusons' concern, the Lower Pecos legacy will reach a worldwide level of recognition.

MARK LANE, *DIRECTOR*

WITTE MUSEUM
SAN ANTONIO MUSEUM ASSOCIATION

F O R E W O R D

ALMOST A QUARTER CENTURY AGO, I fell in love with the rock art, more properly pictographs, left by the Indians of the Lower Pecos region. I set out to preserve the remains of these ancient drawings on film. To date, I have exposed many thousands of negatives in order to have as complete a record of this art as possible. Many of the caves are now beneath the waters of Amistad Reservoir, completed in 1968, and the resultant humidity is deteriorating many more.

Some of these photos are printed in this book and have helped in research on these ancient people. A word must be said about the dustjacket. It represents the awe-inspiring feeling one gets when one realizes that some of the art in these caves is more than 9,000 years old. The artist who drew the pictograph is one of these souls, so long dead. If he spoke to us today, perhaps he would tell us:

These paintings depict who we were, how we lived, what we were like, how we saw ourselves. We had no written language to leave you word of our people, but we had art, primitive to you, historical to us, to tell you of our world. Our lives were simple. We needed shelter, food, water. Our existence depended on them just as yours does, and we spent our short lives attaining them. Our tools were as primitive as our art . . . as our life. We hold no claim to greatness. We were simply the people. We lived, loved, fought, and died just as you do. We left behind these records as our heritage to you.

To those of you who share my enthusiasm about this book I dedicate these photos.

A very special thanks to H. Rugeley and Kittie N. Ferguson, whose generous contribution has made this book a reality. To the other contributors and my staff, my deepest thanks. The following served above and beyond in helping make this book possible—long hours with heavy loads of equipment in the hot west Texas sun, wading creeks, and being camping companions of good spirits: Curtis Tunnel, Mark Parsons, Harvey Smith, George Weynand, Roberta McGregor, "Bo" Bohannon, Clem Spalding, Jr., Kevin Anthuis, Luis Perez, Rue Ferguson, David Gifford, and my patient, long-suffering, dearly beloved wife, Dorothy Zintgraff, who has put up with my zealousness and urged my efforts in all areas.

Jim Zintgraff

ANCIENT

C O N T E N T S

CONTENTS

INTRODUCTION

Faded images in deep canyons where the Pecos and Devils rivers flow into the Rio Grande stand as reminders of an ancient people who lived in this desolate region. Who painted them and what do they mean? Actually, a great deal is known about these strange artistic renderings.

Water is a central need in all cultures. Its location serves as the greatest determinant of settlements. The Rio Grande and the clear waters of the Pecos and Devils rivers provided the original hunters, gatherers, and foragers of the region with a constant supply and a lush environment in an otherwise arid setting. The rugged terrain of the lower canyons contains hundreds of rock overhangs or rockshelters. Some of the most impressive rock art panels occur in these canyons, which were the focal point of a culture that maintained itself for some 9,000 years.

The natural conditions of the region have their roots in the distant geological past. The thick limestone deposits that dominate the landscape and determine the availability of water and the condition of the soil and vegetation were part of an ancient seabed laid down about 100 million years ago. At the end of the age of dinosaurs, about 65 million years ago, the land that was to become central Texas was elevated, and the inland seas retreated toward the Gulf during the next 50 million years. Since then, erosion has been cutting down the exposed land, chiseling and hollowing out the present-day river valleys, cavern-pitted canyons, and underground reservoirs. As the meandering rivers cut through alternating layers of hard and soft limestone, cavities and horizontal caves were formed in the canyon sides. Further downcutting left many of them safely above the canyon floors and provided living areas.

After the last major glacial episode, about 14,000 years ago, the climate was cooler and moister; grass was abundant. Large browsing and grazing animals included mammoths, camels, horses, and bison. Between 12,000 and 10,500 years ago, the first humans ventured into the region. The change at the end of the Pleistocene from a cool, moist climate to warm, dry conditions brought about new plant communities (between 10,500 and 7,000 years ago). The establishment of the arid grasslands mixed with desert succulents such as cacti, sotol, and yucca set the stage for the first human population to settle in the lower canyons. Where these foragers came from is unknown. However, archaeologists have learned much about them in recent years. ■

(OPPOSITE) *Water, sky, and rock etch the Lower Pecos landscape.*

MOON'S BAND
A.D. 210—A Fictionalized Chronicle

The brisk, dry wind had blown from the south ever since the band had arrived at the Place of Shade, a large rockshelter near the River Him. The spirit of this river was that of a man; it was beautiful and clear most of the time, but loud and rough when the rain god was angry. Her, a gentler stream, had mated with Him, and their offspring, Child, was crystal clear. It had been nearly four full moons since the winter solstice, and the first signs of spring were visible. The band had moved southward from its winter foraging grounds in preparation for the warm weather. It was an exciting time, an end to the cold, hungry nights when there was much sickness.

No one had used the shelter for several years. Remains of grass beds littered the dusty cave floor. They would have to prepare new sleeping pits, bring in leaves and grass to cover the floor, and gather firewood. The abundance of wood was one reason Tracks, Moon's husband, had suggested this location for the new camp.

Moon had lived in this shelter one other time— when she was initiated into womanhood. She thought about that time, years ago, of her band and her little brother, who was now with his wife's band. She remembered a cluster of oak trees in a side canyon where she had dreamed as a girl, listening to the birds or to the wind blowing through the deeper canyons. Under those trees she had finished her first coiled gathering tray, which she had carried for years, then used to cover the three-year-old body of her first

child, Thorn, when he was buried.

The noise of the children playing ended her daydreams. She scolded them gently for stirring up the dust, inviting them to go with her to her childhood hideout to gather leaves for the camp. Two of the children, Stick and Flint, eager to explore their new neighborhood, followed closely as she walked along the narrow ledge. Stick, her quiet son, was eleven years old; Flint, her nephew, was nearing manhood at thirteen years of age. They were curious and excited about exploring and indifferent about leaf-gathering. Neither had brought a basket. But both were ready for hunting. Stick carried a small rabbit club, given him by an uncle, and Flint had a lechuguilla stalk and a throwing stick made from a juniper branch.

The ledge passed above a deep waterhole. Flint tossed a rock into the water, startling some canyon wrens and a cottontail. The boys had to run to catch up with Moon, who had rounded a bend and crossed the canyon. The ground beneath the oaks was strewn with leaves. She and the boys quickly filled the basket she carried, and she started back. The boys chose to linger.

Stick spotted a rock squirrel, and both boys gave chase. The squirrel disappeared into a narrow crevice between two boulders, a safe shelter from the predators. The boys, unconcerned about the failure, decided to check the waterhole again. There was nothing interesting at the hole, only a few rock skinks. The boys drank. Flint, impatient, returned to the cave.

Stick remained at the pool, squatting with his bare toes touching the water. He watched the blue sky and clouds on the pond's surface and studied the ripple of

(PRECEDING SPREAD) *Flickering flames light the boys' initiation ceremony as the officiating shaman's shadow blends with painted images lining the shelter walls.*

Moon and boys. Stick and Flint follow Moon as she walks along the narrow ledge leading from the shelter to the side canyon.

a waterbug skating by. He thought of the water spirit, a striped serpent, and wondered where it was. His world was full of spirits, and he knew they were somewhere about this pool; he could feel them.

A hawk's scream broke into his dreaming, reminding him that it was near midday and time to return. Clambering up the rocky slope, he stubbed his toe on the sharp limestone. His fiber sandals gave little protection. He paused to inspect the damage, then limped on. Moon and her half-sister, Onion, were making another trip for leaves when Stick passed them. Moon noticed his bloody toe, but said nothing.

When Stick reached the shelter, he noticed that Feather, Flint's sister, had made her bed in an alcove separate from the main group. He knew that women occasionally did this, but he didn't understand the reason for it. They would build their own campfires and prepare their own food. Sometimes two women would stay together. He knew that before she could rejoin the band, Feather would have to make herself a sweat lodge. Stick had been told that an evil spirit possessed these women and the band had to be protected.

Three men were entering the cave when Stick arrived: Antler, the old shaman; Lizard, Stick's uncle; and Owl, an unmarried man who had become part of the band that winter. Owl's band had joined Moon's for

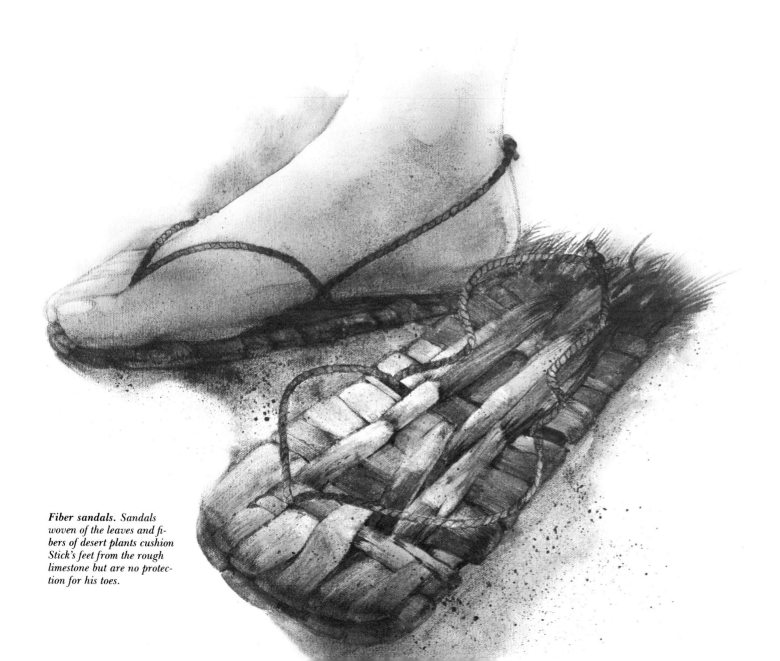

Fiber sandals. *Sandals woven of the leaves and fibers of desert plants cushion Stick's feet from the rough limestone but are no protection for his toes.*

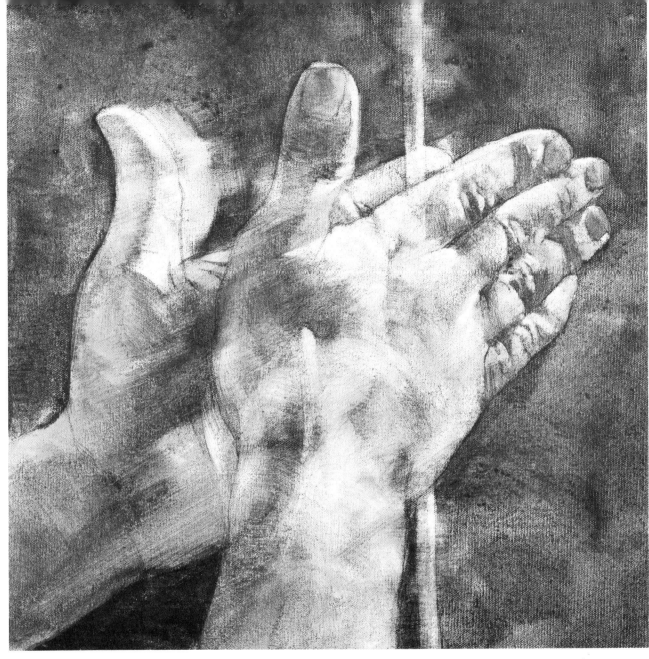

Fire making. Owl works to get a fire started by rotating the fire drill between the palms of his hands.

a communal rabbit hunt, and Owl had become friendly with Lizard; both were skilled hunters. Owl also liked Stick's older sister, Kitten, who had passed into womanhood last fall. At the great mitote, she had been initiated, scarified, and tattooed. She displayed parallel scars beneath both breasts and three blue tattoo lines from her bottom lip to her chin.

The three men had killed a badger and a bullsnake during the morning's inspection of the canyon. Owl carried the dead badger, and Lizard carried the snake. Old Antler brought a bundle of firewood, wrapped in a yucca-leaf sling. Owl found a section of sotol stalk in the debris on the floor. He split it and kept one half. Taking a piece of sharp flint from the floor, he carved

a small cup near one side of the stick and cut a notch in the opposite side, slightly intersecting the cup, to hold his fire stick. The friction from this hand drill caused the dust in the cup to smolder. Owl blew on these tiny embers as they fell through the hole in the cup to a batch of fine fibers lying below. In a short time, he had a good fire burning.

Because Lizard had killed the badger, he could not eat any of the meat; his reward was the skin. He gave the badger to Quail, Onion's mother, to prepare. Using her yucca knife, she skinned the animal, leaving the head, but cutting off the feet and tail. These were left on the skin, which she handed back to Lizard. While Owl made the fire, Quail prepared the cooking hearth. From the front of the cave, she collected flat limestone slabs and placed these in a shallow basin she had scooped in the floor. She gathered dry grass and placed this on the rocks, then added dry sticks to the heap and set it ablaze. When the rocks were hot, Quail placed the skinned badger and the unskinned snake on the coals.

Moon and Onion returned with their leaves. Quail made an offering of meat. Onion's portion was to be divided with her two children, Flint and Feather.

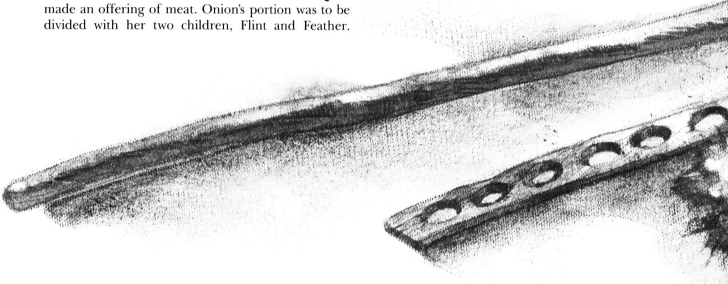

Owl's fire-making kit consists of a fire drill, a split sotol stalk hearth stick, and shredded lechuguilla fiber tinder.

Moon's share was divided among her family. Owl received the remaining bit, a front leg, which he ground between two stones and swallowed without chewing.

Onion took the cooked snake and cut it into sections, putting them in a wooden mortar, along with some leftover sotol cakes. She pounded the mixture together until it became pasty. Wren, Antler's older sister and her stepmother, helped her, using a stone mortar. When finished, they divided the food among other members of the band. Kitten had collected a basket of prickly pear stems earlier in the day, and she steamed these at the fire, singeing off the spines. These, too, were shared and eaten with the paste.

There were no leftovers. The group enjoyed a lazy time. The children played along the ledge. Antler knelt near the bed Wren had made for him, repairing the tip he had broken while trying to spear the badger. He was an accomplished flintknapper, admired for his skill in thinning points to a delicate sharpness. Satisfied with his work, he placed his repaired spear alongside his bed with his atlatl or spear thrower, another spear, and his throwing stick. These made up

the important tools of a man's labor.

The next morning, Tracks and Lizard announced that they were going to fish. Tracks carried his spears and a fishing net. He also carried his rabbit stick, a club, and a small net bag, attached to his rope belt. The bag contained tools to make or repair anything he needed. Lizard also brought along his spears. Flint and Stick followed eagerly. At times the men preferred not to have the children along, but today they needed their help stirring up fish from around the boulders. Onion and Kitten would join them later, when they went to the river to collect wild onions.

The two men paused on the riverbank in silence. The boys stopped about twenty paces behind the men. It was time to pay homage to the water spirit, to ensure his continued generosity. Tracks took four mountain laurel seeds from his hunting bag and tossed them into the stream. They had special powers, and the river spirit would be pleased.

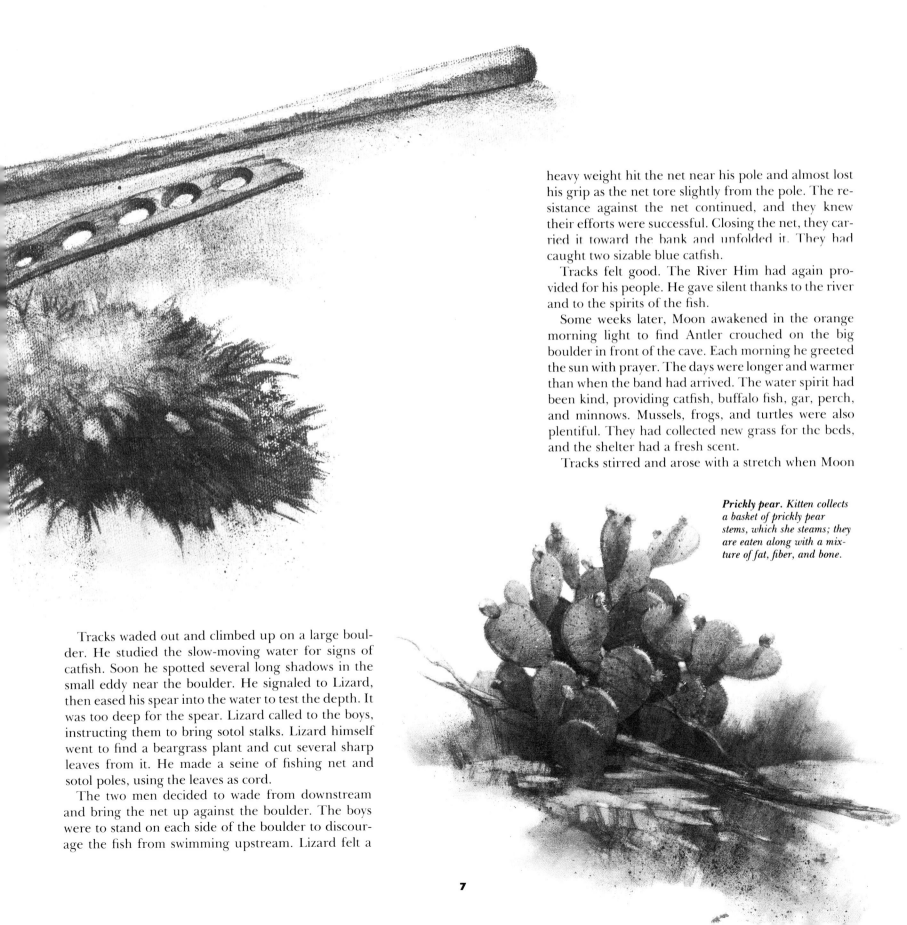

heavy weight hit the net near his pole and almost lost his grip as the net tore slightly from the pole. The resistance against the net continued, and they knew their efforts were successful. Closing the net, they carried it toward the bank and unfolded it. They had caught two sizable blue catfish.

Tracks felt good. The River Him had again provided for his people. He gave silent thanks to the river and to the spirits of the fish.

Some weeks later, Moon awakened in the orange morning light to find Antler crouched on the big boulder in front of the cave. Each morning he greeted the sun with prayer. The days were longer and warmer than when the band had arrived. The water spirit had been kind, providing catfish, buffalo fish, gar, perch, and minnows. Mussels, frogs, and turtles were also plentiful. They had collected new grass for the beds, and the shelter had a fresh scent.

Tracks stirred and arose with a stretch when Moon

Prickly pear. *Kitten collects a basket of prickly pear stems, which she steams; they are eaten along with a mixture of fat, fiber, and bone.*

Tracks waded out and climbed up on a large boulder. He studied the slow-moving water for signs of catfish. Soon he spotted several long shadows in the small eddy near the boulder. He signaled to Lizard, then eased his spear into the water to test the depth. It was too deep for the spear. Lizard called to the boys, instructing them to bring sotol stalks. Lizard himself went to find a beargrass plant and cut several sharp leaves from it. He made a seine of fishing net and sotol poles, using the leaves as cord.

The two men decided to wade from downstream and bring the net up against the boulder. The boys were to stand on each side of the boulder to discourage the fish from swimming upstream. Lizard felt a

got up, but Stick slept soundly on. After using the latrine at the downslope end of the shelter, Tracks walked to the front of the cave toward Antler. He studied the morning. It had not rained for some time, and they had to walk to a small spring in the main canyon for water. Hunting would be good near isolated waterholes away from the river, especially at the Place of Animal Spirits, a large tinaja fed by a seep spring, a day's walk away. They could use the meat, hide, sinew, and bone. Moon needed a new weaving awl; Tracks had no sinew for making spears. Although the men had never returned empty-handed, few deer had been

brought in lately. Tracks began to plan. He needed a new atlatl. He had put off the chore of making one, but he had seen a dry walnut branch perfect for the job near the spring.

Moon watched Tracks leave and knew he would return in time for dinner. She had sotol cakes, but not many. It was time to begin the long task of making a new batch from bulbs pounded into a coarse flour, moistened, and baked. Sotol, lechuguilla, and prickly pear were always available. Their diet was not varied, but they never went hungry.

Tracks moved quietly down the canyon, catching

sight of several wild turkeys. He made no attempt to pursue them because he knew from experience that was not possible while they were off the roost. At the spring, Tracks saw a bounding fox, but that, too, was difficult to catch except with a snare or in the den.

The walnut limb that Tracks wanted was easily obtained. He found a chert cobble on the ground and, with a piece of limestone, struck flakes from one end of it. In moments he had a sharp-edged chopper to cut off the branch. Shaping it would take much longer, so he returned to the shelter. He found two chert nodules and a limestone pebble for use as a hammer-stone. With one long, wedge-shaped flake and the hammerstone, he tapped against the branch until it split. Using one half for the weapon, he whittled it into shape with the second flake. By the end of the day, the atlatl met his standards for a good tool.

When Moon saw Tracks whittling so diligently, she knew he was planning a hunting trip. She went to gather food for him to take along. Their stock of wild plums had been set out in the sun to dry. She would mix these with the last of the sotol cakes.

After dinner that evening, Tracks sat at the fire with Antler and Lizard and discussed the hunting trip.

Moon awakens and sees Antler meditating and paying homage to the rising sun.

9

Tracks making an atlatl. Tracks selects a chert flake and begins to whittle the atlatl.

Antler agreed with his choice of site. They both spoke of past successes at the Place of Animal Spirits. Owl, Stick, and Flint joined the others to listen to the tales. At the end of the conversation, the trip was planned. Tracks would lead Lizard, Owl, and Oak, a young cousin of Moon's who had joined the band two weeks earlier with his pregnant wife, Dew. Antler suggested

that Flint should go, because he was coming of age and had to be trained to hunt. The party would leave in two days.

Lizard and Owl spent the next day refurbishing their weapons. Lizard made two foreshafts from juniper branches, whittling them to the right shape and notching them to insert the stone projectile tips. He had to substitute yucca fiber for sinew in securing the points. He checked his hunting bag and found it complete, containing three projectile point blanks, an antler flaking tool, spare yucca fiber, a squirrel-tooth scarifier and mountain laurel seeds for hunting ritu-

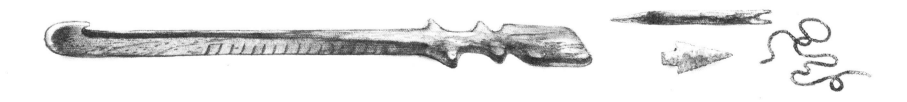

als, a hammerstone, red ochre for body paint, several sharp-edged flake knives, and two spare foreshafts. Owl finished two chert points and retouched the red bands near the knock end of his spears, his ownership mark.

Tracks went to the bluff overlooking the River Him to meditate and fast. He ground several mountain laurel seeds into powder and offered it to the wind spirit to carry to the animal spirits so they would know that the hunters respected them and wished them no harm. It was necessary to take an animal's life for survival, but the animal's spirit was always appeased. Each hunter went through his own personal ritual, except for Flint, who had not yet been initiated.

Antler was still chanting when the hunters left before dawn. It was only a day's walk, but the terrain was rugged and the pace slow. Each carried two spears, an atlatl, and a throwing stick. Each also had a hunting bag with essential tools and medicinal items attached to his belt. Flint carried a digging stick and a bundle of sleeping mats. He had no atlatl or spear, but Antler had lent him a rabbit club.

As an apprentice, he would perform the chores on the trip.

When Tracks reached the top of the divide, he stopped to study the wind: dry, blowing from the southwest. There were a few high clouds in the west, but no sign of a major change in the weather. It was important that the party approach from upwind. Tracks decided to spend the night in a cluster of juniper trees overlooking the canyon. Each hunter foraged on wild plums and cactus flowers along the way, but excitement made them less hungry than usual. They arrived at the juniper stand at sundown.

At the rockshelter, the women were organizing a party to gather sotol and lechuguilla bulbs. Quail (bent with arthritis and crusty with pain), Onion, Moon, Kitten, Stick, and Antler were included. Their

destination was a gentle slope further up the canyon. Wren, Dew, Feather, and Honey, Moon's adopted daughter, were left at home.

The women in the party had their digging sticks and carrying baskets. Stick had a small rabbit club, and Antler brought his atlatl, spears, and net bag. When they arrived an hour later, the women immediately began their tasks. Onion and Moon, the strongest, chopped away at the tight root mass anchoring the plants to the soil, using care to avoid the sharp thorns. Kitten cut some yucca leaves for a makeshift cord, which she used to help Onion, pulling the sotol leaf spray up off the ground as Onion chopped the roots. When the plant was cut, Onion sliced off its leaves, producing a bulb.

Moon was also working on a sotol plant, but discovered signs of a cotton rat nest at the base. Quail and Stick crouched close by with their sticks as she began to take the nest apart. Soon a rat appeared, and Stick quickly killed it. Another

Lizard's hunting bag contains three partially finished points, an antler flaking tool, spare yucca fiber, a small bag of red ochre, a squirrel tooth scarifier, mountain laurel seeds, a stone hammer, and two spare foreshafts.

scampered past Quail, who missed with her first swing, but hit it with the second. Another rat passed Stick and disappeared between two rocks. Moon killed a fourth, then found a nest full of young. She killed each one, biting its head. They would be eaten at dinner.

While the women continued their work, Kitten and Stick went to the rocky edge of the canyon to collect lechuguilla, which was easier to harvest, but smaller than the sotol. They pulled these plants out by their leaves, occasionally digging gently to loosen them. The thick, smooth leaves, tapering to a sharp point, would be used to make sandals.

By mid-afternoon, the women had gathered six

Lechuguilla plant.
Lechuguilla is much easier to harvest, but the bulbs are smaller, and it takes more of them. Flowering plants are avoided, because the bulbs are part of the flower stalk.

ing basket for the lechuguilla. She used the two sticks as a *V*-shaped frame and quickly twilled a conical basket. She then sliced off two yucca leaves; one for use as a trumpline and the other split to tie the trumpline to the frame. With Moon's help, she loaded her basket, and all the women returned to the shelter with filled baskets.

Stick explored the rock bluff above the gathering site. Something in a dark crevice caught his eye: a sleeping porcupine. He motioned for Antler to join him. After studying the situation, Antler decided to use his spear as a jabbing weapon, hoping that he could kill the animal and pull it from the rocks with the barbed tip. Or perhaps he would wound the animal, and it would come out on its own. He thrust his spear into the spiny body as hard as he could. The wounded porcupine retreated deeper into the crevice. Antler tried again, but the spear did not penetrate. Stick noticed that the animal was coming closer to the other side of the rock as it backed away. As Antler continued his efforts, Stick took up a position on the other side, with his club ready. Antler made one last jab, and the porcupine retreated one last time, right into Stick's swinging club.

The women who had stayed behind had spent the day foraging for firewood. The group had used up all the fuel in the immediate vicinity, so it was necessary to look further afield. Wren, Dew, and the two little girls found a large plum tree hidden in a small side canyon. They gathered the plums on the ground and shook off the remaining ones, then they ate their fill and took the rest to the shelter for the evening meal.

The tired gathering party returned to a meal of rats, rattlesnake, snails, porcupine, and wild plums. Tomorrow would be another hard day: they would have to make earth ovens and build fires to cook the sotol and lechuguilla.

Between three juniper trees northeast of the Place of Animal Spirits, the hunters made a small fire, using a hearth stick and a fire drill. Tracks had chosen this location because the smoke would not blow into the canyon from here. Each man slept near the fire on his own mat. Flint made himself a small grass bed.

The men awoke at first light. Tracks presented his strategy. Each hunter made alternate suggestions. The final plan was agreed upon by all. Lizard and Flint would travel east to the opposite side of the canyon from the tinaja from downwind, giving the animals plenty of warning. The animals were expected to make their escape through a wooded side canyon,

sotol bulbs and the children many lechuguilla bulbs with leaves attached. Antler had done little work. His role was to give advice and to kill any animals the women might find. He had gathered a bag of snails and killed a small rock rattler in his wanderings.

Kitten broke two sotol stalks to weave a rude carry-

since the main canyon was blocked. Tracks, Owl, and Oak would be waiting in the wood, concealed by brush and rocks. Lizard and Flint would make their move when the sun was directly overhead, flushing the game toward the waiting hunters by mid-afternoon.

After Lizard and Flint left, the others spread out about a hundred paces apart and began their slow descent into the side canyon. Oak flushed a jackrabbit, but missed with his rabbit club as the animal ran past. Owl, on the right flank, frightened two cottontails and

Kitten helps Onion during their gathering by pulling a sotol leaf spray up off the ground while Onion chops at the roots with her digging stick.

another jackrabbit, but they were not close enough for him to kill. Tracks caught a horned lizard and put it in his bag.

Oak was the first to enter the side canyon as the men came together in single file. They hid in the vegetation and rocks—they did not want to frighten any deer that might still be feeding. Tracks, following the others, decided to circle around a cluster of mountain laurel, persimmon, and walnut trees from the opposite direction. He found two does bedded down in the leafy mulch beneath the walnut trees. They sensed his approach and bounded away. Their line of escape placed them in direct confrontation with the other two hunters. One ran straight at Owl, who stood ready with his atlatl and spear. As the doe turned, ten paces from him, he let fly. The doe jumped aside in the nick of time. Both deer escaped in the direction of the tinaja. Owl found his broken spear tip and joined the others descending into the side canyon. No one discussed the missed shot. It was understood the deer was protected by an unseen force. Every one misses from time to time.

The men drank at a small stream, then settled under a shady vine to wait. Owl took an antler tine from his kit and worked at the spear tip, with advice from Tracks. Oak napped in the shade. Tracks watched the shadows deepen, then rose. It was time to position themselves in hunting blinds.

Oak and Owl hid themselves behind boulders, with a small pile of brush between them and the canyon floor. Tracks went to the other side of the canyon and did the same. Lizard and Flint moved toward the Place of Animal Spirits. Neither had been there before, but they knew where it was from Tracks' directions. As they approached the canyon bottom, the vegetation became thicker and larger. Walnut trees, persimmons, mountain laurels, and mesquites anchored their roots wherever pockets of soil had formed. Canyon grape was everywhere, and seeps along cracks were coated with ferns and moss. Patches of green grass grew along narrow shady banks.

Soon they came to the tinaja, a narrow waterhole with a vertical rock bluff bordering it on one side and a sloping sandy bank on the other. There was a long, shallow rockshelter far above the water. Flint could just make out the painted images on the many-colored wall. For an uninitiated boy, this was a frightening place, and he was grateful for Lizard's company.

Frogs splashed into the water as they approached, and a brown water snake eased off a log into the pool.

Waterbugs broke the polish of the surface as they skated away. The hunters noted many tracks in the moist sand at the water's edge: deer and raccoon mostly, but Lizard pointed out the large paws of a mountain lion. Moving on, they followed a well-marked animal trail through the thick canyon vegetation. They

The spring snare Stick constructed near a small animal run in hopes of catching a cotton rat.

saw a number of rock squirrels, but did not pursue them. They were on another mission. When they heard a noise ahead, they knew they had found deer.

Tracks heard the deer running up the canyon. He crouched in his blind, peering through a small pile of brush, while hidden by the boulder. He saw the first deer, a doe, followed closely by a second. Behind them was a buck. He would try for the buck, hoping the others would go for the does. The deer crashed on, but caught his scent as they were passing. As the buck hesitated, he was struck with Tracks' spear. It penetrated his abdomen and lodged in the muscles of his right thigh. He jumped and fell, dragging his hindquarters. Tracks was on the deer quickly, bludgeoning it to death with his rabbit club.

The does were confused by the turmoil. Owl missed his throw, but Oak hit a doe solidly in the neck. The wounded deer ran past the body of the buck down the canyon with Oak in full pursuit. She did not go far. Oak sang a low chant over his kill: a prayer to the spirit of the doe. Tracks left a small offering of mountain laurel seeds.

It had been a hunting trip they would long discuss. They had killed two deer in a very short time. The men set about preparing their prey. The skin was removed for use as clothing. The sinew was carefully stripped away and laid out to dry. Then, with their flake knives, they cut up the meat, packing it in the skins for transportation home. They also took the buck's head and antlers for use in the fall ceremonial dances. Tracks saved the hind legs, as well, for Moon needed new awls for textile weaving. The remaining bones were left behind. If they had been closer to the shelter, they would have used the entire animal, but this was too far for easy removal.

For dinner that night, the hunters ate the raw stomach, liver, and lungs of their victims. They all slept well, except for Tracks. He was troubled by something moving against his side. Finally, he remembered the horned lizard.

At the shelter, Antler and Stick busied themselves scooping out a large pit where the sotol and lechuguilla bulbs had been left the evening before. They lined it with limestone slabs. Moon, Kitten, and Onion collected firewood. Antler made a fire on the limestone slabs. When it had burned down to coals, the plant bulbs were put on the rocks and covered with ashes and coals for a few hours. They placed green plant material over the bulbs. Yucca and lechuguilla leaves for cordage and sandals were laid on top to be steamed. Then they covered the pit's contents with soil. It would cook for several days.

Stick and Kitten left the women at the pit and checked two deadfall traps Stick had set near rock squirrel dens. One was a fragile figure-four trigger, baited with plum seeds placed beneath a flat limestone rock near a hole. The other was a spring snare placed along a rat run between boulders. The first was tripped, but no animal was caught. The bait had been taken, and Kitten picked persimmons for Stick to use in resetting his snare. A cotton rat was caught in the spring trap. Stick killed it and reset the trap.

When Stick and Kitten returned, they found the successful hunters at the shelter. There was great excitement. Moon took the meat Tracks handed her and parceled it out. She quickly stretched the hide so that it would not become stiff and dry. Owl gave his bundle to Kitten, an obvious gesture of serious courtship. She was flattered but embarrassed. If she accepted the gift, it indicated interest on her part. Rejection of the gift was a final dismissal of all his hopes. She took the bundle and unwrapped it. Old Wren assumed responsibility for portioning out the meat.

That evening, the men gave the full details of the hunt, sitting around the campfire. The listening boys took in every word and stored it away for future reference.

Moon and Onion removed the earth and steamed leaves from the bulbs with digging sticks. Onion took the leaves and set them aside. Moon took out a bulb and tested it, finding it well cooked. The two women stripped the leaf bases from the bulbs, which were then laid out on the rocks to dry in the sun. They set the leaf bases aside to be eaten without further preparation. Onion kept an eye on the drying bulbs. In the afternoon they would be brought in to keep them safe from thieving skunks and raccoons. The next day the bulbs would be set out again to dry until they were ready for grinding.

Onion, Kitten, and Moon pounded the dried bulbs in bedrock mortars, using wooden pestles Moon had cut from a walnut limb. It was a monotonous task, but the women enjoyed the chance to chat. Moon and Onion teased Kitten about her romance and discussed her coming marriage. Later the women were joined by Dew, who was approaching her time. No mention was made of childbirth. By late afternoon, the flour had been ground and collected in coiled baskets.

Stick watched Antler and Oak, who were studying a thunderstorm building in the west. There had been

(ABOVE) *Five foot spear used with atlatl.*

no rain for several moons. Most of the tinajas were dry, and the spring was barely running. Good rains would bring fresh food: vegetables such as onions and greens were important. Even the animals seemed more abundant. Snails appeared on upland plants; millipedes were everywhere. Desert flowers (especially the colorful orange paintbrush) and the scent of cenizo changed the world. Antler noted the density of the rain and the speed of the clouds. He would give this information to the women for use in scheduling foraging trips.

Dew gathered her sleeping mat and some other items: a piece of polished, hollow hawk legbone and a tiny cradle made of twigs twined into a boat-shaped frame, lined with juniper bark and a piece of muskrat

hide. She went upstream a few hundred feet to a small overhang to prepare for the birth of her child. It was a tense time for everyone in the band. Oak was especially nervous, but he tried to appear unconcerned. The success of the birth, the sex of the child, and the speed of Dew's recovery were considered omens.

Dew selected a smooth area on the white cave floor for her delivery. With a digging stick, she scooped out a shallow basin in the floor. She covered this with a piece of matting and a bundle of soft grass. Next to the pit she hammered a wooden stake into the ground. Feeling contractions, she collected several sotol stalks, which she used to construct a lean-to against the back wall to hide her from view. Births were not to be watched by the curious. A midwife would come and

assist if birth was difficult.

As evening came, Dew retired to her rude dwelling. Her contractions gradually grew stronger, and by early morning she knew the time had come. She kneeled over the grass-lined pit and leaned toward the stake. Grasping it with both hands and placing a lechuguilla quid between her teeth, she began to push.

Old Quail, who was serving as midwife, had spent the night outside Dew's hut. She knew when Dew began her delivery, but she would assist her only if she detected some problem. The baby boy was born without complications. Dew delivered the child in the grass-lined pit. Despite her exhaustion, she carried out the process unaided. She used the hawk bone to secure the umbilical cord before cutting it with a flake

knife. Quail entered to check the baby thoroughly, then placed it in the cradle. Dew collected the contents of the delivery pit and took them out of the shelter for burial under a rock. The knife was placed with the grass and the placenta.

Dew took the baby down to the spring, where she bathed him and herself. Quail returned to the band and announced the birth of the boy child. On hearing that he had a son, Oak took his hunting bag and weapons and left the shelter. Antler offered him a mussel shell containing a bitter drink.

Oak went to a low bluff from which he could see Dew's cave. By the time he seated himself, Antler's drink had taken effect. It was a mild poison, made from mountain laurel seeds. Oak wanted his son to be

Form and motion of the atlatl spear thrown by Owl at the doe turning in front of him.

strong. He had to show the gods that the boy's father was strong. With a jackrabbit jaw, he tore deep gashes in his forelegs. He used a flake to cut long gashes across his shoulders, smearing the blood pouring from the wounds into linear patterns across his chest and down his cheeks. Then he began to hallucinate.

The canyon wall changed colors and assumed strange forms. Oak sensed that the spirits were close and chanted.

Antler watched from the shelter. Oak was doing the right thing. Dew had given the band a new hunter. Antler lit a bonfire, and the small band danced throughout

Dew, knowing it is time for her baby to be born, grasps the stake with both hands after placing a lechuguilla quid between her teeth and begins to push.

the night in celebration.

Several weeks later, Tracks announced that it was nearing time for the summer congregation. Small family bands came together each year for dancing, initiations, weddings, games, and warfare at the bountiful time of ripening prickly pear fruit, purple mesquite beans, grass seeds, amaranth seeds, wild onions, persimmons, and hackberries. It was not a time for hunting. The young men fished and trapped, but also had a chance to gamble and go on raids. The older men instructed the novices in initiation preparations. The women were the providers throughout this time, gathering and processing the collected vegetables, fruits, and small game. The older women prepared the girls for puberty rites.

if the little people, the beings that inhabited the rock crevices and played tricks on people, were watching him. He expected them to sneak up and poke him with a thorn. He also imagined hidden spirits watching him as he eased his way along the canyon wall. He saw some rats and several lizards, but made no effort to give chase. He jumped when a dove flittered off her nest, pretending to be injured. Finally, he had an armful of wood and could rejoin the group. As he moved toward them, he looked up the canyon and froze. There were three men with short hair, traditional enemies of Moon's people.

The previous year the men of Moon's group had encountered a group of Shorthairs encroaching on their territory near the River Her. A fight ensued, and a

A light shower
had fallen for two days and a cool,
damp wind blew from the southwest. Onion, Stick, and Honey had gone to look for firewood for the last few days at the encampment. They searched down the canyon near the River Him, finding what they could and placing it along the trail for the trip back. Stick explored the small tributary below the camp's spring, while Honey and Onion stayed in the main canyon.

Stick went into several crevices, inspecting wood rat nests and picking up dry wood from protected dens. For some reason, he felt apprehensive. He wondered

young Shorthair was killed. Stick had heard of that great victory: it was the main topic around the campfire for many months. Now he crouched behind a boulder and watched the three men intently. His duty was to warn the women and divert attention to himself. He knew the route to the shelter, and the Shorthairs did not. He could easily outrun them if they chased him. He stood up and shouted, "Braak! Braak! Braak!" Everyone in the band knew the meaning of this warning call: they were to return to the shelter,

In his search for firewood, Stick jumps a nesting dove, who flutters off her nest feigning injury.

where the men could establish a defense.

The Shorthairs were watching Onion and Honey bundle the firewood and were startled by the boy's call. They all turned toward him. Onion heard the alarm and motioned to Honey to run. When the Shorthairs glanced back to where Onion had been working, they saw that both females had vanished. One of them gave chase. The other two went after Stick, who had almost scaled the wall by this time.

Stick lost his sandals and had to cross the rough

Alerted by Stick's alarm call, Onion flees from the Shorthair warrior.

limestone barefooted. He raced across the flat, making his way through the catclaw, sotol, and lechuguilla like a fox. He did not stop to look back. As he passed the tinaja, he again shouted the alarm.

Tracks was busy making preparations for the band's departure when he heard Stick's call. Lizard also heard it and repeated it for those inside the shelter. The men gathered their weapons and hurried in Stick's direction. Owl was the first to see him. When Stick saw Owl, he stopped and, between breaths, told about Onion and Honey and their peril. Tracks looked across the canyon and spotted the two men who had been chasing Stick. Owl and Lizard bounded down toward the women, while Tracks and Oak went to challenge the strange men, who retreated quickly.

Onion was screaming and shouting. She had been caught and was violently resisting. When he saw the two enemy men, the Shorthair released her to search for his weapons, which he had dropped in the struggle. Onion threw a rock at her attacker, striking him solidly on the chest. The man stumbled, but regained his feet. Onion kept shouting and throwing rocks and twigs while Tracks and Oak stared, each poised with his atlatl ready. Onion stoned her attacker again, this time in the face. As he reeled, Owl released his spear. It penetrated to the right of the man's navel. The two defenders sprang toward him. Onion stumbled down the canyon to find Honey. The Shorthair had caught the little girl first. Onion found her lying on a bed of loose gravel on the canyon floor. She was dead.

The next day Honey was buried at the back of the shelter where Dew had given birth. Wren and Lizard scooped out a small pit. Wren gathered grass and twigs and placed them in the bottom. The little corpse, dressed in a string apron, was placed on a sleeping mat with her knees flexed against her chest. They wrapped the mat around her and tied it with yucca cord, then placed her in the pit. A small carrying basket was laid on top of her. Antler sprinkled ashy powder on the corpse as he recited the death chant, asking the girl's soul to protect the band. Lizard placed several rocks beside the grave. Antler painted two of them with red ochre and placed them on top of the body as a symbol of mourning. Other rocks were placed over the grave, and the pit was filled with soil.

Moon had been sitting in front of the cave for hours, wailing loudly. She had cuts on both arms, and her hair was shorn. The other women were also in mourning, but Honey was Moon's adopted daughter, so her suffering was more intense. Wren made two bundles of

leaves into rude figures, symbolizing protective spirits to aid in warding off witchcraft. The violent death of a member of the band was a cause of concern. The old woman shaman tried to bring stability and prosperity to the band once again. She used these figurines to mark the end of the mourning period. It would normally last for at least three days, but the band was preparing to move.

The men had a victory to celebrate, but they would not do so until they met the others at the congregation. Meanwhile, they made a bonfire and placed the body of the Shorthair on the pile. As the scent of burning flesh filled the air, Antler cut off pieces, which he shared with the other men, ensuring that the dead man's spirit was transferred to the victors and

Moon mourns over Honey's corpse, now wrapped and ready for burial.

21

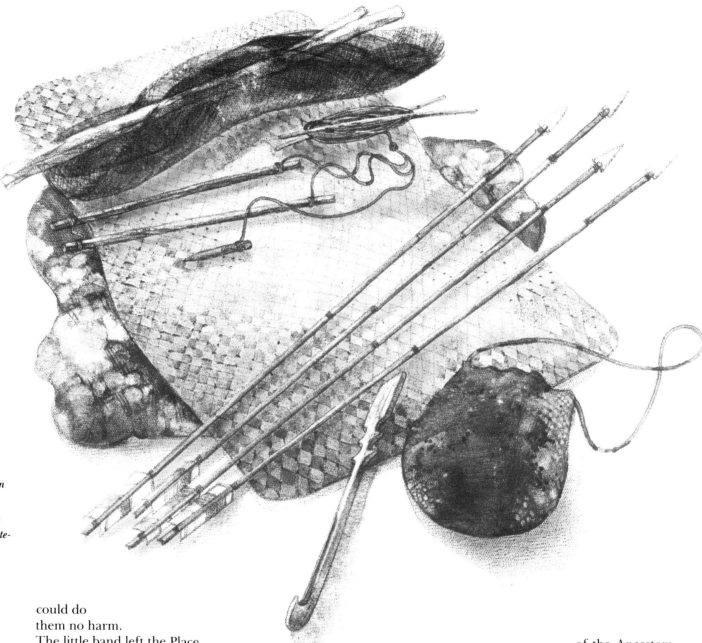

Each man carries his own sleeping mats, rabbit-fur robe, hunting/fishing net, snares, spears, atlatl, and bag of personal and maintenance tools.

could do
them no harm.

The little band left the Place of Shade the next morning. Their destination was only about twenty miles distant, but they had to cross rugged terrain to get there.

The great congregation was the time when most of the bands of Moon's people came together to celebrate the rainy season. Usually it was held near the confluence of the rivers Him and Her, where there was plenty of shelter space and open terrain. One popular place was a long winding canyon known as the Place of the Ancestors.

People told many myths about the spirits dwelling in it. There were numerous large shelters for dances and rituals. These displayed several generations of paintings made during initiation ceremonies and mitotes. Some of the bands would choose to live in the shelters, but most would be camping in rudely made structures on the broad flats.

Moon and Feather chatted as they trekked across the rocky slopes. Most of the travelers were silent, but

Each woman takes along her sleep mats, net carrying bag, several baskets, a sotol knife, bone awls, sandals, and a digging stick.

the men could be heard joking from time to time. They teased Owl about the upcoming mitote. Their pace was slow. They passed old campsites littered with chipped flint and mussel shells. Everyone carried his or her own possessions. Each man carried weapons and a tool kit, a bundle containing sleeping mats, a fur robe, a fishing net, and snares. Some things had been left hidden in their last shelter. The women carried digging sticks, baskets, sleeping mats, sotol knives, net bags, sandals, trail food, and everything else needed for the trip. They walked along a large, flat area of exposed rock. Stick saw strange figures carved into the surface. He recognized some of the symbols, like circles within circles, a sign for pregnancy. Stick asked Antler about the other marks. Antler did not know what they were, but attributed them to ancestor spirits.

In the afternoon of the third day, they encountered a related band. There was much shouting. The women stood at some distance. The men approached each other, carrying their weapons. Formal greetings were

23

in order: an exchange of spears. Once this was concluded, the women joined the group. The verbal exchange was noisy, filled with gossip, bragging, and jokes. Feather, an uninitiated female, hid her face in modesty. Children stayed close to their parents at first. But they soon began to mix and play. The men sat around the campfire exchanging tales throughout the night. The children, fascinated by the stories, squatted in the shadows until they dropped off to sleep.

Onion and Moon got up early to build their houses. Soon Wren and Kitten arose and assisted, collecting sotol stalks to construct three semicircular lodges. First, they made a framework of stalks tied at the top and a latticework of stalks and branches. Over this they placed sleeping mats and brush. A small, basin-shaped fireplace was positioned just inside each entrance. They arranged grass sleeping beds along the back wall of the huts. In a few hours the new households were set up.

Meanwhile, the old men were meeting to make plans for upcoming social events. Old Bear, a crusty shaman who had seen many rainy seasons, arranged the rituals. The first celebration was a victory dance, commemorating the killing of the Shorthair. The purpose of this event was twofold: to revel in triumph over the enemy and to absorb strength from the dead man's bones, which were ground and consumed in a drink.

The camp grew quickly. Within a week, there were about one hundred and fifty people in thirty huts arranged in a broad arc. Others were in an adjacent canyon. In all, there were about four hundred noisy people. Women went foraging together to catch up on the news. Men visited in small groups, swapping stories. The children played. Several little girls made dolls from sticks and grass leaves and built doll shelters. Some boys wrestled, while others threw spears at a makeshift target. One popular sport was running and throwing a spear through a rolling hoop, made of grapevine.

Onion and Moon construct open-air shelters for the band to stay in during the summer congregation.

Grown men played games of chance. One game used sections of reeds, open at one end and painted to distinguish value. These were divided into pairs of "old people" and "young people," with each marked "male" or "female." A small mountain laurel seed was placed in one, and all were then filled with fine soil. The object of the game was to guess which reed contained the seed. Each counted a certain number of points, the "old man" being the most important. Points were scored either by successful guessing or by skillful hiding. The losers had to sing the reed game song to the winners.

Lizard and Owl were teamed against two men from another band. Lizard was an expert at the game and sized the others up as overconfident. Quiet and patient, he never took his eyes from his opponents' hands as they moved over the reeds. Owl, less experienced, was learning from his partner. The game lasted all morning, becoming more intense. Lizard and Owl finally won and challenged a new pair of opponents for an afternoon game.

The adolescents were nervous about their upcoming initiation. The girls were gathered from time to time for instruction by an old female shaman, who observed them critically. Feather was followed by an old woman constantly, being scolded for laziness and incompetence. Fortunately, this lasted for only one week. Then she was tattooed to indicate familial affiliation, and a dance was held.

For the boys, initiation was more stringent. Shamans taught them who they were, how they came to be, what their relationship was with the natural world, and in what ways they could maintain that balance. The boys lived separately in a small shelter near the mouth of the canyon, chaperoned by Turtle, a shaman. They were trained for a month, fasting, running naked through cactus, sitting for hours without moving, listening to stories, and being scarified and tattooed.

One important ritual for the boys was calling upon animal spirits to look after the initiates. Antler and another shaman led Flint and the other initiates down into the canyon to a rockshelter with colorful paintings covering the back wall. The shamans chanted until darkness fell. The boys were given a drink made from peyote, which caused them to vomit. Flint thought he was going to die, but then he began to see strange images and many colors. They were led into the world of dreams for the first time.

The flicker of light from the campfires illuminated a colorful, distorted image of the animal spirit, glowing first in red, then in yellow, then in black as the light reflected on the painted body of the dancer, whose head was hardly distinguishable, except for antlers. He carried weapons, an atlatl and spear in one hand, a rabbit club and extra spears in the other. Deer tassels hung from each arm, and feathers dangled from his waist. Flint felt a strong gust of wind as the spirit's image loomed large. The essence of the spirit was projected along the back wall of the shelter as it moved behind the fire.

The deer was a semidivine animal. The shamans knew how to appease and influence the deity, bringing it to life in ritual and dance. Opposite the deer in the spiritual world was the panther, the hunter. The deer was the sun: the panther the moon, moving at night, stalking the deer. The real power was in the deer.

It took the boys two days to recover from this experience. Then the shamans took them back to the shelter. It was daylight, and one of the shamans was painting a figure bearing a strong likeness to the spirit. The painting commemorated their entering into the dream world. This would be their personal shrine for life, to which they could return at any time.

At the time of the new moon, some of the families decided to take part in a rabbit drive, an event that would net numerous cottontails and jackrabbits with relatively little individual effort. Rabbit drives occurred at various times and could be done with as few as four people. But a group of twenty to thirty made the event more exciting. The best time was at the new

moon, when the nights were dark and rabbits foraged in the early morning and at dusk. Shortly after rains, when the shoots were coming up, the rabbits were concentrated in the grassy areas.

Lizard, Stick, and three men and two boys from a related family band spent the following morning joining several hunting nets to make one long one. Onion and some other women also helped, making some nec-

essary repairs. At mid-afternoon, the men walked two miles to a grassy flat. They placed the net across a low draw, anchoring each end with a sotol stalk secured by rocks. The net stretched about one hundred paces.

The drive began at dawn the next day. A group of men, women, and children assembled to take part. The men leading them took care to skirt the grassy flat, forming a broad arc. When all were in place, they

On the grassy flat, rabbits scamper away from the approaching line of noisy humans toward the net stretched to cut off their flight.

began to walk toward the net, making noise and beating the ground with sticks. The men were at the end of the arc. As the line closed in on the flat, the rabbits scampered away from the noise. Their escape route took them directly into the net. As the hunters converged on them, over twenty rabbits were caught. The men ran them down and clubbed them. Boys and girls gave chase to those that managed to elude the men.

The moon was three nights from full when Old Bear announced the annual mitote to celebrate the harvesting of the desert fruit. They all took part in this major event. The shamans prepared mixtures of peyote and mountain laurel leaves for the male dancers. The women also danced, but took no drugs. Fasting for everyone began the morning after the announcement. The women gathered wood for the dance fire and prepared food for the feast that followed the dancing.

Dew was frightened and kept her distance from the men, especially the shamans. Old Bear would choose an infant for sacrifice, and no one knew what might influence his choice. The men, reluctant to appear stingy, said nothing about the selection.

By mid-afternoon of the second day, the congregation had gathered around the wood pile. The shaman had placed antlered deer heads around it, which had special powers for hunting and curing. Two shamans, one painted red, the other red and black, served each man his portion of narcotic. At dusk, the fire was lit. Male and female shamans began to chant to the rhythm of rasps and bone flutes. Three dancers circled the fire, each wearing rattles around his knees or ankles, made of the dew claws of deer. They carried spears, atlatls, clubs, and sotol stalks with seed tassels and were adorned with feathers in their hair and feather fans around their waists. Red, yellow, and black stripes were painted on their bodies. The lead dancers were joined by couples who snaked around the bonfire in a long line, tossing offerings into the fire as they danced past.

Old Bear approached a seated woman holding an infant and wrenched the baby from her arms. The mother began to scream, but he carried the baby to the fire. The singing became louder. Old Bear stood with his back to the fire, then turned, holding the baby high above his head. The chanting stopped as he recited a prayer and laid the baby into the fire. With an upward sweep of his arms, Old Bear encouraged the smoke to spread toward the spirits, so that they would feed on the food and the child offered in sacrifice.

Some dancers dropped out, exhausted from the tension of the ceremony. Others continued throughout the night and into the day. By midday, it was over; the bonfire was ashes. The shamans gathered the bones of the charred infant to grind them for consumption during the ceremony that ended the initiation of the boys.

Stick felt shaken. He could not understand what had happened. He escaped to a place on a bluff, where he sat listening to the wind moaning through the canyon. The September heat stirred the air and formed a whirlwind that drifted toward the camp. He wondered why the wind spirit was seeking out his

Deer heads with antlers attached, believed to have special powers for hunting and curing, are placed around the woodpile by the shaman.

*Old Bear **holds the infant's body** high above his head, reciting a prayer before laying the baby in the fire.*

Three painted pebbles are used to recite the people's relationship with the animals in the supernatural and natural worlds. One represents the spirit of the animals; another, the various trails leading to Moon's people; and the third, the spirit of the hunter.

Moon's band departs with Hawk, as Flint is named after his initiation, eagerly making his way among the other men (**OPPOSITE** *).*

people. Perhaps it had to do with the sacrificed child.

The initiates were brought to a sheltered recess. Antler explained their relationship with the animals, natural and supernatural. In his instruction, he used three painted pebbles; one represented the spirit of the animals, another the trails leading to Moon's people, and the third the spirit of the hunter. Following the narration, Turtle made painful slashes in the thighs of the young men. Then each boy's face was painted with charcoal mixed with possum grease. A round spot was made on each cheek and on the chin: from the lip down was solid black. Antler then used a mesquite thorn to prick three lines down their chins and circles on their cheeks. Each initiate now assumed a new name, which identified him with the animal world. Henceforth, Flint would be known as Hawk. Tracks, the family representative, gave him a spear and an atlatl. Hawk was now a man.

The composition of Moon's family band changed. Old Wren chose to remain in the Place of the Ancestors. Her time was near. Sparrow joined the band. She was angry with her husband, who had slept with another woman, and had decided to separate from him. Badger and Doe, who had once been with the band, returned with their baby. Kitten got married, but not to Owl. Another young man had left several jackrabbit carcasses before Tracks' hut as an indication of his interest. Tracks accepted the gift. Kitten collected her personal belongings and joined the young man, who had already built a hut. Owl had found another girl at the congregation, and the two of them joined Moon's group.

By the time the boys' initiation was concluded, many of the bands had moved on. Moon's band stayed on until mid-October before leaving for their fall encampment in the Valley of Nuts. Many bands would camp there to take advantage of the pecans, acorns, and walnuts and of the good deer hunting for which the valley was known.

The group abandoned the huts, strewn with the debris of their congregation activities. Moon was saddened by Wren's decision to stay behind. A few other old people were also staying, including Old Bear, who was unable to walk with his group. One by one, these elders would die in their shelter. As Moon's group left, the men were joking among themselves about the events of the past few months. Stick looked forward to the clear waters of the River Child, toward which they were heading. Hawk was proud as he eagerly made his way among the other men. ■

THE LOWER PECOS ENVIRONMENT
Evolution of the Present Landscape

Low vibrations of thunder seemed to shake the very rocks of the Pecos River canyon as dark clouds rolled through the skies. Winds spurred by the approaching thunderstorm produced a low groan as air moved through willows along the sandy riverbank. A roaring sound echoed down the canyon as the gusts passed through the narrow corridor, stirring up bits of dust that bombarded the bluffside and tore tiny particles of soft limestone from the eroding rocks. A premature darkness came upon the canyon. Large raindrops formed by melting hailstones began to fall from the turbulent clouds, and soon a gray wall of water descended as the storm drifted northeasterly across the late afternoon August sky.

The bare limestone hills and bluffs were coated as if a giant paintbrush had swathed a sheet of water across the landscape. Every recess in the limestone became a bowl full of water that quickly overflowed. The waters first trickled off the higher rocks, forming tiny drainages, which merged to form larger networks of rushing white water descending toward the Pecos River.

The rainstorm lasted only about forty-five minutes. By early evening, the running waters had found their way into the lower canyons and to the river itself, leaving behind thousands of small puddles in the bare limestone, ranging from teaspoon size to tinajas several feet across. Evaporation of the water in the next day's sun would leave the landscape mostly dry again, but the standing water in the potholes and tinajas, by dissolving the limestone bedrock ever so slightly, was undoing nature's own handiwork begun more than 100 million years ago. Tiny particles loosened by this process would eventually be carried away and dissolved or deposited into the sands and gravels along the stream courses. The waters of the Pecos River continued their endless and ageless action of dissolving and abrading the bedrock riverbed and slowly deepening the canyon.

The archaeologist was sitting on a low limestone shelf just above the clear waters of the Pecos River, studying the fluted channels in the shallow bottom formed by the eternal flow of the river's waters. He was resting from a strenuous climb down from the top of the canyon before scouting the nearby overhangs for traces of rock art. He looked up at the high bluff across from him, studied a hawk as it glided in the updrafts of the canyon winds. His eyes focused on the various white and gray layers of limestone that formed the bluff face and the more gently sloping terrain above the bluff. The stratigraphy was impressive. He thought of the millions of years it took for all of this limestone to form in layers and then for the river to slice through it like a blade. He imagined the shallow seabed on which he now sat and the eons-long sequence of inundation, sedimentation, uplifting, mountain-building, and erosion that had created the physical setting he was now observing. It took so much time to create this place in which time seemed to stand still.

The processes that he imagined had also molded the setting for the ancient people who lived in the can-

(PRECEDING SPREAD) *The lower canyon area about 10,000 years ago when Paleo-Indians first entered the region. Species shown: a group of Jefferson's mammoths, lacking the heavy coats of their northern counterparts; a sabertooth cat, a direwolf, and three camels; a herd of "antique" bison; two flat-headed peccaries.*

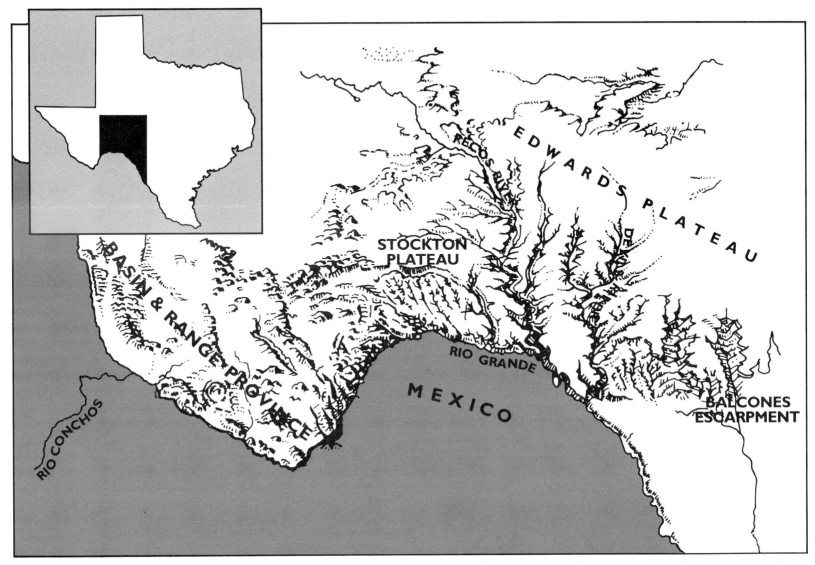

The geography and physiography of the Lower Pecos River region are highlighted by the deep canyons of the Pecos and Devils rivers where they join the Rio Grande.

yons and left their handprints painted on a rock recess not far from where he sat. What did they think of this world of deep canyons and the forces of the winds, rains, and moving water? Certainly they had not formulated the kind of geological understanding taught by modern science. But perhaps their appreciation of this environment was expressed in a different manner through their cave art.

Geology

The lower canyon region under consideration is defined by the Pecos River to the west, the Devils River to the east, and the Rio Grande to the south. This area occupies the southeastern portion of the Edwards Plateau region and, west of the Pecos, the Stockton Plateau, which together form the southernmost ex-

tension of the Great Plains Province of North America. To the west, beyond the Stockton Plateau, lies part of North America's Basin and Range Province. To the north, the lower canyon area grades into the southern High Plains or Llano Estacado (Staked Plains). Here the High Plains do not form the distinct eastward-facing Caprock Escarpment so characteristic of their separation from the Central Plains region further north. To the east, beyond the Devils River, the lower canyon country continues into the southern edges of the Edwards Plateau, as defined by the Balcones Escarpment, the plateau's geological demarcation from the Coastal Plains Province.

The formation of the present-day landscape began during the later part of the Lower Cretaceous over 100 million years ago. The continents then were not

35

in their present position, and the area that would become the lower canyon region lay just north of the equator. It was part of a continental shelf covered by a shallow sea. Near the shore, rivers and streams were depositing their loads of sand and silt; more limy sediments were being formed further down on the sea floor. By the end of the Lower Cretaceous, thick deposits of mixed sediments had formed what would eventually become the Glen Rose Limestone. This was the age of dinosaurs; many of these huge creatures left their footprints in the limy tidal muds that were incorporated into this formation.

The sea continued to encroach in this area, and limy deposits accumulated to become the Edwards Limestone and Georgetown Limestone and the Upper Cretaceous Eagle Ford Formation. Silicates in these deposits congealed to form the beds, nodules, and seams of fine chert that came to be so economically important to the ancient hunters and gatherers who would later forage on the uplifted surfaces of these limestone outcrops.

By middle and late Cretaceous times, the eastern edges of the region were subsiding toward the Gulf of Mexico, resulting in faulting and volcanism along what is today the Balcones Fault Zone. Shallow seas then reached all across Texas and joined another inland sea that had invaded North America from its Pacific borders. Toward the end of the Cretaceous (between 75 and 65 million years ago), the western portion of this area was affected by the plate tectonic events along the Pacific coast that led to the beginnings of the Rocky Mountain Province and the Basin and Range Province.

By the beginning of the Tertiary Period, some 65 million years ago, the dinosaurs were gone and the environmental setting was favorable to the development of mammals and modern birds. Over the next 10 million years or so, mammals filled the niches left vacant by the dinosaurs, increasing in variety and size. From humble insectivores and possumlike beginnings arose a variety of archaic mammals, some of which eventually led to the ancestors of our modern forms.

After regression of the late Cretaceous seas, this area (together with the rest of Texas) became a dry upland. Rivers draining south and southeastward over the next 60 million years began to deposit the sediments that form Texas' present Coastal Plain beyond the Balcones Escarpment. Major volcanic activity occurred in the Trans-Pecos region west of the lower canyons during the Eocene epoch of the Terti-

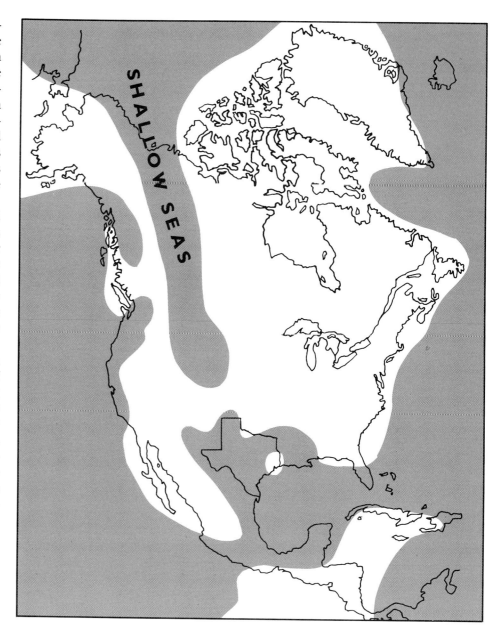

Southwest Texas was part of an ancient shallow sea encroaching from the Gulf of Mexico 120 to 100 million years ago, during Early Cretaceous times (RIGHT). During the Late Cretaceous, 100 to 65 million years ago, the area became part of a mid-continental seaway stretching from Alaska to the Gulf (ABOVE). Gradual uplifting of the land and stream erosion led to the landscape we know today.

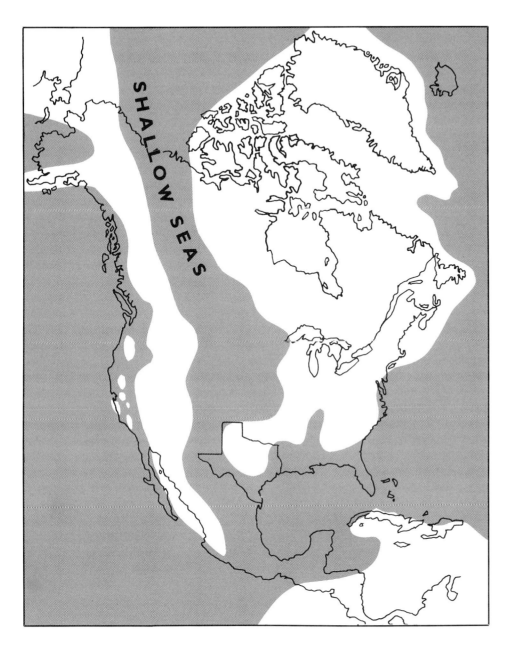

SHALLOW SEAS

ary Period (from 58 to 37 million years ago). By that time most of the archaic mammals that followed the age of dinosaurs had become extinct, and the early ancestors of our familiar plant and flesh-eating forms had come on the scene. Fossils from the Big Bend region of Texas substantiate these changes.

Volcanic activity continued into the Oligocene epoch (from 37 to 25 million years ago), when the bulk of the block faulting resulting in the present Basin and Range Province occurred. This entire region underwent major uplifting during the first half of the subsequent Miocene epoch (from 25 to 5 million years ago) due to these events.

The formation of today's Rio Grande and the Conchos River in Mexico can also be traced back to the Miocene. The ancestral Rio Grande followed a southerly course only and did not include its current southeasterly extension beyond present-day El Paso. It was during this time that the Conchos River was developing most of what was to become the extended Rio Grande system into the Gulf. It was also during the early Miocene that renewed movement along the Balcones Fault Zone formed the present-day escarpment that separates the Edwards Plateau from the lower Gulf Coastal Plain to the east and south.

The Pliocene (from 5 to 2 million years ago) witnessed renewed uplifts in the Rocky Mountain and Basin and Range areas and the final elevation of the bordering Great Plains that came to lie in their rainshadow. Major rivers carrying sediments from the Rockies began forming and dissecting the Great Plains, including the Edwards Plateau. The Devils River was probably formed at this time and drained the central portion of the Edwards Plateau. Drainage in the Basin and Range Province consisted mainly of closed systems until the Rio Grande cut its basin southward and captured the Rio Conchos opening to the Gulf.

It was during the early Pleistocene (about 1-½ million years ago) that the Pecos River was formed. In the Pliocene, the rivers that later became the Canadian, Brazos, and Colorado drained directly out of eastern New Mexico across Texas toward the Mississippi River and the Gulf of Mexico. This drainage pattern was changed by headward erosion of the Pecos River, which captured the major mountain headwaters of these rivers and channeled them south across the Great Plains/Basin and Range boundary into the Rio Grande.

Late Pliocene and Pleistocene times also saw the arrival of many of the large mammals that were to dominate the North American continent until their extinction about 10,000 years ago. Among the immigrants were mammoths and bison that crossed the Bering Strait land bridge from Asia and groundsloths, glyptodonts, and giant armadillos that made their way north from South America. The new arrivals joined an already existing megafauna of native camels, horses, mastodons, sabertooths, direwolves, and giant beavers. There were even vultures of outsized dimensions.

The Pleistocene was an age of glacial advances and melting. Four major glacial episodes are recorded, with three interruptive interglacial stages, but there were many smaller fluctuations within these larger divisions. The modern age, commencing 10,000–12,000 years ago, after the melting of the last major continental ice sheets, is considered an interglacial stage by many geologists. During the glacials, ice covered the northern half of North America and Eurasia, and the lands south of the glaciers (for example, Texas) were considerably cooler and moister than today. Animal populations, depending on their degree of adaptation to Arctic and cold-weather conditions, moved north and south with the fluctuating ice sheets.

Today the majority of exposed rocks in the lower canyon area are of Lower Cretaceous age, although there are a few remaining Upper Cretaceous "islands." Erosion has worn away all post-Cretaceous sediments and chiseled deep canyons pocked with solution hollows along their sides. These caves provided convenient homesites for the human populations that moved into the region during the last days of the Pleistocene megafauna.

Formation of the Lower Canyon Environment

The lower canyon region's present semiarid environment (the region forms the eastern portion of the Chihuahuan Desert) has been developing for thousands of years. The area's temperature and moisture gradients responded to changes in weather patterns brought about by the melting of the glaciers of the last Ice Age to the north. This marked the onset of modern weather patterns determined mainly by its two flanking ocean systems—the Gulf of Mexico to the east and the Pacific Ocean to the west—and the effect of intervening mountain ranges. We can begin to trace specific environmental changes from about 25,000 years ago in the late Pleistocene.

Starting then and into the Holocene, or Recent, the physiographic setting of this area resulted in a clinal distribution of rainfall that is reflected in the distri-

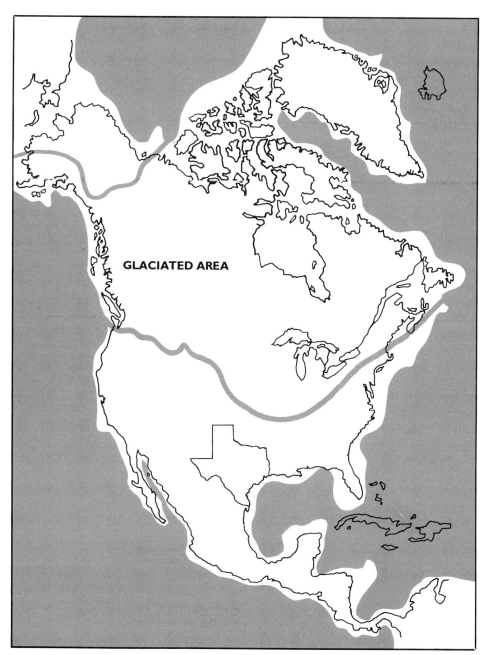

GLACIATED AREA

Glacial ice masses covered much of North America at the full extent of the last Ice Age, blocking the route for human migration across the continent until the melting of the ice sheets about 12,000 years ago.

bution of its plant and animal life. The cline, or gradient, of increasing rainfall runs from southwest to northeast. Less rainfall occurs in the western portion, since it is separated by substantial distances from either of the major ocean systems. This, combined with the rain shadow effect of the Mexican Pacific coastal mountains, produces a much more arid climate than toward the east. Plants and animals found here tend to be more adapted to desert conditions. As one travels eastward, rainfall increases and plants and animals typical of a relatively moist environment become more common. There are, of course, localized variations due to elevation differences; sheltered canyons also create special environmental situations favoring certain species of plants or animals.

The north–south temperature gradient is enhanced by the generally flat terrain of the Llano Estacado and Edwards Plateau, which provide no obstruction to cold winter air masses sweeping down from the north. There are also no major obstructions to hot air blowing out of Mexico in the summer. These summer and winter temperature extremes affect the north–south distribution of local plants and animals. In addition, plants that occur over the entire region, such as mesquite and prickly pear cactus, mature more rapidly in the southern portion of this area. This undoubtedly had a significant effect on the foraging movements of the ancient hunters and gatherers.

The general climatic trend of the region since the last glaciation (the Wisconsin Fullglacial) about 14,000 years ago has been toward decreasing moisture and increasing temperature. The net effect has been the gradual movement of cool- or moist-adapted species to higher elevations in the mountains or down into the wetter, sheltered canyons. Species that required mean temperatures cooler than found in the mountains or more moisture than available in the canyons either became extinct or migrated to cooler, moister environments. Plants and animals suited to the hotter, drier climate that developed migrated into the area from the southwest or south and took over the newly opened ecological niches.

Scientists have used the microscopic fossil pollen preserved in the sediments of ancient lakes and river terraces to reconstruct the environment. Additional sources of information are found in fossil woodrat nests. These curious animals gathered plant debris and twigs from vegetation near their nests, thus preserving a remarkable record of the environment at the time the nests were built. The nests were often tucked

Prickly pear cactus plant (**RIGHT**); *flower* (**ABOVE**). *The pads and fruits (pears) of several species of prickly pear cactus (*Opuntia *sp.*) *were a mainstay in the Lower Pecos diet for thousands of years.*

away in dry crevices and small caves and were preserved for scientists to find and date by the radiocarbon method. Other environmental information comes from the archaeological sites themselves. People, acting somewhat like the woodrats, brought into their homesites vegetation and animals that occurred in the vicinity. Paleontologists can study the preserved bones and plants left by the human occupants. These scientists also study fossil deposits, determining the occurrence of specific kinds of animals and plants for the given area. When information from the pollen record, woodrat investigations, and paleontological studies is combined, scientists can piece together major environmental trends for a remarkably long period of time. Subtle or short-term fluctuations may not be recognizable, but certainly the long-term trends are clearly detectable. The paleoenvironment of the lower canyon region can be traced back to the time just prior to the last major advance of the northern glaciers, during an interval called the Wisconsin Interpluvial.

Spring flowering plants of the lower canyons. (Many flowers were used for food as well as for their medicinal properties.)
(ABOVE LEFT) *Feather dalea (Dalea formosa);* **(CENTER)** *Blue curls (Phacelea congesta);* **(RIGHT)** *Eryngo (Eryngium leavenworthii); and* **(BELOW)** *Yucca (Yucca sp.).*

Wisconsin Interpluvial (33,500–22,500 Years Ago)

The fossil pollen studies of playa lakes in the Llano Estacado indicate that the general environment on the High Plains was a cool, moist grassland, mostly without trees. This type of environment probably extended into the lower canyon region. The nearby mountainous regions were more wooded. Some areas adjacent to the grassy plains were covered with parklands of spruce, pine, and juniper.

The animals in this region probably included many of the now extinct species of Pleistocene megafauna as known from the High Plains as well as species still in existence: mammoths, mastodons, horses, camels, giant bison, ground sloths, giant armadillos, peccaries, deer, elk, and antelopes. Among the carnivores were sabertooths, giant jaguars, mountain lions, lynx, and bobcats, as well as direwolves, coyotes, several kinds of bears, raccoons, weasels, badgers, and skunks. Jackrabbits and cottontails, along with pocket gophers, ground squirrels, beavers, and many kinds of mice and rats, constituted the smaller herbivores of the mammalian fauna.

Wisconsin Fullglacial (22,500–14,000 Years Ago)

More information is available for environmental reconstruction for this period than for the preceding interpluvial. Pollen data are more diverse, and the information is supplemented by studies of fossil woodrat nests. The Wisconsin Fullglacial period was sub-

stantially cooler and wetter than any time before or after. The vegetation consisted of scattered Ponderosa pine/spruce parklands with intervening sections of grasslands and scrub grassland across the Edwards Plateau and Stockton Plateau. This vegetation pattern did not quite extend into the lower canyons, but ran just north of them, probably due to the north–south temperature gradient.

In the higher-elevation area of west Texas, such as the Guadalupe Mountains and Chisos Mountains, the forest cover was denser, and the elevations above 4,000 feet were dominated by Ponderosa pine/Douglas fir forest with intermixed hardwoods. In the elevations below 4,000 feet, the vegetation consisted of a mosaic of pinyon pine/oak parkland, scattered grasslands, and scrub grasslands. This type of vegetation also characterized the areas of high open ground in the lower canyon region. The canyons supported a mixture of deciduous trees and pinyon pine along the permanent waterways and on the gentler canyon slopes.

This extremely cold period of the Pleistocene added significantly to the formation of sheltered locations by accelerating the processes of limestone erosion. Moisture contained in tiny cracks in the limestone became frozen during intensely cold spells, expanding to cause spalling (thin sheets falling off). Thick layers of limestone spalls can be seen in numerous rockshelters in deposits that underlie the preserved archaeological materials of the early Holocene. The degree of spall-

ing can be used as a rough measure of temperature extremes for extended periods of time.

The diversity of habitats is reflected in the diversity of animals represented. Animal species ranged from open parkland herbivores such as Jefferson's mammoths (a true elephant), mastodons, *Bison bison antiquus* (a long-horned form), camels, horses, and their predators to riverine forms such as muskrats, otters, and beavers.

Limestone caves and overhangs in the canyons provided ample dens and protection for animals such as wolves, bears, cats, sloths, flat-headed peccaries, and packrats.

The lower canyons were at their biological maximum in terms of diversity and carrying capacity for plants and animals during the Wisconsin Fullglacial. The region would never again support that amount of biomass.

Lateglacial Period (14,000–10,000 Years Ago)

This period marks the beginning of the gradual trend of increasing mean annual temperatures and decreasing rainfall that has characterized the lower canyon environment since the Wisconsin Fullglacial. Pollen studies show a rapid decline in the pines and the almost total disappearance of spruce by the end of the period about 10,000 years ago. This change was accompanied by an increase in the grasses and herbs. The Fullglacial parklands and forests shrank into small island communities in the higher elevations, while the scattered grasslands and scrub grasslands extended to cover most of the Llano Estacado and Edwards Plateau.

In the lower canyon area, Lateglacial changes include a thinning out of the pinyon pine woodlands.

Two essential plants for food (the buried bulbs) and fiber (the leaves) were (**LEFT**) *Sotol (Dasylirion wheeleri) and* (**ABOVE**) *Lechuguilla (Agave lechuguilla).*

The Rio Grande (INSET). *An aerial view, unavailable to the original settlers, of the junction of the Pecos River and Rio Grande. The rocky shoals of the Rio Grande served as ancient corridors for people passing north and south.* (RIGHT) *Blue waters of Lake Amistad fill the Rio Grande canyon today.*

These were changing into open parklands with grass and herb cover much as exists today in relic stands of pinyon found in the Edwards Plateau north of Brackettville, Texas.

The end of the Lateglacial Period marked a dramatic episode in the development of North American animal life. It was then that most of the Pleistocene megafauna died out, in the canyons as well as in the rest of the continent. This was also the time when many species left the canyon area for moister environments and new, more arid-adapted species came in from the south and west. These changes occurred over some 5,000 years, a very long period of time in terms of human lives, but a mere blink in terms of geologic time.

There has been a long-standing debate between two schools of thought over what caused the extinction of the Pleistocene megafauna. One claims that the extinction occurred as a result of major climatic changes that affected vegetation patterns, resulting in the destruction of many of the habitats essential to the various members of the Pleistocene megafauna. The other school thinks that climatic change was not sufficient to account for the wholesale extinctions and that overkill by Paleolithic hunters was the primary cause.

It was during these extinctions and the shift in remaining faunas that the first humans entered the lower canyons. The area still contained a relatively rich and varied assemblage of animals and must have presented an attractive environment for hunting and

gathering peoples. The climate was moderate, there were good sources of water, and shelter was available in the form of caves and rockshelters to weather the occasionally bitter-cold winters of 10,000 years ago.

Early Postglacial Period (10,000–7,000 Years Ago)

The environment of the lower canyons during the Early Postglacial was one of gradual change. Pollen and fossil plant parts recovered from archaeological sites and animal remains brought into the sites by human predators all attest to the gradual drying trend that followed the end of the Pleistocene.

Plains and plateau highland areas were becoming grassland and scrub grassland communities as the pinyon pines, oaks, and junipers retreated to higher,

moister areas. The Ponderosa pine/spruce communities had already become restricted to the high mountain areas of west Texas and northern Mexico. The pinyon pine parklands now also retreated northward, away from the lower canyons. Their place was taken by scattered oaks and juniper parklands with grass and herb cover. The erosional areas along canyons and arroyos became footholds for small communities of mesquite, ocotillo, yucca, prickly pear, sotol, lechuguilla, and mountain laurel. The river terraces were still rich with mixed stands of willow, pecan, walnut, cottonwood, some conifers, and a wide variety of wildflowers.

A broad range of animals occurred in these habitats. The plains/plateau parklands were utilized occa-

The Pecos. The majestic beauty of its blue-green waters and deep limestone canyons gives the Pecos River a deceptively complacent character.

43

sionally by bison (now represented by the modern variety), but were permanent homes for deer, antelope, coyotes, gray foxes, gophers, wolves, prairie dogs, jackrabbits, and various small rodents. The erosional breaks were inhabited by rabbits, rodents, and reptiles, and smaller predators such as bobcats and skunks. Along the rivers were found beavers, deer, gophers, amphibians, turtles, and other moist-adapted species. Abundant species of fish were available in the rivers and tributary streams.

The Early Postglacial Period in the lower canyons was one of relative abundance in terms of plant and animal habitats available for exploitation. Although the biomass of the region was reduced from that of the previous Lateglacial due to the final extinction of the Pleistocene megafauna, the absence of this fauna provided resources and space for many smaller species. The human component of the ecosystem was able to adapt gradually and naturally to what really were slow changes in terms of human life spans.

Middle Postglacial Period (7,000–4,000 Years Ago)

The continuation of the general drying trend that began with the end of the last glacial period can be traced through the Middle Postglacial. The emphasis is on the word *trend*. There were probably periods of reversal to moister and cooler conditions, but these are not easily detectable in the archaeological and pollen records. The general pattern since the Pleistocene was a decrease in the frequency and intensity of such reversals.

The evidence for the drying period comes both from plant and pollen materials and from animal remains recovered from archaeological sites. Grasses predominated on uplands and open plains. The arid-adapted plants gained footholds on the open slopes and the erosional breaks that are characteristic of the lower canyon region. Moisture-dependent plants were even more closely confined to the river floodplains and the higher elevations. The distribution of animal species followed the vegetational pattern. As the areas of occupation of specific species became more closely defined, the human inhabitants had to become more in tune with the spatial and seasonal distributions of food resources. Since this gradual drying trend occurred over such a long span in terms of human generations, it probably was not even recognized by the ancient foragers of the region. Actually, their resource base had expanded, with new desert plants and animals added to a restricted but still available supply of the more moisture-dependent species. As the zones of resource distribution became more closely defined, regional differences in the types of resources exploited became more apparent in the archaeological record. Conditions were approaching the anything but homogeneous environment we find exemplified today in the marked differences between the arid Pecos River drainage and the comparatively moist Devils River watershed.

Late Postglacial Period (4,000–100 Years Ago)

The gradual drying trend for the region continued during the Late Postglacial, and the specific biotic zones and communities that we see today were becoming better defined. Open grasslands in upland areas were firmly established, along with the specific wet/cool-adapted communities in the river bottoms, shaded canyons, and higher mountains. Plants adapted to the encroaching desert conditions made the most rapid gains, including such species as mesquite, agave, sotol, acacia, prickly pear, cenizo, and creosote.

There was little significant change in the kinds of animals endemic to the area. However, as plant communities became more sharply defined, so did their animal components. Almost all of the present species of animals found in the region were present during all or most of the Late Postglacial. There were, however, two exceptional periods. One happened about 2,500 years ago— botanists identify a short-term shift to cooler and wetter conditions, possibly triggered by an

Arctic interval comparable to a mini–Ice Age. Large herds of bison were attracted into the region. Not since the Pleistocene had the area been so populated by herds of large mammals. The bison ranging into the area may have been driven southward from their more central or northern Great Plains habitats by unusually cold conditions.

The archaeological result of this otherwise minor climatic reversal was that the bison also attracted predators, especially humans. Hunters from central Texas may have ventured into the area, as suggested by the style and materials of the projectiles recovered from Bonfire Shelter, where hundreds of the large animals were driven into a cleft and conveniently tumbled into the adjacent shelter. The bison disappeared from the area again, and the post-Pleistocene drying trend continued. While this climatic interval may have brought outsiders into the area, their impact on the arid-adapted lower canyon people was not significant.

Another reversal in the drying trend seems to have started sometime after about A.D. 1300 and lasted into historical times. The change again brought bison close to the lower canyons. In fact, much of Texas east of the

The Devils River (OPPO-SITE & ABOVE). The turquoise waters of the Devils River, the youngest of the three streams, contrast sharply with the white limestone through which it cuts its course. The rivers and their tributary canyons provided sources of water, shelter, and ecological opportunities that nourished and protected the ancient people for 9,000 years.

Pecos River seems to have been overrun by herds of bison. This is borne out both in the widespread occurrence and quantity of bison bone in archaeological sites and in descriptions by Spanish explorers and missionaries. Juan Mendoza, for example, who traversed the northern portion of the area in 1684–1685, mentions repeatedly how they killed fresh bison almost daily to fill the needs of their expeditionary party. Possibly, as before, the appearance of bison over much of Texas during this time was due to unusually cold Arctic weather, pushing the bison southward. The possible intrusion of bison hunters is documented in subtle ways in the lower canyons after A.D. 1300, mainly in the depiction of bisonlike animals in late pictograph panels at several archaeological sites such as Meyers Springs and Castle Canyon.

How this last reversal affected the flora and fauna of the Pecos River area is unknown. Bison bones are very uncommon in lower canyon archaeological sites (Bonfire Shelter is a truly exceptional situation), and no deposits have been isolated that demonstrably date after A.D. 1300, although they surely occur. Recently recorded circular stone alignments, pottery, arrow points, and small end scrapers (indicative of hideworking) at the Infierno Site may indicate a campsite of intrusive bison hunters, possibly dating from after A.D. 1300. However, because of the generally poor stratigraphic separation of archaeological deposits late in the cultural sequence, environmental changes, if any, cannot be determined.

Late Historic Period (1880–Present)

When the first Europeans ventured into the lower canyon area, they found the uplands covered with extensive grasslands fringed by low stands of stunted woody plants. Larger trees were confined to the rocky slopes, mesas, erosional breaks, canyons, and floodplains of the major streams. In essence, it was much the same environment that was described for most of the Late Postglacial Period.

Removal of the native Indian populations by 1875 and the eradication of the southern buffalo herd in 1874 eliminated the two major factors that maintained equilibrium and stability in the southern High Plains environment of which the lower canyon grasslands are an extension. Periodic range fires, many probably set by the Indians in efforts to drive deer, antelope, or possibly even bison in the northern fringes of the region, helped to keep woody plants such as mesquite from encroaching on the grasslands. The

The stark beauty of their environment must have helped shape the emotional and spiritual world of the ancient inhabitants of the region. The harsh appearance of the landscape (OPPOSITE & RIGHT) is deceiving to the modern viewer. To the hunter and gatherer, the deep canyons were sources of water, food, and shelter as well as avenues to upland tributary canyons and the plants and animals found there.

Large stands of sotol, lechuguilla, and prickly pear occurred in the uplands away from the rivers.

buffalo herds, which generally ranged north of the lower canyon area but extended at times as far south as present-day Crockett and Sutton counties, helped to keep the grasslands thinned and the upper soil layers churned and fertilized. Such maintenance of the sod layer sustained the grasslands and helped protect against·the encroachment of woody shrubs and cactus.

With the buffalo gone, the grasslands at first experienced a burst of increased growth and expansion. However, it was not long before European ranchers moved into the region. The completion of the Texas and Pacific Railroad in 1883 brought domestic cattle, sheep, and goats in great numbers and made it possible to ship livestock and animal products to market. A classic example of overexploitation of an environment resulted.

Within a few years, the grasslands were almost completely destroyed. Unlike the intermittent winter grazing of bison herds, the constant grazing pressures of fenced cattle, sheep, and goats removed the grass cover of the upland landscape, accelerating erosion of the sod layer. Soil erosion and the elimination of

range fires opened the way for woody shrubs and cactus to invade the former grasslands. Also, eroded soil does not hold moisture, and during severe rainstorms huge quantities of water are flushed into the lower canyons, scouring away anything in their path. In many rockshelters in Seminole Canyon and elsewhere, entire shelter deposits built up over thousands of years have been removed by such massive flash floods. The land practices responsible for these unwelcome changes continue into the present.

Native animal life, too, has obviously been affected. Most of the larger carnivores have been hunted or trapped out of the region. Beaver and muskrat populations have been depleted due to environmental damage as well as trapping. However, other species, such as the collared peccary and armadillo, have moved in from the south over the last hundred years.

The construction of the Amistad Reservoir in 1968 —backing water some eighty miles up the Rio Grande, twenty miles up the Pecos River, and thirty miles up the Devils River—has obviously affected the surrounding landscape and its flora and fauna. Many of the lower canyons are now permanently flooded, providing new environments for some species and eliminating habitats for others. This construction has also had both positive and negative effects for archaeologists. The major effort made to retrieve archaeological remains from areas threatened by the reservoir resulted in important advances in our understanding of the human cultures of the area. But many potential sites must have been flooded and lost forever to science. ■

Stream erosion and weathering created the overhangs and sheltered recesses used as homesites by the lower canyon people. (**ABOVE**) *View of Fate Bell Shelter, a rich archaeological site.*

POLLEN
Nature's Tiny Capsules of Information

by Vaughn M. Bryant, Jr.
TEXAS A & M UNIVERSITY

Most people think of pollen as the tiny specks of yellow dust that cause hay fever, yet that is only one of the many routes that pollen grains can take after they are released. Some pollen grains reach their intended goal, complete fertilization, and produce next year's crop of seeds. Other pollen grains are the main food source for some insects and animals. All of the rest of the pollen either falls to the ground and becomes buried in the soil or floats away in streams and rivers and eventually becomes part of lake or ocean sediments.

Today a small group of scientists, called *palynologists*, devote their careers to unlocking the secrets left behind by pollen grains. Most palynologists are trained as geologists, work for the petroleum industry, and are directly involved in the search for oil, gas, and coal resources. Fossil pollen studies are important to those industries, since the many different types of pollen and spores are used to identify the stratigraphic zones in oil and gas wells and to trace coal seams in mines. Some petroleum palynologists are also involved in basic research focused on using the fossil pollen record to predict where oil and gas deposits might exist. Other palynologists have their basic training in

botany and spend most of their careers using the fossil pollen record to reconstruct past vegetations and to speculate on how and why ancient vegetations may have changed. When possible, they also use the fossil pollen record to determine what types of climatic cycles led to vegetational changes. Finally, there is an even smaller group of palynologists trained in archaeology who use the fossil pollen record to determine prehistoric diets, understand the function of certain types of artifacts, calculate seasonality or site occupation, and determine a variety of cultural traits and rituals involving the use of pollen.

Unlike geology and botany, which represent the parent disciplines from which the field of palynology evolved, the application of fossil pollen research to the field of archaeology is fairly recent. Within the last several decades, archaeologists have found that fossil pollen trapped in the floor surfaces of pueblo sites offers clues to whether those rooms were used for ceremonies, food preparation, living quarters, or the storage of food. In a similar manner, fossil pollen trapped in the cracks and crevices of rock surfaces used for grinding seeds often reveals the kinds of seeds that were ground into flour. Samples of dirt containing pol-

len from the soils underneath or directly on top of buried skeletons suggest that ancient cultures often used flowers and/or pollen as part of their burial ceremony. Pollen recovered from the inside bottom portion of ancient pottery vessels and from between the weave of prehistoric baskets tells us what kinds of plant foods were carried or stored in those containers. In some cases, fossil pollen has even been recovered from the cutting surfaces of flint knives and has provided an indication of the kinds of plants that may have been cut by those stone tools. Finally, fossil pollen recovered from coprolites (preserved feces) of past cultures has given us some of the best clues about ancient cooking habits and diets.

Geologists, ecologists, and archaeologists are able to use fossil pollen to help them answer questions about the past because pollen grains are among the most durable plant materials that exist. The outer walls of pollen (produced by flowering plants) and spores (produced by nonflowering plants) contain a long-lasting compound called *sporopollenin* whose chemical structure has only recently been decoded. So durable is this material that it has remained unaltered in fossil spores preserved in rocks dated as being over 2.2 bil-

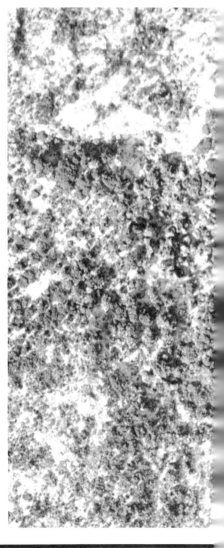

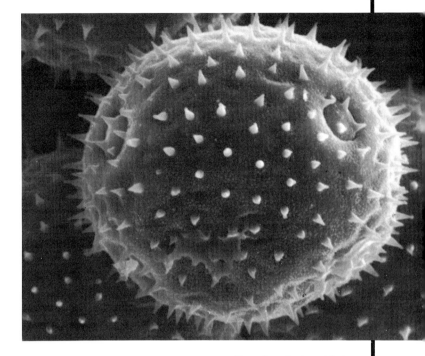

Scanning electron photograph of Cucurbita foetidis-sima—*buffalo gourd (1,600x).*

lion years old. Those spores offer us one of the oldest records of life on earth. The durability of pollen walls also prevents the destruction of fossil pollen in the laboratory when palynologists use caustic chemicals such as hydrochloric, hydrofluoric, sulfuric, and nitric acid to separate the pollen grains from their matrix of soil, rock, or sand. Once separated and concentrated, the fossil pollen can be examined, identified, and analyzed using various kinds of microscopic techniques.

In the field of archaeology, one of the primary uses for fossil pollen research is to determine the paleoenvironment in which prehistoric people lived. This aspect of archaeology is important, since it helps determine the range of natural limitations that could have restricted diets and migration and influenced cultural changes. In addition, that type of paleoenvironmental information also helps answer questions about how artifacts recovered from the prehistoric sites may have been used.

Fossil pollen analysis can help us reconstruct past environmental conditions because of our knowledge of a number of aspects of pollen and how it is released into the atmosphere. We know, for example, that many plants produce great quan-

tities of pollen or spores, which are dispersed and carried by wind or water currents or are transported by various types of insects and animals. Wind pollination is a chancy process; it is therefore not unusual for some wind-pollinated plants to produce several billion pollen grains each season. The enormity of pollen production capacity among some plants is exemplified by the conifer forests of middle and southern Sweden, which are estimated to produce more than 75,000 tons of airborne pollen annually.

Plants that rely upon insects or animals (such as bats or hummingbirds) to carry their pollen produce far fewer pollen grains—no more than several thousand per flower—since insect pollination is much more precise than wind pollination. In addition, since those pollen grains are designed for insect travel, they are generally covered with sticky oils that hold them tightly to the flower anther until they become attached to some insect. Thus, few of these insect-carried pollen grains are ever released on wind currents; they are, therefore, less likely to fall to the ground to become part of the fossil record.

Ecologists have long noted that most plants are restricted to certain habitats and are most abundant in regions that meet their optimum needs. Thus, we should expect to find the largest concentrations of certain types of windborne pollen in the regions where the plants they represent are the most abundant. In general, that concept is valid and is used by palynologists once certain other aspects are recognized and their effects are calculated. Different plant species generally produce different amounts of pollen. For example, we know that some wind-pollinated plants, such as pines, produce more pollen grains per tree than do the oaks. Therefore, if a forest contained equal amounts of pine and oak trees, that equality would not be reflected in the amount of pollen one would find in the soils of that forest. Another complicating factor is that certain pollen types tend to fall rapidly to the ground, while others are light and are often carried for great distances. Spruce and fir pollens are large and heavy and generally fall to the ground within a few miles of the tree that dispersed them. Pines, on the other hand, produce small, light pollen grains that sometimes travel for thousands of miles. That is why studies of ice deposits in the Arctic often contain a few pine pollen grains, even though the nearest pine trees may be a thousand miles away.

Experiments that compare the vegetational composition of a region with the percentage of pollen that falls to the ground have shown that pollen is a useful tool for reconstructing the past vegetational conditions and provides a reasonably accurate image of the regional, wind-pollinated vegetation within a radius of approximately thirty miles. Again, however, there are a number of variables that must be considered before one is able to determine the actual past vegetational composition of a region based upon the fossil pollen record. In an area such as a desert or a tundra, where there are few plants and where many of them are insect-pollinated, much of the airborne pollen that is deposited comes from sources that may be hundreds of miles away. This type of phenomenon can be recognized by conducting a test for pollen concentration. In other words, knowing approximately how many fossil pollen grains occur in each cubic centimeter of soil, one can determine, in general terms, the type of vegetation that probably existed in the past. For example, a forest with many wind-pollinated tree species generally produces high volumes of pollen per cubic centimeter of soil. In some cases, these concentrations may number in the hundreds of

thousands of fossil grains per cubic unit. In a grassland, the concentration of pollen tends to be much lower; and in desert or tundra soils, the concentrations may not exceed more than a few thousand pollen grains per cubic unit of soil.

Finally, one of the essential reasons that palynologists are able to use fossil pollen to reconstruct past vegetations is that each plant species produces a distinct type of pollen. In other words, we know that the morphological characteristics of a pollen grain from a particular plant species (i.e., live oak, loblolly pine, cattail, century plant) are always identical, regardless of where the plant grows. Likewise, the pollen grains from other plant types are different, so that no two species of plants have identical pollen types. This last aspect is critical to the whole field of fossil pollen studies, since without it the palynologist would not be able to identify the plants represented by the pollen in the fossil record.

By this point, some readers might be wondering how a palynologist is able to sort through all the variables in order to arrive at a logical reconstruction of past vegetational conditions. In some cases, it is easy; but in others, there are so many variables that it becomes a complex and difficult task. In those instances, the palynologist often must turn to other types of available evidence to help recognize all of the potential variables. For example, in trying to reconstruct the past vegetations for the Lower Pecos region, it has been necessary to rely upon available botanical, geological, and paleontological evidence in order to interpret the fossil pollen findings.

The fossil pollen record from locales in the Lower Pecos region has provided us with many clues about the paleoenvironment and ancient cultures of that area. The oldest pollen records from the Lower Pecos region come from deposits in Bonfire Shelter, located near Langtry, Texas. In the lowermost sediments of that site there are thick layers of limestone spalls that geologists believe came from the walls and roof of that rockshelter. Those deposits are not dated, but many believe that they originated around 20,000 B.C., when continental glaciers still covered most of Canada and parts of the northern United States. When the spall zones formed, the Lower Pecos region's summers averaged at least 5° C cooler, and colder winters froze water that seeped into the cracks of limestone shelters, resulting in spalling. The fossil pollen trapped in the spall zones at Bonfire Shelter consists mainly of pinyon pine pollen

and lesser amounts of oak and grass pollen. This information suggests that around 20,000 B.C. the Lower Pecos region probably contained a mosaic vegetation consisting of pinyon and scrub oak woodlands in the protected canyons and north-facing slopes. During that same period, the upland regions probably consisted of scrub grasslands containing isolated stands of pinyons, oaks, and junipers.

Lower Pecos deposits dating from the later part of the Paleo-Indian era (ca. 11,000–9,000 years ago) contain faunal remains of large extinct animals such as horse, giant bison, and camel, and the earliest cultural remains in that region. The available fossil pollen records from that period indicate that the region was undergoing a subtle change in vegetation. The evidence suggests that the scrub grasslands in the upland areas were expanding and that the wooded areas were thinning, both probably caused by a warmer and drier climate. It was also during this period, around 10,500 years ago, that ancient hunters stampeded herds of giant bison over cliffs at Bonfire Shelter. Why Paleo-Indian groups did not use that hunting technique any earlier in the Lower Pecos region is unknown, but it is likely that, prior to 10,500 years ago, the

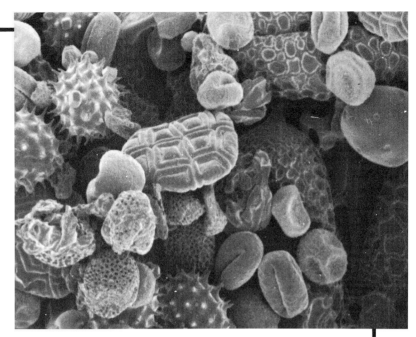

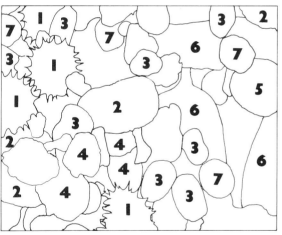

Scanning electron photographs of pollen types often found in deposits of the Lower Pecos region of Texas *(875x).* **KEY TO PHOTOGRAPH:** *(1), Helianthus annuus—***common sunflower;** *(2), Acacia berlandieri—***guajillo;** *(3), Quercus virginiana—***live oak;** *(4), Brassica hirta—***white mustard;** *(5), Juglans microcarpa—***Texas little walnut;** *(6), Agave lechuguilla—***lechuguilla;** *(7), Juniperus ashei—***Ashe juniper.**

amount of scrub grasslands in the Lower Pecos region was not sufficient to attract bison herds. Until then, these beasts probably roamed mainly to the north, where there were ample grasslands.

During the last 10,000 years, the vegetation in the Lower Pecos region gradually changed from plant types that preferred cool and moist conditions to types that were able to survive in hot and dry, desertlike conditions. To the generations of people who lived through this long time span, the changes in vegetation and climate would not have been apparent, since both were very gradual. However, when we look back over the whole period, we can see the results of the changes that must have occurred. For example, during the first 3,000 years of that period (10,500–7,000 years ago), the Lower Pecos region began to support many plants that tend to grow best in warm and dry regions. We suspect that many of those desertlike plants (such as cacti, yucca, agave, and sotol) migrated into the region from warmer areas to the south. Evidence for the early arrival of these desertlike plants is not well documented in the fossil pollen record, since those plants are insect-pollinated and thus their pollen is rarely found in sediments. However, leaves, fruits, and

seed remains of these plants found in archaeological deposits and human coprolites dating from this period confirm that these plants not only were present, but were also becoming important food items.

The period 7,000–4,000 years ago in the Lower Pecos region marked a time when the vegetation continued to become more desertlike, and we suspect that the climate was continuing to get warmer and drier. The fossil pollen record for this period shows increases in grass pollen and decreases in pollen from various types of trees, suggesting that a drier climate was favoring the expansion of grassland regions. In addition, coprolites and soils from archaeological sites that date from this period contain high percentages of pollen from desertlike plants, such as sotol, agave, and cactus, indicating that those plants were being heavily exploited for food. Also, the coprolites from this period show that the people were depending more heavily upon meat protein from small animals such as mice, woodrats, and lizards instead of the deer and rabbits that had been more important food sources earlier. This shift may reflect a sudden scarcity of deer and rabbits caused by a loss of scrubby habitats attractive to those animals.

One of the most interesting aspects of the end of this period was a series of severe floods preserved in the sedimentary record of archaeological sites located along the Rio Grande and Pecos River. Evidence records twenty-two major floods along those rivers during the last 4,500 years, with one-half of them occurring between 4,500 and 3,200 years ago. What caused those severe floods is not fully known, but we can use the available geologic and pollen records to speculate on some probable causes. One possible explanation is that rises in summer temperatures or periods of drought led to a denuding of the upland vegetation, causing rapid runoff during rains and higher levels of river discharge. Another possibility is that changes in existing wind patterns may have brought new types of frontal systems into the Lower Pecos region that were heavily laden with moisture from the Gulf of Mexico or Gulf of California. The resulting rainfall from such systems could have filled streams that were normally dry and caused major erosional activity along both the Rio Grande and Pecos River systems. Regardless of the cause of the increased flooding, these events were catastrophic as far as the people of the region were concerned and may have led to new cultural practices to cope with their unpredictable nature.

Perhaps the most significant information provided by the fossil pollen record in the Lower Pecos region is about climatic events occurring around 2,500 years ago. The archaeological record from numerous Lower Pecos sites suggests that bison were not exploited as a food source between 10,500 and 2,500 years ago. Then, during one brief period around 2,500 years ago, a significant number of bison were stampeded over a cliff above Bonfire Shelter. This happened on at least three separate occasions that may have spanned a period of several hundred years.

Archaeologists could not find a reason for the sudden exploitation of bison from the available artifacts and had difficulty trying to understand why bison were not hunted either before or after. However, the fossil pollen record showed that around 2,500 years ago the climate suddenly favored cooler-adapted plants such as pinyon pines and that the area covered by grasslands in the Lower Pecos region had also increased. Other fossil pollen evidence from regions north of the Lower Pecos suggests that the brief climatic cooling was widespread around 2,500 years ago. If that as-

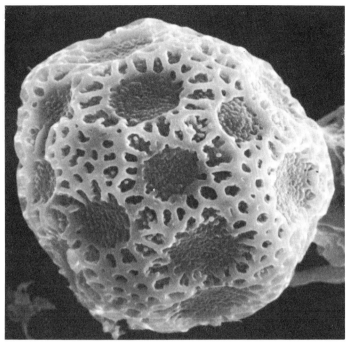

Scanning electron photograph of Opuntia lindheimeri—*nopal prickly pear (1,800x).*

sumption is correct, then perhaps heavier than usual snowfalls in the grassland areas immediately north of the Lower Pecos region may have forced bison herds unusually far south in search of winter feeding grounds. Once in the Lower Pecos region, the bison could have been exploited by peoples living there or, more probably, were killed by skilled bison hunters from the north who had followed the herds. In either case, it was the fossil pollen record that provided the clues as to why the bison briefly visited the Lower Pecos region at that time.

Soon after the brief cool period came to a halt, the Lower Pecos vegetation again favored those plants that were best adapted to living in a semiarid environment. The pollen record of those last 2,500 years shows a continuation of the previous 10,000-year trend toward warmer and drier desertlike environments.

It is apparent that pollen studies have become one of the techniques archaeologists in the Lower Pecos region can use to interpret the events of the past that influenced and shaped ancient cultures. Like most other disciplines, palynology alone certainly does not provide all of the answers, but it must be apparent that pollen serves more purposes than merely creating headaches for thousands of modern hay fever sufferers. ■

CHAPTER THREE

NINE THOUSAND YEARS OF OCCUPATION
The Cultural Sequence

When did the first human groups enter the lower canyon region? This is a question not easily answered, since the record of their appearance is obscured by both the effects of time and the litter of many subsequent generations. In an effort to answer the question of when the lower canyons were first visited, it is necessary to trace the appearance of the first human groups in the New World.

Peopling of the New World

Archaeologists generally agree that the first migrants into the New World entered via the land mass between Alaska and Siberia called the Bering land bridge. This passageway existed during glacial times when the sea levels were lowered. With the rise of the sea following the melting of the glacial ice, the Bering land bridge, like the continental shelf, came to lie as it does today beneath the shallow waters of the Bering Sea. This cycle was repeated throughout the Pleistocene.

There are essentially three schools of thought on when the first migrants came into the New World. One contends that the first humans came over more than 30,000 years ago (i.e., before the last, or Wisconsin, glaciation), citing several localities in North and South America where claims—all of them, however, highly disputable—have been made for excessively ancient finds. Other scholars take a more moderate view, suggesting several different periods when migrant groups could have entered into the New World

during the glacial period between 30,000 and 12,000 years ago. The third school contends that the oldest acceptable and demonstrable evidence of occupation of the New World is no older than about 12,000 years, during the waning stage of the Wisconsin glaciation. This last approach is the one taken here.

However, it is reasonable to assume that several separate migrations of small nomadic groups could have penetrated deeply into the North American continent well before but left no concrete trace of their existence. Some of these groups may not have survived; others may have established a fairly settled hunter-gatherer way of life; still others may have pursued a nomadic existence based on the movements of large game animals similar to their Old World predecessors. Descendants of the last group would later become identified as the first big game hunters in the New World.

Late Pleistocene Mammoth Hunters

The repeated association of human artifacts with now extinct animals occurs about 11,300 years ago. These finds follow a similar pattern and stand as the first clear example of an established way of life for the New World that spread across most of the continent. The animals hunted were mostly mammoths (close relatives of living elephants) and bison. The last small herds of native camels and horses may also have fallen prey to the ancient hunters. From careful recent studies, we now know, too, that many of the smaller animals along with plant foods were essential components of the big game hunters' diets.

Archaeologists refer to this first recognizable an-

(PRECEDING SPREAD) *Outdoor campscene. In the foreground, two women cut and gather sotol. Toward the rear, children and old people bring firewood to the lodges.*

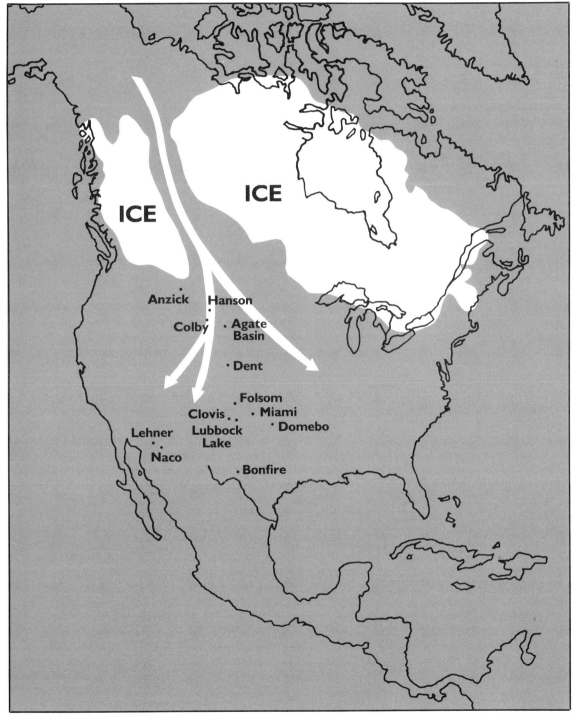

Melting of the glacial ice about 12,000 years ago opened a corridor into previously uninhabited North America. Clovis hunters spread quickly to hunt the last of the Pleistocene big game and to populate much of the continent within a thousand years.

cient culture or way of life in the New World as the *Llano* (after the Llano Estacado) or *Clovis* (after Clovis, New Mexico, where the first finds were made in the 1930s). We do not know much about the Clovis people and their way of life. What is known, however, is sufficiently distinctive to stimulate the imagination of even the stuffiest archaeologist. The stone implements of the Clovis hunters have been found with the bones of Jefferson's mammoth, the largest land animal in North America during the last Ice Age. These finds have been made in the southern High Plains east of the Rocky Mountains and in the American Southwest.

How does a group of hunters armed only with spears and rocks kill a huge mammoth? The mystery is magnified when the bones of several mammoths are found at one place, suggesting that not one animal but a small herd was killed at one time! How many hunters were involved? We know surprisingly little about these hunters other than that they made distinctive stone tools and also shaped mammoth bones to their needs. We do not know, for example, if they took up mammoth hunting and began to chip their distinctive stone points after arriving in the New World or if the mammoths were perhaps the reason they came in the first place. It is possible that mammoths became extinct or rare earlier in the Old World than in the New and that diminishing supplies forced the hunters to seek new lands. We know that Old World woolly mammoths were extensively hunted in what is now western Russia and Czechoslovakia near the end of the Pleistocene.

The hallmark of the Llano or Clovis culture is the distinctive stone projectile point that was used to tip the spears. In silhouette it resembles the shape of a rowboat; it was chipped on both sides and had a distinctive flute, called a *channel flake*, removed from the base down the center of the blade for about one-third of its length. The scars that resulted from the channel flake removals are called *flutes*, and the term *fluted point* is used to describe this Clovis artifact.

The distinctive chipped stone spear points of the Clovis hunter have no antecedent in America. However, the chipping technique of removing the channel flakes does have an Old World analog. The similarity lies with the so-called core-flake or Levallois technique: a core of flint or chert was shaped and trimmed by removing flakes—usually from both sides, creating a biface—with some type of hammer. Then a flake of a desired form and thickness was removed by striking a prepared platform at one end of the core. This flake became a ready-made tool requiring little if any additional chipping. The Clovis point can be compared to the Levallois core, since it is essentially a triangular biface fashioned with a thick cross-section whose final form was achieved by removing a channel flake on each side.

Another element in the Clovis stone technology common to late Pleistocene big game cultures in the Old World is a technique whereby long, parallel-sided flakes are produced. The term *blade* is used to refer to

these specially made tool blanks created by striking long parallel-sided flakes from a core or mass that, as in the Levallois technique, was preshaped. Usually several blades were struck from a single core. Blades make highly efficient knives in that they offer a maximum amount of cutting edge with a minimum amount of mass. The blades can also be converted into several other tools, including scrapers and borers.

Like the fluted points, the blades have no antecedent in the New World prior to about 11,500 years ago. Since the Clovis people had a sophisticated stone technology, aspects of which do have Old World counterparts, many archaeologists believe that the Llano/Clovis culture represents a movement of people from eastern Asia into the game-rich, unglaciated parts of North America about 11,500 years ago. A find at the Anzick site in Wyoming is particularly significant: Clovis points and bifaces of exceptionally colorful stone were found in the burial of two children; in addition, a red mineral pigment was sprinkled over the bodies. Such findings of artifacts and red pigment are similar to Paleolithic burials from Siberia.

*Hunters of mammoths and giant bison fashioned the distinctive Clovis projectile points (**LEFT**). A particular characteristic of these points is the long flake removed from the base, creating a **flute** down the middle portion of the blade. The fluting was presumably done as an aid in hafting. Born out of the original Clovis populations, Folsom hunters continued to fashion a smaller version of the fluted point (**CENTER**) to hunt a now extinct form of bison and other big game. Fluting was not essential to kill large game. The Plainview hunters effectively killed big animals using an unfluted point (**RIGHT**).*

Coexisting with the last of the big game hunters of the southern Plains were people in Texas who lived more by hunting and gathering. Their characteristic points mark where people went and where they camped. Shown above are four such points representing three styles: Scottsbluff, Meserve, and the Texas version of the Angostura point.

Numerous finds from about 11,000 years ago in and near the southern High Plains made it likely that early Indian groups were present in the general lower canyon region soon after that time. These were the waning days of the soon-to-be-extinct native mammoths, horses, and camels of the late Pleistocene. Best-known, perhaps, is Blackwater Draw, just across the Texas border in New Mexico. This important site was located along marshy springs and ponds of the ancient Brazos River. The water and vegetation had attracted big game for centuries, along with animal and human predators. Clovis people hunted and camped here, as did the other big game hunters that followed.

Were the first visitors to the Lower Pecos canyons Clovis people? We have reason to believe that they were, although no actual Clovis sites marked by the distinctive spear points have been found. A deposit of camel, horse, and mammoth bones was found in Bonfire Shelter, a site used by post-Clovis big game hunters for mass kills. Datable charcoal was found with the bones, but no stone tools were recovered. The ex-

cavator, David Dibble, did find several stream-worn cobbles among the bones and speculated that these may have been brought in by human predators or scavengers.

Chance surface finds of Clovis points have been made north and east of the lower canyons. One mammoth kill site, Miami, is located about 400 miles north of the mouth of the Pecos River. Three Clovis projectile points and a flake knife were found among mammoth bones recovered from an adjacent area. We have proof, then, that Clovis hunters were in the general region. It is more than likely that they ventured into the canyons as opportunity presented itself. With luck, perhaps someday archaeologists will find one of their campsites.

What happened to the Clovis people? Their association with mammoth bones is clear. When the mammoth became extinct, where did the Clovis people go? Chances are that they stayed right where they were and simply changed to hunting the kinds of game still available. However, what we call the Clovis culture disappeared. The change is recognizable in the archaeological record, where a new pattern emerges. Extinct species of bison became the major big game, and a slightly different spear point style serves as the diagnostic marker of this succeeding culture. The new pattern is given the name *Folsom*, after the chance find by a black cowboy near Folsom, New Mexico, in 1926 that provided the first conclusive evidence of human artifacts with extinct animal bones in the New World.

Ancient Bison Hunters of the Southern Plains

While some of the large animals such as the mammoth, horse, and camel died out at the end of the Pleistocene, the people who hunted the diminishing herds did not. They continued their nomadic way of life in pursuit of the one large animal, the bison, that managed to survive the rigors of the changing glacial environment to propagate into huge herds that blackened the landscape. The successful adjustment to changing environmental conditions guaranteed the survival of the ancient hunters and set the stage for a population explosion that filled many of the major environmental niches in the New World within 3,000 to 4,000 years. The bison represented a major food and material reserve for the human groups that shared the plains and prairies with them. These animals also provided an important minor source of food and hides for those who lived in the periphery of their range. There may have been problems locating a steady supply of animals; but once they were found, the hunting technology was both efficient and deadly.

Regrettably, we know as little about the Folsom way of life as we do about the Clovis, except for the constant pattern of chipped stone artifacts that appears at each site. The characteristic Folsom point, like the Clovis from which it most assuredly is derived, is usually fluted on both sides, although not all points found in Folsom layers are fluted. The variation in Folsom specimens is as great as with the thicker and usually longer Clovis. Although there is some size overlap between the two, many Folsom points stand out as uniquely refined elaborations of chipped stone art. The channels usually extend the entire length of the points, with the edges delicately crafted to a remarkably even angle and outline. Moreover, there appears to have been a deliberate selection of colorful raw material for many (although not all) Folsom points. (This has also been noted to a lesser extent for Clovis points.) Many of the Folsom points are reworked, which probably accounts for the wide range in size. Reworking was necessary since sources of stone were often far away.

Folsom points are recovered from both campsite locations and kill sites in direct association with bison remains. Because the points occur in different kinds of sites, much has been learned about how they were made and how and why many were broken during the course of manufacture. Folsom campsites such as the Lindenmeier Site in Colorado and Adair-Steadman near Abilene, Texas, and kill sites like Blackwater Draw, Lake Theo, Lubbock Lake, Bonfire Shelter, and the Folsom type site in northeastern New Mexico provide the basic information about these nomadic peoples. We know that they followed the extinct long-horned bison at least during certain seasons of the year. The geographic range of Folsom sites may be less than that of Clovis materials, which are found not only with mammoth remains in the southern Plains and the Southwest, but also in numerous locations in the eastern portion of the United States. Folsom sites extend as far north as Wyoming and possibly into southern Canada, but they are confined to the known geographic range of the extinct bison.

The importance of the long-horned bison to their way of life is also underscored by their other stone tools, such as small end scrapers (most likely attached to wooden handles) and oval flake knives (identical to those seen in the Clovis materials) that were resharpened by removing a series of flakes from one edge along one side. These oval flake knives, often mistakenly referred to as "side scrapers," bear a remarkable resemblance to the ulu knives used by Eskimo women in ancient and recent Arctic households.

The ulu is an all-purpose knife, but is especially useful in processing the carcasses and hides of whales, walruses, seals, and caribou. That is not to suggest that Folsom people were Eskimos or hunters of marine mammals—rather, the Clovis/Folsom tool kit, like the Eskimo's, was adapted for use on large game animals and was derived from Old World counterparts.

Another Folsom tool characteristic is a small point chipped on the corner of a flake or scraping tool. Although these are usually called "gravers," their function is unknown, as are the processes that formed them. We do not know if they were deliberately shaped or were accidentally formed by the way the flake tool was used.

What types of weapons did the Folsom people use to kill the large bison? Probably their most effective weapon was knowledge about how the animals herded and reacted when frightened. We can be sure that the

Folsom hunters had come to know their prey well and knew where they would be located at given times. This was as crucial to their way of life as the handmade weapons that they carried. The large numbers of animals killed in drives and traps at one time suggests cooperative hunting by a number of individuals, taking advantage of such factors as wind direction, topography of a specific locality, and the bison's habit of following blindly behind a leader. A carefully planned kill included coaxing the bison into a situation where the desired number were cut from the herd and driven into a trap or over a bluff. Wounded animals were slaughtered using rocks or spears thrown with a throwing stick (atlatl).

Were these stout, stocky people similar to the Paleolithic hunters of the Old World idealized by artists? We suspect that they were a relatively small people overall, although only one possible example of a Folsom burial is known. This is the gracile skeleton of a young woman found in the sand dunes near Midland. The geological level of the bones is the same as for the site's Folsom point specimens. The burial was badly disturbed by the shifting sands; consequently, nothing is known about how she was buried and what, if anything, was buried with her.

Neither the Clovis nor the Folsom people left a record of art in the form of carvings or paintings. This is unusual, in that big game hunters in other parts of the world such as those who once lived in western Europe, Africa, and the Arctic left remarkable records of representational images of the animals that they hunted. The skill displayed in the manufacture of many of the delicate Folsom points, however, leads us to speculate about some of the nonmaterial aspects of their way of life. Why did they go to so much trouble to make a small projectile point that involved so many highly complex steps? A simple pointed flake or chipped point would seemingly have sufficed for practical purposes. People who are familiar with the technique of stone tool manufacture marvel at the technique and deliberate care of many of the Folsom stone workers. Perhaps there is a parallel between the Folsom hunters and the Eskimo big game hunters using similar types of weapons. The Eskimo took great care in manufacturing and elaborating the weapons that would be used to kill their prey. After all, the animal was going to die so that they could live. There was a concern with the animal's spirit; when it was killed, a void was left in the universe, and they feared that something evil would take its place. There-fore, by showing reverence to the animal through prayer and the elaboration of weapons used to kill it, forces over which they had little or no control might be appeased. Perhaps the Folsom flintknapper was prompted by similar motives.

Quantitative estimates have been made by archaeologists of Folsom social groups, based on the size, frequency, and density of campsites in the southern High Plains and in the basins south of the southern Rocky Mountains. The groups were probably composed of family units and single individuals numbering from about 25 to 150 people. Such groups are called *bands*, implying the lack of any rigid political structure and organization. Band membership is generally fluid, in that families or individuals are not tied to a specific group and can break away and join other related bands as they wish. Cooperative activities, such as those that would be called for in carrying out a large bison kill or communal gathering, required food sharing. Family members' responsibilities were to their immediate kin, but mutual sharing among all members of the band was essential.

Our information on the Folsom way of life is biased toward materials associated with hunting; we have not found or recognized any perishable remains attributed to this culture. Most known Folsom campsites occur either on the periphery of the southern High Plains or in the basins of Colorado and New Mexico, where a variety of plants as well as animal resources would have been available to them. However, we know virtually nothing about what kinds of plants they gathered, how the plants were prepared, and what they were used for.

In the lower canyon area, Folsom hunters took advantage of a natural trap in Mile Canyon near Langtry to slaughter dozens of bison in one single kill. This event took place about 10,500 years ago at Bonfire Shelter, where bison were stampeded into a blind cleft that emptied onto the floor of the huge rockshelter below. The wounded and dying animals were killed and butchered in the shelter. Archaeologists have excavated a portion of this site and found partly articulated bison skeletons along with the bones of butchered carcasses and a few Folsom stone tools, including a Folsom point.

The same location was used shortly thereafter to carry out two additional and almost identical bison kills. It is estimated that in all about 120 animals were killed in the three episodes. The only observable difference between the three kills is that the latter two were made by hunters who used a very similar point form except that it was not fluted. Whether these people were descendants of Folsom people or were hunters who lived at the same time is not known. At Blackwater Draw, for example, where there is a similar sequence of big game hunting finds, the unfluted points occur stratigraphically above the Folsom horizon and hence are generally regarded as being more recent. One other locality in the lower canyons has yielded traces of the Folsom people; this is a small Pleistocene terrace in Dead Man's Canyon, where the wife of a local rancher discovered a Folsom point.

We have been identifying Folsom and Clovis sites and localities mainly on the basis of the presence of characteristic points. Can we identify a particular tribe or linguistic group based on a projectile point style such as Folsom? A particular artifact style such as a projectile point is not a reliable criterion for this purpose. Certain aspects of technology—such as the manner of hafting, which may govern the shape of a point— frequently transcend group or language differences. Similarities in technology are often conditioned by similar use rather than by social or ethnic affiliation. Despite the many different language groups among the Indians who lived in the Great Plains region in the nineteenth century, there was a remarkable similarity in the tools that they used to hunt bison and process the carcasses.

When we speak of the Clovis or Folsom culture, then, we are addressing the material similarities that are recovered in the archaeological record. Fluted points occur over much of the North American continent after 11,000 years ago; surely these are not all part of the same tribe or language group. Furthermore, a shift in technology does not necessarily mean that a new group of people has moved into a particular region. People do change the way they customarily do things under certain conditions. The elimination of the mammoth, for example, made it necessary for the Clovis people to make an adjustment in their way of life. When the environment changes, so do the habits of the endemic people. They adapt by learning to exploit more efficiently the plants and animals that remain.

The Folsom people lose their identity in archaeology when they cease to make the telltale fluted point, but that is not to say that they did not continue as a breeding population. Other people who hunted the now extinct longer-horned bison (*Bison bison antiquus*) may have coexisted with the Folsom groups. Also, vir-

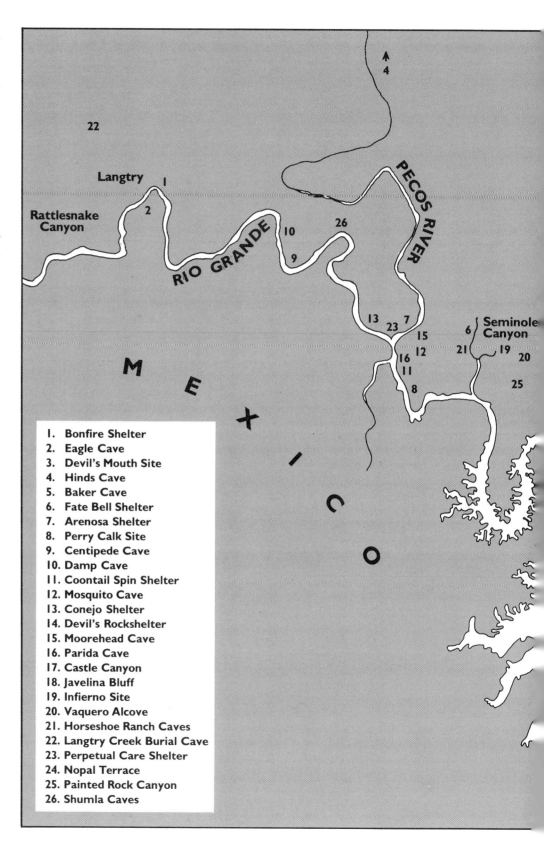

1. Bonfire Shelter
2. Eagle Cave
3. Devil's Mouth Site
4. Hinds Cave
5. Baker Cave
6. Fate Bell Shelter
7. Arenosa Shelter
8. Perry Calk Site
9. Centipede Cave
10. Damp Cave
11. Coontail Spin Shelter
12. Mosquito Cave
13. Conejo Shelter
14. Devil's Rockshelter
15. Moorehead Cave
16. Parida Cave
17. Castle Canyon
18. Javelina Bluff
19. Infierno Site
20. Vaquero Alcove
21. Horseshoe Ranch Caves
22. Langtry Creek Burial Cave
23. Perpetual Care Shelter
24. Nopal Terrace
25. Painted Rock Canyon
26. Shumla Caves

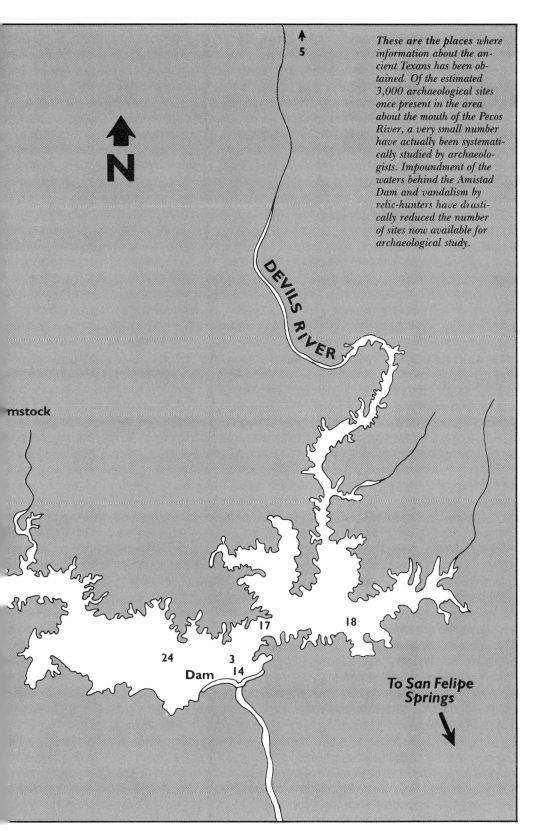

N

DEVILS RIVER

mstock

5

24
Dam

17

3
14

18

To San Felipe
Springs

These are the places where information about the ancient Texans has been obtained. Of the estimated 3,000 archaeological sites once present in the area about the mouth of the Pecos River, a very small number have actually been systematically studied by archaeologists. Impoundment of the waters behind the Amistad Dam and vandalism by relic-hunters have drastically reduced the number of sites now available for archaeological study.

tually identical ways of life are suggested for the bison hunters who used the unfluted, lanceolate point forms recognized by archaeologists by such names as *Plainview*, *Midland*, and *Firstview*, among others. We can be fairly certain that some of these were Folsom descendants who continued to hunt the bison on the High Plains until 9,500 to 9,000 years ago. Other groups were settling into well-watered river valleys in central and southwest Texas. Perhaps these, too, were descendants of the Folsom people who continued to make occasional hunting forays onto the Plains while spending most of the year gathering and foraging in the lush valleys. The shift in their way of life was probably brought about in part by the warming and drying conditions that led to the formation of the vast grasslands of the Great Plains and provided an ideal habitat for the American buffalo. Although we do not know the range or the population density of the longer-horned bison during the period immediately following the Folsom, finds in the northern Plains in dicate that, as the glaciers receded, this bison's range was extended northward. Southern Plains groups who had extensively hunted bison were presented with two choices: either to move with their game animal or to adjust to the changing conditions. These choices were conditioned by the given territorial range of each population and how each had come to utilize local plant and other animal resources. To be sure, bones of the extinct bison disappear from archaeological sites for a long period after 10,500 years ago. Either the bison's range edged northward away from the southern High Plains periphery, or the hunters made seasonal treks to where the bison were, leaving little evidence of this activity in their campsites along the river valleys. The result was that between 9,500 and 9,000 years ago, a shift from hunting highly mobile herds of big game to gathering locally among abundant plant and animal resources occurred among some of the people living on the edges of the southern Plains. The first hunters and gatherers who ventured into the lower canyons to stay and live off the land were in all likelihood descendants of the very people who had hunted the bison a few generations earlier.

Settling into the Lower Canyons

Sometime between 9,500 and 9,000 years ago, the first hunting and gathering groups to claim the lower canyons as their territorial domain appear in the archaeological record. These people, like those that fol-

*Golondrina Complex.
Hunting, cutting, and chopping tools provide clues as
to how the people of the Golondrina Complex lived.
Projectile point shapes reflect
a development from the earlier Clovis and Folsom traditions. The edge-sharpened
flake knife indicates a shift
to plant collecting, particularly desert succulents such
as prickly pear, sotol, and
lechuguilla. The triangular
tool was an adze for shaping
wood and other mundane
uses.*

lowed for the next 8,000 years, selected rockshelter locations, such as Baker Cave and Hinds Cave, that provided ample space and protection from the winds, sun, and rain for living quarters. Outdoor locations on stream banks, like those available at the mouth of the Devils River, that led easily to the river waters and to the uplands were also used from time to time as campsites. No big game remained by this time, not even bison. White-tail deer, which had survived the Pleistocene, were thinly scattered throughout the canyons and uplands, but attention had to be focused on really small game as a source of meat. Snakes and lizards, along with mice and snails, became important dietary items. Our best picture of what these people were eating comes from Baker Cave, where Thomas R. Hester found a large hearth that yielded an impressive list of small game that had apparently been captured and eaten by these early hunters and gatherers. Hester's term *Golondrina Complex* is used to designate this archaeological assemblage.

The first hunters and gatherers of the Golondrina Complex continued to use spears thrown with the atlatl and tipped with a lance-shaped chipped stone point. This point style is reminiscent of projectile heads used to hunt the extinct bison, but these points are not fluted and are generally not as well made. The largest game animals hunted in the lower canyons by the Golondrina Complex people were deer. Archaeologists use the names *Golondrina*, *Angostura*, *Plainview*-like, among others, in reference to these projectile points from early sites of this period in central and southwest Texas. Other stone artifacts include notched or grooved pebbles that may have been used in hunting certain kinds of game. These stones are thought to have been attached to thongs and used as bolas, which, when thrown, tangle or snag the prey's legs or wings, temporarily disabling it. Another common artifact is a triangular chipped stone tool with a wide scooplike beveled or tapered "bit" end. This particular tool is a basic adze or multipurpose chopping and cutting tool; it occurs in many different forms around the world. Other articles include flakes of chipped stone with one end rounded by knapping along one side of the flake. These are small hide scrapers.

The Golondrina Complex tool kit is one geared for gathering and for hunting small game. It is possible that these people also occasionally ventured several hundred miles north to hunt bison in the manner of their contemporaries at Blackwater Draw, Lubbock Lake, and other localities on the southern High Plains.

Some of the projectile point forms found in the early hunting and gathering sites of central and southwest Texas are almost indistinguishable from some of those found in the High Plains.

Among the stone tools used in gathering and food processing are oval cobbles abraded on one or both sides. These are often partially shaped by pecking, a technique whereby a stone is shaped by gradually chipping away little bits of rock with another stone. These artifacts are called *manos*, the Spanish word for "hand," meaning hand stones or grinding stones held in the hand. (Later in the archaeological record, manos were used with *metates*, or stationary grinding slabs.) The most common stone tool found in the early levels at the Devil's Mouth Site, where the largest collection of Golondrina Complex tools has been found, are oval flake implements sharpened along one edge by chipping tiny flakes from one side. These tools, similar to the ululike tools described for the big game hunters, were knives and not hide scrapers, as they are often described. The form of these tools and their use scars are identical to those found in younger layers at such sites as Hinds Cave, where the residue of the plants they were used to cut still adhered to the surfaces of the stone blade.

A chance find at Baker Cave yielded an incredible treasure of plant residue and small animal remains. This feature was a large hearth whose contents, carefully collected and meticulously examined, were found to include identifiable remains of twenty-four differ-

Devil's Mouth Site. This triangular plot of terrace at the confluence of the Devils River and Rio Grande was a popular prehistoric campsite for thousands of years. Repeated occupations were sequentially buried by overflow deposits from both rivers, giving archaeologists a historical sequence of buried campsite remains.

ent plants, portions of which had been collected and brought into this ancient household. Equally fascinating were the faunal remains, which included rabbits, rodents, reptiles, and fish but no game larger than the gray fox. This impressive list provides the best information available on the diet of these early hunters and gatherers.

No burials have been found for this period in the lower canyons, but two examples of burials have been discovered in central Texas. Both occurred at levels in the respective sites that represent what is essentially the beginning of the long hunting and gathering sequence in central Texas, which is in many ways quite similar to the sequence in the lower canyons. The most spectacular of these burials was at Horn Shelter, where a child and a man were placed beneath a rock overhang above the Brazos River near Waco. The man was buried with a necklace of canine teeth and shell beads, several turtle shells, and a kit for making chipped stone tools. The other find was that of a female burial at the Wilson-Leonard Site north of Austin. The only artifact found near her was a combination grinding tool and chopper.

The Horn Shelter burials, while lacking the red pigment noted at the possible Clovis burial at the Anzick Site in Wyoming, may have represented a continuation of ancient Paleolithic burial practices, particularly when the associated artifacts are taken into account. Unfortunately, these three examples do not give us a very good picture of what these people were like physically. Nor do they give us any good indication of their religious practices.

The first inhabitants who established a home territory in the lower canyons may have come from the more arid regions to the south, simply following the marginal desert environment as it slowly encroached northward following the recession of the glaciers. By 9,000 years ago, the marginal desert vegetation was already established along the Pecos drainage, as findings at Hinds Cave have shown; the Devils River drainage was less arid than that of the Pecos, much as it is today. The ancient people probably had brought with them established and sophisticated methods of processing plant fibers from certain yuccas and lechuguilla (a dwarf agave akin to the century plant), which marks the northern fringe of the Chihuahuan Desert today. These fibers were woven into a variety of textiles; some of the more complicated weaves occur at the very beginning of the hunting and gathering sequence.

Horn Shelter (**LEFT, ABOVE**). *Paleolithic rituals are preserved in the remains of this double burial of an adult male and a child in a rockshelter along the Brazos River near Waco, Texas. The find, dated about 10,100 years ago and representing one of the oldest human burials in the Americas, was made and meticulously documented by avocational archaeologists Frank Watt and Al Redder. Accompanying the male was a flint-knapper's tool kit, a necklace of shell and canine beads, bone implements, and turtle carapaces, probably used as rattles. Texas' most famous "first" women (**BELOW**) are "Midland Minnie," found in the sand dunes near Midland, and the "Leander Lady," shown here. The Leander discovery was made by archaeologists from the Texas Department of Highways and Public Transportation while testing an archaeological site near Austin. The "Leander Lady" had been carefully placed in a semiflexed position in a shallow pit dug from deposits that date in excess of 9,000 years.*

Textile technology had obviously been around for a long time, but simply did not survive in the archaeological record until the great rockshelters in the lower canyons were occupied in the early Holocene period. If the first populations came from the south, where did they learn their textile technology? This question becomes more complicated because we know that the cooler and wetter conditions two thousand years earlier did not favor desert plants. However, there are many plants other than desert species whose roots, barks, or stems can be beaten, pounded, stripped, and shredded to produce fiber. The source of the fiber is not the issue here, but rather the weaving technology. It is the latter that most likely had long traditional roots. Perhaps the technology came from the Paleolithic of eastern Asia and textile parallels in some of the drier caves of that region will be found. Woven fiber sandals and other textiles have been recorded from dry caves in the Cascades of the northwestern United States that date about 9,000 years ago. It would be far-fetched to think that the earliest migrants learned textile crafts after they arrived in the New World.

By 8,500 to 8,000 years ago, the ancient hunters and gatherers had clearly established themselves in the lower canyon country. They had successfully adapted to the area by scheduling their hunting, and especially their gathering, in accordance with seasonal fluctuations. The warm season began in late March with the first flowering of yucca and extended through most of October. It was during this season that the greatest variety of foods was available—especially in the summer and early fall months. The cool season, by contrast, was one of deprivation, particularly during the coldest months, when food resources were at a minimum and the climate was harshest.

The human population density was low, probably no more than 1,000 people over the 10,000 to 14,000 square miles encompassed by the lower canyon country, and remained low throughout the next 8,000 years. Density was determined largely by the number of people that could be supported by the technology and food resource base during the cool season. Social units must also have been small. We guess them to have been family-size groups or bands of extended families consisting of several generations, including the families of married brothers and/or sisters. Such small groups probably did not number more than 25 or 30 individuals. If the Lower Pecos canyon people were anything like other hunters and gatherers of semiarid lands, smaller groups would combine at

times for occasions of celebration and feasting. These events were of special importance, because they included storytelling, play, gambling, and opportunities for young adults to meet mates. They were also significant because of the information learned and shared through stories and songs.

Family bands scheduled their movement and settlement in accordance with the seasonal availability of resources. They also foraged opportunistically, taking advantage of exceptionally good yields and second fruitings, fish trapped in a pothole after a flood, or the sudden appearance of a bison herd on the grassy uplands. Raw material needed for making digging sticks, carrying baskets, nets, knives, and choppers such as stone, wood, and fiber was only a short distance away. The essential tools and equipment were always carried wherever they went. Carrying containers were light, as were most other tools used in daily tasks. Many items were made as needed and simply thrown away when their usefulness was over. Individuals had few personal possessions. A man might carry his spear thrower, a couple of spears, a curved flat stick used for many purposes but especially as a rabbit club, and a small net bag with a basic flintknapping kit—including an antler section, a limestone hammerstone, several chosen flakes, and some unfinished blanks—along with a variety of other small treasures. Women carried their newborn children in cradles and used carrying baskets made of a wooden frame and a body of sotol or yucca leaves. A tumpline was placed around the forehead to leave the arms free. Each woman also carried a digging stick and a stone knife hafted much in the manner of the Eskimo ulu or the Pima agave knife.

Material Evidence of the Hunters and Gatherers

Tangible evidence that hunters and gatherers either roamed permanently in the area encompassing the lower canyons or frequented the area regularly can be seen in many forms. Conspicuous indications of their presence are the accumulations found beneath many rockshelters or rock overhangs in the limestone canyons. That these deposits are attributable to human activity is clearly shown by the presence of fire-fractured limestone rocks, dark gray ashy soil, charcoal, bits of chipped stone, discarded stone, bone, shell, and often fibrous material. Soot stains occur on the ceilings of many of the rockshelters, attesting to the smoky fires that once burned on their floors. Faded pictographs or paint stains also show that some of the walls had once been adorned with bright painted symbols. Bedrock exposed in many of the shelters or on stone ledges and boulders near waterholes often display deep conical depressions worn by hours of pounding fibrous foodstuffs with a stone or wooden mortar.

Other accumulations of fire-fractured rock occur on stream banks or on slopes, usually where the canyon gently grades toward the uplands. These accumulations are known as *burned-rock middens*, since they are interpreted as discarded piles of heat-fractured rock removed from repeatedly used hearth areas. Limestone slabs were used to retain heat for earthoven baking, a process described below. Usually seen among the burned slabs are discarded chert tools and flakes, snail and occasionally mussel shells, and, more rarely, pieces of bone. Such sites are thought to be the result of repeated use by groups that camped for several days while the baking process was underway. Isolated pieces from burned-rock concentrations and single finds of a chert tool or flake can occur almost anywhere one walks in the lower canyon.

Cultural Sequence and Stylistic Change

Repeated visits to a specific campsite by hunters and gatherers resulted in noticeable accumulations of trash and other residue left after each visit. Time reduced much of the organic refuse if the campsite was in the open, but when well protected beneath deep overhangs, much of the organic trash stayed preserved for remarkably long periods. Repeated uses of a campsite usually resulted in mixing the trash of previous visits with that of subsequent visits. When this happened, there is little an archaeologist can do to sort the materials left from one visit from those of another. In instances where the use of a rockshelter occurred over long periods of time and the trash has accumulated to considerable thickness, changes over long-term intervals can be detected. Short-term changes such as two separate groups using one rockshelter or open site for entirely different purposes normally cannot be distinguished, because the deposits of those two visits are likely to be mixed.

Nature sometimes provides a helping hand in working out changes in the archaeological record by depositing a layer of sediment between layers of human trash. This process occurs when a campsite location along a stream bank becomes flooded and a thin layer of sand or silt is deposited on top of the trash or midden accumulation. Sometimes the campsite is scoured by the moving waters, displacing some materials from their original location. The important thing, however, is that natural forces play a major role in separating the various layers of cultural trash and allow us to see more finite divisions than would otherwise be possible.

For example, let us assume that the Devil's Mouth Site was visited by three different bands on separate occasions over a period of fifty years with a total of twenty visits overall. The trash left by each of these visits would become intermingled with that of subsequent and preceding ones, leaving a thin layer of ash, burned rock, discarded animal bones, mussel shells, snail shells, chipped stone residue, and discarded or left-behind tools. The chipped stone residue from one time simply could not be separated from that of another; that is, the layer of human cultural material represents a composite accumulation of twenty separate cultural events. Then a tropical storm drifted into the Edwards Plateau, and the Devils River experienced a major flood. The floodwaters scoured the surface of the terrace, displacing some of the light refuse, and deposited a thin layer of silt over the dark ashy and burned-rock layer. The site was again visited by bands over the next fifty years, leaving another thin layer of trash. If any change occurred in the tools used at the site in the twenty visits before or in the twenty visits after the flood, then it may be possible to recognize these changes in artifacts thanks to their separation by natural flood deposits. Had the flood not occurred, then one mixed layer representing the garbage of forty visits would be facing the archaeologist.

Nature does not always work to the archaeologist's advantage. While the natural shelters do provide a good potential for organic preservation for a period of time, the once organic-rich deposits are eventually compacted into mostly mixed layers of nonorganic burned rock and ash. Two excavated shelters, Hinds Cave and Mosquito Cave, can be used to illustrate this archaeological problem. Hinds Cave is a large amphitheaterlike overhang that had a deposit of almost pure cultural material nearly two meters thick. Much of this deposit was composed of organic remains such as plant residue. These perishable remains extended back about 8,500 years and have provided perhaps the best sequence of perishable artifacts and plant remains recovered from the lower canyon caves. The upper half of the Hinds Cave deposits was composed of layer upon layer of plant materials accumulated from many (perhaps hundreds of) separate visits to the site. Because the fibrous layers were thick, it was possible to separate and excavate individual layers

Hinds Cave stratigraphy (RIGHT, ABOVE). *Keeping floors clean was never a concern of the ancient shelter-cave dwellers. They set up their housekeeping on the trash left by the previous occupants. Unusually dry conditions prevailed inside shelters such as Hinds Cave, excavated by Harry J. Shafer and Vaughn M. Bryant of Texas A & M University. Such rockshelters often protected plant and other normally perishable materials from deterioration, giving archaeologists not only a layer-cake deposit of separate prehistoric households, but an unusually complete view of their way of life. At Hinds Cave, plant foods and artifacts of fiber, leather, wood, bone, and stone were preserved.*

View of Arenosa Shelter (RIGHT) *during excavations conducted by Dr. David Dibble of the University of Texas at Austin in 1966. The archaeologists found cultural sequences separated by layers of sand and silt deposited during floods.*

and to examine this part of the stratigraphy at Hinds Cave in the finest detail. In the lower half of the deposits, however, the layers of organic residue were often separated by layers of trash and decayed plant materials. The deposits were more compacted because of the gradual decay of the organic materials, making the separation of individual layers virtually impossible.

At Mosquito Cave, deposits were about as thick as at Hinds Cave, but consisted mostly of compacted ash and burned rock resulting from the removal of organic materials through decay. In addition, the human factor had mixed previously deposited materials with the remains of subsequent visits—only the grossest changes could be detected there.

Careful archaeological excavations at open campsites (such as Devil's Mouth Site, Arenosa Shelter, and Nopal Terrace) and at rockshelters (such as Hinds Cave, Baker Cave, Devil's Rockshelter, Conejo Shelter, and Coontail Spin Shelter) have resulted in the documentation of a long history of cultural activity in the lower canyon area. What has been demonstrated is a remarkable similarity in the general composition of tool kits through time, on one hand, and changes in the specific style of certain tools, on the other.

The archaeological record shows that the sequence of human occupation in the lower canyons was continuous. There is no evidence at the present time to suggest abandonment of the region for any detectable period of time. It is possible that some displacement took place during the 9,000-year sequence. If this was the case, however, the replacement population must have come from nearby regions where similar resources were used with a similar technology. Such a replacement might show in the archaeological record as a minor style change. (This is only one of several possible explanations for style change mentioned in the next chapter.) Lacking clearly defined layers of cultural differences that would serve as distinct markers to separate one series of deposits from another, a series of arbitrary divisions has been defined. These time intervals, mostly referred to by local place names, are called *Baker*, *Pandale*, *Devils*, *Comstock*, and *Historic*. They range from early to late in what is regarded as a continuous archaeological sequence.

Baker Interval (8,500–5,000 Years Ago) A significant portion of the deposits produced by human activity in many sites in the lower canyon region accumulated during this period. Perishable remains are absent in most of them, and artifact collections are not as complete as for later periods. Excavated sites yielding materials of the Baker Interval are Fate Bell Shelter, Devil's Rockshelter, Eagle Cave, Hinds Cave, Baker Cave, Moorehead Cave, the Shumla Caves, and Arenosa Shelter. Open-air campsites include Devil's Mouth Site and sites along San Felipe Creek east of the Devils River and Sanderson Canyon west of the Pecos River.

Key diagnostic artifacts are primarily projectile point forms and fine-line painted pebbles. Less diagnostic stone artifacts are oval unifacial tools identical to those described for the Golondrina Complex, milling stones or manos, milling basins or metates, bedrock mortars, hammerstones, and scratched pebbles probably used as hammerstones in the process of thinning bifaces. Common in these and all subsequent deposits are discarded bifaces, many of which never achieved final form and represent manufacturing failures. The residual flakes and discarded cores from the production of a variety of chipped stone tools litter deposits in sites occupied during this time. Many flakes display evidence of short-term or single-purpose use such as cutting, slicing, or scraping some perishable object. Such tools underscore the expedient day-to-day technology of these people. Raw materials for a multitude of tools and other items were readily at hand when the need arose. The natural abundance of excellent chert made it unnecessary to carry reserve supplies of raw material and heavy stone tools from place to place. Chipped stone tools could be made as needed and left at the place where they were used. Likewise, raw materials for making carrying baskets, mats, sandals, and the like could be had virtually anywhere in the region.

The use of leaves and fibers from desert succulent plants such as yucca, sotol, and lechuguilla is demonstrated in textiles recovered from deep deposits at Hinds Cave. Basketry was of two kinds. The first employed the technique of coiling, where frame elements were linked into a more or less continuous coil and stitched together with fibers stripped from plant leaves. The second technique was plaiting, where whole or split leaves of yucca, sotol, or lechuguilla were woven over and under to form a container or mat. Plant fibers were extensively used to make cordage and string, and analysts distinguish the various types on the basis of direction of twist of the elements (usually two or three strands) and the direction of twist of the elements (if there are more than one) of each strand.

Ten different types of cordage have been recognized. Cordage was widely used for making nets, snares, basketry, sandals, and aprons, for wrapping working ends of tools, and probably in many other ways that we have not as yet seen in the archaeological record. Netting was exclusively knotted and was used to make throw and fish nets and also small bags and large carrying containers. Sandals display a variety of manufacturing styles, including a plaited form and another style of shredded fibers occurring only during this period.

Animal bones found in ancient campsites are usually attributable to the hunting and dietary practices of the people. However, archaeologists need to be cautious in this assumption, since animals can die naturally in shelters or along stream banks where human groups have camped. Caves used as shelters were also used as dens by predators, who left the residue of their meals on the floor. Recovered bones showing systematic breaks (to obtain the marrow) or charring clearly point to human involvement, as do bones found in former hearth areas.

Bones of animals butchered and eaten by the ancient lower canyon people during this period include (in order of frequency) several species of rodents, lizards, snakes, birds, rabbits, fishes, turtles, and whitetail deer, and carnivores such as coyotes, foxes, ringtails, raccoons, and skunks. Shells of river mussels and land snails show that these sources of meat were not passed up when available.

A rare opportunity to gain direct information about lower canyon diets presented itself at Hinds Cave, where desiccated human feces were found in the deepest cultural layers. Fossil feces, called *coprolites*, are frequently found in the dry caves of the lower canyons, sometimes in great abundance. Many archaeologists in the past viewed such objects, along with the preserved plant remains they had to sort through, with idle curiosity and passed them by for the sake of more aesthetic items. When interdisciplinary teams of scientists started to investigate the relationship between the lower canyon people and their environment—that is, the human ecology—the botanists and zoologists in these teams looked upon the feces and the masses of preserved plant remains as a gold mine of information.

These scientists were able to identify the plants and animals that the people were collecting and eating. Not all plants collected were eaten; some were used

Baker Interval artifacts. Ancient traditions can be identified by the kinds of artifacts that occur together. However, when a lifeway changes only slightly over the centuries, archaeologists have little to identify periods of occupation. For reasons archaeologists cannot explain, the ancient men of the Lower Pecos area changed their projectile point styles; the women's tools (edge-sharpened flake knives, bottom two items), however, remained basically the same. Among the earliest tool assemblages found in the Lower Pecos area sites are those of the Baker Interval. Projectile point types characteristic of the Baker Interval are Baker (top two) and the delicately made and barbed Bandy (center and left of middle row and at bottom) and Bell (middle row, right), and an early triangular form (not shown). The barbed points were made from thin biface preforms (center) using limestone pebbles as hammerstones. Bone awls were used to fashion textiles. Painted pebbles decorated with fine-line designs represent the earliest rock art in the area.

for bedding, others for flooring, still others for tools, tool parts, and fiber. This kind of information provided a real turning point in the study of the lifeways in the lower canyon area. No longer did research center solely on the stone, bone, and fiber tools and articles left behind; archaeologists became interested in everything left at the site.

Botanist Janet Stock studied coprolites from two early levels at Hinds Cave, one group from about 8,200 years ago and another group from about 7,500 to 6,800 years ago. Plants identified in the fecal samples include prickly pear fruit and stems, walnut hulls, persimmon, wild onion, mesquite, and the seeds from the weed *Chenopodium* and from several different kinds of grasses. The animal bone fragments included rats, mice, jackrabbits, cottontails, fish, snakes, and white-tail deer. Other animal parts remained unidentified because of their fragmentary and pulverized condition and the impossibility of identifying species from hair alone.

A more ambitious dietary study was done by Glenna W. Williams-Dean. She analyzed a sample of one hundred coprolites from a single latrine deposit at Hinds Cave dated about 5,800 years ago, during the latter part of the Baker Interval. Twenty-three different kinds of animals and twenty-two different plants were among the food items found in the feces. Rats, mice, cottontails, jackrabbits, raccoon, deer, coyotes (or dogs), snakes, birds, lizards, and fish were among the animals eaten. Plant foods included prickly pear stems, fruit and seeds, lechuguilla bulbs, persimmon, mesquite, hackberry, grapes, onions, possibly *Chenopodium*, *Amaranthus*, grass seeds, sotol bulbs, and yucca.

Plants were either eaten raw, as with certain vegetables or fruits, or processed, perhaps by drying and grinding. Baking was done either over a fire or in earth ovens where limestone rocks were heated. Shallow, basin-shaped hearths lined with slabs of limestone are commonly seen in buried deposits in the lower canyons. This technique of baking—where the oven was repeatedly used and limestone rocks that became thermally fractured were replaced by new rocks—produced the earliest burned-rock middens and burned-rock scatters found in the Lower Pecos River region. The earth ovens were used to bake the bulbous portions of desert plants such as lechuguilla, sotol, and possibly certain yuccas. Although Stock did not positively identify the remains of all of these plants in her coprolite samples from Hinds Cave, burned lechuguilla bulbs were found among burned

rock accumulations at Hinds Cave dated to about 6,500 years ago. Baker Cave also had deep burned-rock midden deposits, indicating that these baking practices were widespread at this time.

Hunting was done using a spear propelled by an atlatl, fending sticks or rabbit clubs, traps, snares, nets, and bare hands. Scavenging natural "dieoffs" or kills by other predators was also a likely practice.

Due to a lack of datable burials from this time, we know little about funeral practices. However, we have learned a great deal about the housing arrangements of the Baker Interval people. At Hinds Cave, shallow, basinlike pits were lined with layers of twigs, grass, and prickly pear stems or other flat materials such as discarded sandals and basketry fragments. These lined features occur in the habitation areas of the cave near the back wall and probably represent bedding places. Two separate floored areas, both composed of prickly pear stems, are found in early deposits at Hinds Cave. These areas were presumably constructed to make the dusty caves more habitable. The occurrence of floor features and the observation that coprolite deposits (marking latrine areas) were segregated from other areas within the rockshelter indicate a compartmentalized use of space. Rockshelters can be viewed as natural housing arranged much as our own homes are into specific activity areas.

Pandale Interval (5,000–3,000 Years Ago) Most archaeological sites in the lower canyon country that contain accumulated cultural deposits were used as campsite locations during this period. Rockshelters, campsites on riverbanks, dome-shaped burned-rock middens located on upland surfaces adjacent to shallow canyons, and many surface locations near permanent sources of water have yielded materials diagnostic of this period. The intensity of use in excavated rockshelters such as Eagle Cave, Baker Cave, Centipede Cave, Damp Cave, Arenosa Shelter, and the outdoor Devil's Mouth Site are notable for the sheer amount of fill resulting from human occupation during this period.

While dietary studies are currently lacking for the Pandale Interval, an inspection of food residues shows little indication of any dramatic change in the way of life from the previous period. Deer may have been killed more frequently by the people who lived in Hinds Cave, but this may not be an overall trend. The list of reptiles, fish, rodents, and other mammals remains essentially unchanged. There is one notable

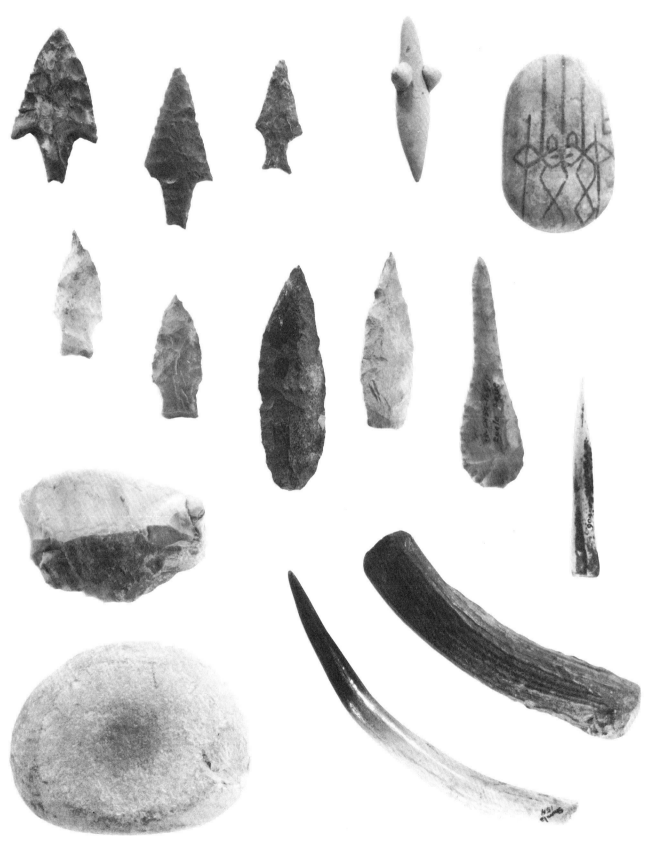

Pandale Interval. Change and stability are both indicated in the Pandale Interval artifact assemblage. The twisted blade and stem of the Pandale point type serve as a distinctive departure from the carefully thinned points of the preceding Baker Interval. Unfinished bifaces reveal that the efforts to create the twisting effect occurred early in the manufacturing sequence (right two specimens on the bottom row of points). A change back to a thin preform and point style is shown by the Langtry (top row, left two) and Val Verde (top row, third to the right). Edge-sharpened flake knives, grinding tools such as the mano, awls of bone and chipped stone, and antler tools were all part of the everyday tool kit of the Pandale Interval people. Painted pebbles become more established in style, with bolder lines. Unfired clay figurines made by rolling the clay between the hands reflect a growing symbolic expression. Perhaps the earliest recognized Pecos River pictographs were painted by these people.

Devils Interval. Stability in human adaptation to the desert landscape is reflected in the Devils Interval artifacts. Projectile point styles Montell (bottom), Shumla (third row, second row), Frio (first row, right), and Ensor (first row, center and left) indicate stylistic shifts through time. Other tools such as edge-sharpened flake knives and awls of stone and bone show little change. Archaeologists have detected a slight increase in the use of fish during this interval. This shift in subsistence may be reflected in the occurrence of bone spatulas made of deer ulna, possibly used for net tying, and cobble tools used for fiber shredding. Painted pebble styles continue to change, and the Pecos River pictographs may have reached their zenith during this interval.

change in the plants used; the occurrence of lechuguilla dropped significantly from the previous period, being replaced by sotol. This shift in plant use from one bulbous desert plant to another cannot be viewed as particularly significant in the economy of the people. The tools used to harvest, bake, and prepare the two plants would be the same.

The textile industry is especially diverse. Basketry is represented by examples of both simple and diagonal twining, coiling, and simple and twill plaiting. Cordage is much like that of the previous period and includes at least twelve structural types. Knotted netting continues, and knotless netting—widely used to make small carrying bags for personal possessions—appears for the first time. Knotted fibers representing the discards of single-purpose wraps and bundles are common elements (as, indeed, they are in the perishable artifact sample throughout the sequence).

Sandal styles also show changes from the previous period. A dominant style involved first laying two lechuguilla or yucca leaves parallel to each other to form warps and then bending the ends down between the bases. Additional leaves were then woven across the frame to form the body of the sandal. This frame style is called *opposed warp* and appears for the first time in the sequence. A more unusual style, also a two-warp frame, has a figure-eight wrapping to form the body of the sole. This style has been found only in the early portion of the Pandale Interval. Weaving was done using awls made of bone and probably also sharpened sticks. Highly polished pointed bone awls made from the upper leg bones or long bones of deer are commonly found. Occasionally bones of smaller animals or lateral spines of fish show evidence of use as awls.

The stone tool complex indicates stylistic changes that bear comment. Projectile points made during the early part of this period are usually chipped in such a way that the blade twists to the left. Archaeologists have used the local place name *Pandale* to refer to this particular projectile point style. The stems of the points are chipped so that they twist the opposite way. The purpose or the advantage of this twisting effect is not known, but it was extremely popular for nearly a thousand years. The stoneworker who made a Pandale point began shaping the blank with a twist at the very beginning of the chipping process.

Later in the period, flintknappers made two separate styles of projectile points with very thin, flat blades. The two styles occur together in the deposits.

The stem of these points shows two basic forms. One is beveled much in the form of the Pandale type, but the stems are longer and thinner; this style is called the *Langtry* type. The other form, called *Val Verde*, is formed by broad, shallow notches chipped in the corners of the blade. Both types are expertly thinned by using a flaking technique requiring a hammer softer than the chert being flaked. In skilled hands, the result produced is a thin, delicate point that markedly contrasts with the thicker Pandale type.

Why did the hunters change the style of their points, especially when the change required learning a totally different manner of chipping? Style change through time is a constant aspect of human culture, but the reasons for it are many. For example, a change in a component of a composite tool such as a spear thrown by an atlatl could carry a significant technological advantage. A spear is composed of three major parts: the main shaft, the foreshaft (one end pointed and inserted into the end of the main shaft and the other notched to receive the stone point), and the projectile point. A change in the way the point is secured to the foreshaft may have called for a change in the design of the point itself.

Other stone artifacts found in the deposits of this period are similar to those described for the Baker Interval. Unifacially chipped cutting tools are not as frequent during the early portion of the Pandale Interval, but increase notably later, when sotol becomes common in the shelter deposits. The slicing tools show clear indication of their use for cutting silica-rich desert plants such as sotol. Repeated contact between the stone tool and the plant leaves a characteristic sheen on the blade. Even though plant remains may not be preserved in the deposits, the stone tools clearly indicate the kind of plants harvested. Manos, mortars, flaked cobble chopping tools, residual flakes and cores from chert tool production, scratched pebbles probably used as hammerstones, and fine-lined painted pebbles are all part of the Pandale Interval artifact complex.

Devils Interval (3,000–1,000 Years Ago) The prehistoric archaeological remains show their greatest degree of variation during this period. The fluctuations do not appear to reflect any significant long-term changes in the overall regional way of life and may be related to the effects of a short cold interval about 2,500 years ago. This climatic reversal to cooler, moister conditions temporarily disrupted the ongoing warming and drying trend and favored the reestablishment of grassy uplands. In turn, large herds of bison were once again attracted into the region. Archaeological evidence of this event is clearly present at Bonfire Shelter. Once again the unique setting of this shelter was used as a blind trap and fall, into which an estimated 800 animals were driven either in one major or several successive drives. Bison bones do occur separately at other sites (e.g., Eagle Cave and Arenosa Shelter), but bison do not represent a major dietary element for the region as a whole. Notably absent, too, is any consistent occurrence of the kinds of tools associated with bison exploitation—the end scrapers and stone awls designed for working hides that are found over most of the Great Plains. The projectile point styles recovered from among the bison bones at Bonfire Shelter are not like those made locally. Large bison herds always attracted hunting groups from wide areas, and it is likely that the Bonfire Shelter hunters originally came from central Texas. (Warfare depicted in Pecos River Style rock art in several locations could document violent encounters with outsiders encroaching upon the local people's territory.)

The brief bison interlude is an exception to the traditional way of life of the lower canyons. Dietary studies from coprolites, animal bones, and perishable plant remains (from deposits at Parida Cave, Conejo Shelter, Hinds Cave, and Baker Cave) virtually duplicate those reported earlier. Plants such as lechuguilla, sotol, prickly pear, wild onion, mesquite, hackberry, and persimmon are all present. An increase in fish remains can be noted at some sites, perhaps related to increasing efficiency in fishing techniques.

A succession of projectile point style changes occurs during the Devils Interval. One distinctive tool appears for a brief span: a knife carefully fashioned from a cobble or large flake blank. The butt end is unworked, but the blade is expertly thinned to a rounded tip. The function of these knives is unknown, but they may have been designed for everyday household use, again much like the Eskimo ulu. It is also interesting that the knives occur in the sequence at the same time that bison appear at Bonfire Shelter. The new knives may represent a tool form introduced by outsiders.

Other stone artifacts show little notable change from previous intervals and underscore the continuity of the general way of life. Oval, single-edge unifaces are more common at this time than ever before. Organic residue preserved on such unifaces at Hinds Cave show that these tools were used to slice the leaves from bulbs of lechuguilla and sotol preparatory to baking. The manner of hafting is known from preserved examples from Shumla Caves. The sharp oval flakes were inserted into the side of a grooved or split stick so that the handle extended on both sides of the blade. Once hafted, the blades were sharpened by chipping tiny flakes from one side of the dulled edge. Visible wear patterns on most of the "sotol knives" indicate a consistent pattern of use.

Flaked cobble choppers or planes, scratched pebbles or hammerstones, manos, metates, an assortment of bifaces resulting from failures in projectile point manufacture, and waste flake debris from flintknapping are all found in deposits dating to this period. Fending sticks or rabbit clubs, atlatls of at least three basic kinds, spear shaft fragments, digging sticks, fire hearth sticks, fire drills, snare and trap elements, fire tongs, and mortars and pestles have all been found made of locally available woody materials.

Painted pebbles show evolutionary changes from the preceding period but clearly display a stylistic continuum. Bold-line designs display more distinctive anthropomorphic (humanlike) motifs at one end of the pebble. Unbaked clay figurines representing female forms occur infrequently, and some are decorated with punctuated, incised, or painted designs.

The Pecos River Style pictographs can confidently be placed in this period, although older styles may extend back into the preceding interval. The stylized polychrome anthropomorphic figures characteristic of this art style are often depicted holding or throwing an atlatl. This feature clearly places the art in pre-bow-and-arrow times.

The basketry assemblage shows little notable change from the preceding period. Simple plaiting and twill plaiting were used to construct mats of various sizes; flexible baskets were manufactured by twining. Coiling is not common and, as during previous periods, was restricted to the construction of large parching trays (flat containers for drying seeds and fruit). Cordage is represented by at least six structural types, including a three-ply yarn that was introduced in the previous period. Nets were exclusively of the knotless variety. A small net bag recovered from Fate Bell Shelter contained a mano. The three sandal types found in this period are distinguished on the basis of their frame construction. Awls used in textile weaving were made of split deer and other animal bones. Bone beads, antler tine artifacts, and worked mussel shells also occur. There is notably little

The remains of circular and crescent-shaped accumulations of fire-fractured rocks (called burned-rock middens) are the result of the repeated use of earth ovens for baking desert plants. The crescent-shaped middens first appear during the Devils Interval of the Lower Pecos cultural sequence.

change in these aspects of lower canyon technology from preceding periods.

Personal items are occasionally discovered hidden in shallow pits in rockshelters or tucked away in obscure crevices. Two almost identical wooden mortars and pestles were found hidden away in protected niches. A large cache containing several sticks, including a beveled-end digging stick, and at least two carrying baskets of twine was found in Hinds Cave. One of the baskets contained several prickly pear nodes. A similar but smaller bag containing a pair of sandals was found at Horseshoe Cave on the old Martin Kelly ranch. Another twilled carrying bag at the same site contained the following items: two bundles of deer sinew, a buckskin thong, pink pigment, three apparently unfinished chert bifaces, one nearly complete chert projectile point, three deer antler flaking tools, a scratched limestone pebble hammerstone, a small perforated terrapin carapace, a mussel shell, ten unifacially worked oval flake tools, eleven left jackrabbit

mandibles, and over a hundred mountain laurel and buckeye seeds. This interesting find may give some idea of the contents of a portable tool kit likely to be carried by a man. The items, taken together, could be used to manufacture virtually any kind of tool needed to exploit the resources available in the region's environment. Although this is often described as a "medicine bundle," the mundane functions of most of the items suggests a more practical interpretation.

The manner in which space was used inside the rockshelters shows little change from previous periods. Grass-lined beds, rock pavement hearths, and established latrine areas show the same spatial pattern. One notable change in cultural practices seen for the first time is the burial of the dead in rockshelters. (At least this is the first time that burials can be dated to a specific period.) We do not know if the people buried their dead in shelters they were occupying at the time or in nearby abandoned shelters.

What did the people do with their corpses before?

Burials are occasionally found in vertical shaft caves or in horizontal solution caves without any artifacts diagnostic of a specific time. These burials either may be of an earlier period or may represent alternate burial locations during the Devils Interval. If burials had been made in rockshelters before this interval, surely some of them would have been preserved and found. Presumably some other mode of disposal was used—perhaps the above-mentioned shaft graves. Occasional scaffold burial, leaving the corpse in a crevice or on the surface, and depositing it in the river are other possibilities. With any of these methods, the bones would have long since been removed from the archaeological record.

The known burial pattern for the Devils Interval was to wrap the partly clothed, flexed corpse in a twilled mat and place it in a shallow, oval pit near the back of a rockshelter. The body was then covered with a layer of flat limestone rocks capped over with the original pit fill. Red ochre is sometimes found covering the rocks. The sheltered burial localities include extensively occupied sites (such as Moorehead Cave, Coontail Spin Shelter, and Conejo Shelter) and also isolated shelters or vertical shaft caves (such as Perpetual Care Shelter, Langtry Creek Burial Cave, or the Perry Calk Site). Rarely are artifacts found accompanying the skeletons or partly desiccated corpses, although a few bone beads and shell ornaments have been recovered. What is found is the corpse's clothing, such as sandals, fringe or string aprons, and blankets made of strips of rabbit fur twisted around a net frame.

A new type of site occurs in the region during the later portion of this interval about A.D. 700. This is the crescent-shaped burned-rock midden, in addition to the exclusively ring- or dome-shaped midden of earlier times. Middens resulted from the repeated use of earth ovens. Continually using the same slab-lined cooking pit and replacing fire-fractured rocks used for heat-conducting purposes resulted in mounded accumulations of discarded burned limestone rock fragments. This method of earth-oven baking had been in use for thousands of years, but, for unknown reasons, crescent-shaped middens first date from this interval. Charred remains of lechuguilla and sotol found in the pit features leave little doubt as to what was being cooked in the crescent-shaped midden sites, which are found by the thousands in southwest Texas. They may occur literally anywhere on the landscape where there was sufficient soil depth for the pit to be dug, including rockshelters.

The activities of earth-oven baking took some time, so people temporarily camped and foraged around the oven locations. Evidence of campsite activity is usually provided by a modest number of chipped stone tools or debris and snail and mussel shells (either mixed with the burned rock or scattered on the surface). The snails were gathered as they became seasonally available and, like the mussels, were probably steamed on the hot rocks. Since the focal point of the group's activity around these sites was plant processing, few hunting tools occur at the middens.

Baking of agave and other bulbous desert plants was commonly practiced among Indians who lived in the marginal deserts of northern Mexico and in the southwestern United States. The process of preparing the baked foods is well documented. It was a group effort involving both men and women. The basic chores were digging the pit and gathering rocks, firewood, and the plants to be cooked. The latter task was not easy if sotol was one of the plants. The sotol bulb was trimmed of its many sawtooth-spined leaves and pried from the ground, and the heavy bulbs were carried to the baking pit. Lechuguilla, a much smaller plant, was detached from the ground simply by pulling, or with a minimum of prying with a digging stick. It has fewer leaves than does sotol and is much safer to handle. The leaves were sliced near the base of the plant, however, before baking.

When the proper number of plant bulbs had been gathered and trimmed of their leaves, the cooking process began. A large fire was built to heat the limestone slabs placed around and under the wood. After the fire had burned down and sufficiently heated the rocks, the coals were removed. The bulbs were placed in the basin-shaped pit and covered with the green leaves cut from the bases and soil dug from the pit itself. The bulbs were allowed to bake several days. When sufficient time had elapsed, the pit was opened and the cooked bulbs were removed from the oven, partly pounded, and allowed to dry in the desert sun. Once dried, the baked bulbs were pounded in mortars to a coarse flour and mixed with water to make flour cakes, completing the processing cycle. The crescent- and ring-shaped midden sites clearly represent the prehistoric traces of a very similar sort of earth-oven baking.

Comstock Interval (1,000–400 Years Ago) Capping the cultural deposits in some of the rockshelters is a thin veneer of refuse that contains small stemmed

Comstock Interval. *The most dramatic changes since the hunters and gatherers first settled in the Lower Pecos canyons occurred about A.D. 1000 with the arrival of the bow and arrow. This new weapon brought about changes in hunting strategies and certainly in warfare as well. Changing ecological conditions of the southern Plains also brought bison much closer to the region. All of these changes are seen in the Comstock assemblage. Arrow point types Toyah, Livermore, and Perdiz hafted on wooden foreshafts and inserted into cane shafts demonstrate a change from the atlatl-thrown spear. End scrapers and edge-sharpened knives made from large thin bifaces argue for a shift from plant processing to flesh processing. Other knives made from long, prismatic flakes show a basic change in lithic technology. Plant fibers and foods were not totally ignored. The cobble scraper planes were still used for shredding fiber. The latest painted pebbles show the most realistic patterns. The Red Monochrome Style, showing use of the bow and arrow, is a complete departure from the Pecos River Style art tradition.*

projectile points and, when the preservation conditions are suitable, cane arrow shafts. These artifacts indicate that a change in weaponry occurred about A.D. 1000. The basic economy seemed to continue for the most part, and there is no evidence of any major qualitative shift in the way of life from that of the preceding period. Other lithic tools, such as the oval flake hafted knives used in slicing the leaves from edible desert plants, remained the same, and ring- and crescent-shaped burned rock middens continued to accumulate. So far, none of the rockshelter deposits from this late in the archaeological sequence have been analyzed by biologists; neither have coprolites been recovered.

A new type of site, marked by circular stone alignments, pottery, and stemmed arrow points, may hint of intrusive groups shifting into the area near the end of this interval. An example is the Infierno Site. Pottery occurs rarely in open sites (having been found only at the Javelina Bluff Site and Devil's Mouth Site), and the vessels are typically bone-tempered—that is, when the potter mixed the clay, ground, burned bone was added to the paste.

Two new pictograph styles appear in the lower canyon region after the introduction of the bow and arrow: the Red Monochrome and the Red Linear. The Red Monochrome Style depicts anthropomorphic and zoomorphic (animallike) motifs that, although more naturalistic than those of the Pecos River Style, somehow retain similarities to the earlier designs. Negative handprints are also present, as well as other symbols that may indicate the presence of more than one group. The striking aspect of the Red Monochrome Style is the clear illustration of the bow and arrow, allowing us to place this style no earlier than about 1,000 years ago.

The much different Red Linear Style is a clear departure from the Lower Pecos River rock art tradition. The known sites are few, and the pictograph panels are small, consisting of numerous stick figures, mostly males, in various scenes. Some may depict rituals, while others may record historical events. The Red Linear Style clearly dates after the Pecos River Style, and reports of bows pictured in the hands of some figures (which have since been destroyed) would also place these paintings sometime within the last 1,000 years.

There is no strong indication of bison being exploited in the lower canyons, although their presence is well documented across much of central and southwest Texas at this period. Certain zoomorphic picto-

graph motifs may symbolize bison, deer, turkeys, catfish, turtles, and jackrabbits. The faunal remains from a small rockshelter in Sanderson Canyon included rabbits and other small game, together with occasional deer bones. It seems that the basic subsistence patterns changed little from the preceding period. The advantage of the bow and arrow over the atlatl-propelled spear may have provided more opportunities for harvesting larger animals, but the same species were exploited. The continued use of earth ovens to process desert succulents and the list of economic plants present at Gobbler Shelter in Crockett County indicate the ongoing importance of desert succulent plants in the economy.

The occurrence of burials virtually on the surface of some rockshelters may signify a continuation of preceding interment practices. These burials cannot be precisely dated, however, because of the absence of associated materials that would convincingly place them into this time slot. It is also not possible to list diagnostic textiles of this period because they have not been successfully segregated stratigraphically from those of earlier deposits. This is especially unfortunate, since there is some hint that intrusive human groups had shifted into the area prior to the coming of Europeans; we have no way of identifying who these people were.

Historic Interval (400–150 Years Ago) Several Historic Indian groups have been recorded in the Lower Pecos River canyon, including Coahuiltecans, Lipan Apaches, Tobosos, Jumanos, and Comanches. No archaeological sites have been found that can be identified as belonging to any one specific group, however. Indeed, the traces of Indian activity subsequent to the appearance of Europeans are meager. Several Red Monochrome pictographs in the area depict Historic motifs (horses, non-Indian human figures, churches). A church, vaqueros roping longhorn steers, and non-Indian dress are depicted at Vaquero Shelter in Val Verde County. At Meyers Springs in Terrell County, churches, horses with and without riders, buffalo, guns, and priests are shown.

Two sites in the lower canyon area have yielded artifacts that can be assigned to the Historic period. The Fielder Canyon Cave, located in a tributary canyon of the Pecos River, contained wooden arrow shafts with barbed metal points, several hundred conical metal objects and strips of flat hoop iron and tin from which the conical objects were made, glass beads, scis-

sors, a buckle, and buttons. This site is an Historic Indian cache.

Another cache of Historic artifacts was found under a pile of rocks in Pecos County. This stockpile contained several pouches of dressed bison, deer and antelope hides, stone ornaments, and a fire drill, in addition to such "European" items as calico cloth, gunpowder, lead, an iron axe, and tobacco. This hoard would seem to date to the early nineteenth century at a time when Comanches were the dominant group in the southern Plains. However, it could have belonged to any one of a number of late Plains Indian groups known to have passed through this region of Texas, including Lipan Apaches, Tonkawas, Kiowas, and Kiowa Apaches.

These two sites mark a major change in the material culture of the Indian groups who frequented the area: use of materials obtained from European sources. Historically, the Lipan Apaches made extensive use of desert succulents, and it is from ethnographic accounts of their techniques of earth-oven baking that archaeologists reconstructed the methods of their predecessors in the area. Lipan Apaches, however, were at least partly equestrian and also made extensive use of the bison. Since their stay in the region was

short (at most 150 years) and their lifestyle far more mobile than that of the indigenous hunters and gatherers, few identifiable traces of Lipan occupation would be expected. Likewise, the Comanches were even more mobile, and their major home range was to the north, in the southern High Plains. Their presence in the Lower Pecos River area was basically transitory, going and returning from raids into Mexico.

The indigenous populations of the Lower Pecos area disappeared without much notice. Some may have joined other native Texas Indians attracted to the Spanish missions of northeastern Mexico and southern Texas; others may have been drawn to the Mexican settlements along the upper Rio Concho in Mexico or even further south; still others may have been absorbed into the intrusive Lipan Apache bands and contributed to the latter's almost immediate adaptation to the arid southwest Texas environment.

The indigenous occupation of the lower canyon country probably did not last beyond the early 1700s, bringing an end to some 9,000 years of occupation. The same resources that successfully sustained these people remain in the region today, largely untapped by the new settlers who first claimed the lands in the 1800s. ■

BAKER CAVE
A Rich Archaeological Record

by Thomas R. Hester
THE UNIVERSITY OF TEXAS AT SAN ANTONIO

The Setting

In 1984 and again in 1986, the Witte Museum, in collaboration with the University of Texas at San Antonio (UTSA), Center for Archaeological Research, carried out archaeological excavations at Baker Cave in Val Verde County, Texas. The site is a dry rockshelter perched high in a canyon wall on a tributary of the Devils River. These recent excavations by the Witte-UTSA archaeological teams were designed to explore in more detail research questions raised by earlier fieldwork at Baker Cave.

The first excavations at the site were done by avocational archaeologists, under the guidance of James H. Word of Floydada, Texas. Word's research began in 1962 and continued until 1966: his findings were published in 1970 by the Texas Memorial Museum. Following this initial project, John W. Greer, then a graduate student at the University of Texas at Austin, carried out excavations at the rear of the cave in 1968. Eight years later, in the summer of 1976, the author, along with Robert F. Heizer and a UTSA-Earthwatch team, dug at the site. These excavations in the 1960s and 1970s, combined with the more recent field-work, have provided a rich body of data on the ancient inhabitants of Baker Cave. Such a continuing research program is rare in the Lower Pecos. Unfortunately, sites are often dug once by archaeologists, only to be subsequently destroyed by relic-collectors, who use no scientific controls in their efforts to recover artifacts for private collections. But Baker Cave is an exception. It was protected from such looters, initially by the late Jim Baker and in recent years by Mary and Les Hughey. Without their vigilance, Baker Cave would surely have been destroyed long ago.

The Site

Baker Cave is technically a large solution cavity formed in the limestone walls of Phillips Canyon. It is a medium-sized rockshelter, in comparison with others in the Lower Pecos, about 120 feet long and extending 56 feet from the mouth of the shelter to the back wall. The shelter's overhanging roof, coupled with the dry Lower Pecos climate, has preserved the remains of more than 9,000 years of prehistoric Indian habitation.

Just getting to Baker Cave is quite an experience. After an hour-long ride across rugged ranch terrain, the site can be seen in the west canyon wall, over 200 feet above the floor of the canyon. It is a spectacular view, although the exhilaration of the moment is sometimes tempered by the thought of the descent, along narrow canyon ledges, down to the cave.

Once in the cave, a dusty deposit of prehistoric occupational debris can be seen. Excavations have shown this to be from nine to eleven feet thick. The roof and walls of the site are of very soft limestone; as they weather, a fine deposit of dust falls to the cave floor below. This appears to have been the pattern for thousands of years. Indeed, when the cave (or parts of it) was not being used by Indians, the limestone dust sometimes accumulated in layers several inches thick. This factor, coupled with the continuing, perhaps seasonal, reuse of the cave by ancient Indian groups, has created a series of layers—or stratifications—consisting of deposits of human refuse separated at various levels by zones of limestone dust.

Digging Baker Cave

Excavations in a rockshelter present the archaeologist with a number of problems concerning logistics and strategy. At Baker Cave, logistics is a particular concern: all excavation

equipment has to be carried down a steep slope—and then, at the end of the project, back up again! This requires not only safety procedures on the part of the field team, but also a lot of planning so that only needed equipment gets carried to the site. Also, in most rockshelters the very dry conditions cause a choking cloud of dust as the excavation begins, requiring team members to wear dust filter masks. Fortunately, this kind of equipment is not necessary at Baker Cave because of a continuous breeze coming down the canyon, forming an updraft that carries the dust, in a large swirl, up and out of the excavation areas.

The scientific information provided by dry rockshelter deposits is rich and diverse. Practically all of the materials used by the Indians in their daily activities are still preserved. As animals were butchered and plants were processed, and as these items were eaten and discarded, a vast amount of residue was formed—plant leaves, tiny seeds, nut shells, fish bones, bits of bone from deer, rabbits, rats, snakes, and lizards, feathers, and other fragile material. These food remains— along with the discarded artifacts used by the Indians, such as projectile points, pieces of baskets and mats, worn-out sandals of plant fiber, and rocks used in cooking— are all part of the archaeological deposit in the cave. The remains accumulate both vertically and horizontally, and it is the archaeologist's challenge to record and recover materials from the deposit in a fashion that will tell the story of how ancient Indians lived in the cave. The *vertical* patterns that show up during the excavations enable us to see what has gone on through time, from earliest to latest. The *horizontal* patterns permit us to determine how space within the shelter was used during a given time span—where they cooked, slept, manufactured tools, processed desert plants, and so forth.

Archaeologists usually lay out a series of square excavation units, called *grids*. This allows control over the horizontal and vertical patterns that might be exposed. All of the excavations at Baker Cave have used such grids, although they have not been directly related because of the long time gaps between major projects. However, the grids can be correlated, as Mary F. Chadderdon has done in her study of Baker Cave, so that documentation of much of the excavated deposits is assured. Various excavators have used different strategic approaches. For example, James H. Word dug both by six-inch levels and by natural stratigraphic levels as revealed in the deposits. In the recent Witte-UTSA work, emphasis has been on excavation of the natural layers within the deposit, although at times "arbitrary levels," usually 10 cm increments, have to be used to ensure the best possible vertical control. Where possible, the excavations in 1976 and in 1984–1985

Baker Cave, Val Verde County, Texas. This important site has deposits that date back as far as 9,000 years ago. First excavated in the 1960s by amateur archaeologists, the site was later the scene of excavations by the University of Texas at San Antonio (1976) and the Witte Museum–UT San Antonio collaborative projects of 1984, 1985, and 1986. Phillips Canyon can be seen on the left, winding its way downstream to the Devils River.

have plotted artifacts and clusters of materials (such as plant-processing areas, cooking pits, ancient latrine areas) in place, so that we have full horizontal and vertical controls. In 1976 and 1984–1985, a reference point, or datum, was established on the back wall; vertical and horizontal measurements were made from that spot, using steel metric tapes and a transit-and-stadia rod.

In excavating a dry deposit like that at Baker Cave, the major problem that confronts archaeologists is what to keep and what to discard. Unlike open campsites where only stone and bone tools might be preserved, the dry deposits of rockshelters contain an overwhelming array of residue and artifacts. In general, as much material as possible must be documented and saved; once a deposit is dug, it is forever lost. This means, at Baker Cave, the collection of vast quantities of plant remains—seeds, leaves, stems, roots—left behind by the ancient occupants. Also, the screening or sieving of the excavated deposits must be done in a special way; normal ¼″-

mesh screen will recover only part of the artifacts, such as bones and other debris. In 1976 and 1984–1985, we used window-screen mesh as our bottom screen; over that, we placed ¼″ screens. Thus, the larger materials could be collected from the upper screen and the fine materials from the one below. We then bagged all the residues left on the screen, for further analysis in the laboratory. At intervals, "bulk" samples of unscreened deposits were taken from excavation units or features, for detailed constituent analysis back at the lab.

The fragile nature of many of the materials in the deposit required patience and care in excavation. When a sandal or piece of basketry appeared, great care was taken to expose the specimen—usually with delicate brushes and by blowing away the adhering dust with an ear syringe or plastic blowing tube. Once cleaned, the specimen is best preserved by gently placing it in a plastic bag, along with an identifying label. Sometimes a fine mist of preservative can be applied in the field,

although this is usually best done in the laboratory.

Another example of situations that must be faced in excavations at Baker Cave is the loose, unconsolidated nature of the cave fill. Straight and neat walls, so dear to most archaeologists, simply cannot be maintained. The walls of the excavation pit have to be sloped to prevent collapse—which would result in the loss of much information and danger to the excavator in the pit. In 1984, the deep excavation block dug by the Witte-UTSA team had to be shored up with plywood sheets and two-by-four braces.

By the end of the summer of 1985, several major areas of Baker Cave had been fully or partially excavated. The central portion had been dug by Word in 1962–1966, while excavations at the rear of the cave were carried out by Greer in 1968 and Hester in 1976. In 1984, the Witte-UTSA team dug toward the front of the cave, just southeast of Word's original excavation area. Then, in 1985, work was begun in the remaining block between the central and back parts of the shelter. Through these series of excavations, much has been learned about the antiquity of human use of the cave, as well as how different parts of the cave were used for a variety of activities through time.

Summary of Findings

Excavations have demonstrated that prehistoric Indians lived, at times, at Baker Cave for more than 9,000 years. The earliest habitation, first found by Word in the 1960s, is radiocarbon-dated to 7,000 B.C. and is known in the archaeological literature as the Golondrina Complex. This represents human use of the cave after the end of the Pleistocene Ice Age. The deposits of this period lay on the bottom of the cave; distinctive Golondrina projectile points,

Harvey P. Smith, Jr., a participant in the 1976 and 1984 projects at Baker Cave, kneels by a stratigraphic profile exposed in the 1976 excavations. Round labels designate individual strata. Fiber lenses represent occupations in Middle to Late Archaic times; in between are zones of dust—much of it from the cave roof—accumulated during times when the cave was unoccupied.

chipped stone tools, and animal bones are found.

One of the most striking features of this original occupation was a cooking pit found in 1976. All of its ashy contents were bagged and then fine-screened in the lab, yielding a vast array of materials, which were preserved primarily because they had been burned or slightly charred. A number of experts have worked with these materials, identifying more than twenty species of plants (notably absent are some of the common desert plants of the region, suggesting that the climate was perhaps moister around this time), eleven species of mammals (all modern species), six species of fish, and eighteen species of reptiles. Of the latter, there are sixteen species of snakes—from large rattlesnakes to very small nonpoisonous snakes that could have been found only if the Golondrina Complex peoples were literally turning over every rock in search of this food source!

Following the Golondrina Complex, there is a thick deposit linked to Early Archaic hunters and gatherers, between 6000 B.C. and 3500 B.C., based on radiocarbon dates. Desert plants such as sotol and lechuguilla make their appearance, and we believe that the environment at that time must have been much as it is today. Though the Early Archaic deposits, and those of the underlying Golondrina Complex, are very loose and dry, there is little preservation of sandals, basketry, and other fiber and skin artifacts: these deposits appear to be too old for preservation of such materials.

The Middle and Late Archaic deposits, however, contain a tremendous wealth of plant remains and perishable artifacts. Also, many activity areas and features are identified from this era, dating roughly from 3000 B.C. to the early centuries A.D. During the latter part of this

View of excavations and screening operations at Baker Cave, during the Witte Museum–UTSA excavations in 1984. Materials being excavated in the center right are screened at the mouth of the cave; two sets of ¼″ and ⅛″ screen ensure maximum recovery of seeds, tiny animal bones, and other clues to the nature of the human occupation of the site.

time span, we can begin to see how Baker Cave was "divided up" by its Indian inhabitants in terms of certain activities. For example, based on Greer's work in 1968, the rear of the cave seems to have been used as a sleeping area. Toward the front, there were large cooking areas, as seen in Word's excavations and in the 1984 Witte-UTSA research. In the 1984 excavations, a vertically distributed series of at least five overlapping cooking pits was found. The earliest pit goes back to at least 5000 B.C. and the latest, to early in the Christian era—indicating that this one section of the cave was used for specialized cooking tasks for 6,000 or 7,000 years. Adjacent to the cooking area to the west was a Middle Archaic living area, with small pits, a

latrine area, sotol and lechuguilla leaf and bulb processing areas, and, next to a large block fallen from the roof, a basin-shaped, grass-lined sleeping area or bed. Just to the north, in 1985, the Witte-UTSA crew dug part of a very large rock-filled pit, perhaps used for baking plant foods, and the artifacts from it indicate use into Late Archaic times, perhaps 1200–1400 A.D.

Baker Cave is remarkable for its preservation of the human presence over some 9,000 years—a span that can be divided into periods by stylistic differences in various artifacts, yet one that basically records an unchanging way of life over its total extent. ∎

BONFIRE SHELTER
An Ancient Slaughterhouse

by Solveig A. Turpin
TEXAS ARCHAEOLOGICAL RESEARCH LABORATORY

The earliest people of the Lower Pecos River region, the Paleo-Indians, entered a habitat considerably different from that of today. A vast parkland savannah supported herds of now extinct large game such as elephants, camels, horses, and bison and their human predators. The most dramatic mark of their tenure was left at Bonfire Shelter, the oldest and southernmost example of the jump technique of bison slaughter in the New World.

This shelter lies hidden behind a massive roof fall in a deeply entrenched box canyon, tributary to the Rio Grande near the historically famous hamlet of Langtry. About 10,500 years ago, the expert hunters of the Paleo-Indian period stampeded herds of now extinct giant bison, *Bison b. antiquus*, over the cliff, driving them to their death on the rocks below. The house-size boulders blocking the shelter mouth diverted the falling animals into the cave, where they were systematically butchered under the protective overhang. At least three separate episodes garnered over 120 animals, providing literally tons of meat, hides, and bone. The butchered carcasses and the presence of tools used for that purpose demonstrate that these drives were the work of humans and not accidents of nature.

Among the stone artifacts are the distinctive Folsom and Plainview dart points, time-markers of the Paleo-Indian period. Radiocarbon dating of charcoal from small hearths in the bone-bearing level places these events at about 10,500 years ago, just prior to the mass extinctions that were to eradicate these species from North America.

Although Bonfire Shelter is the only mass-kill site known this far south of the southern Plains, the big game hunting strategy and the Folsom projectile point are similar to those found across great expanses of North America at this time. Thus, Lower Pecos lifeways were part of a widespread tradition of exploiting the large game animals of the last Ice Age. Soon afterward, increasing aridity and rising temperatures forced Lower Pecos populations to migrate or adapt to the encroaching desert habitat, laying the foundation for the Archaic stage, marked by small game foraging and plant gathering, that was to prevail with only one interruption until Historic times.

Some 8,000 years later, Bonfire Shelter was once again the scene of mass bison drives, this time by Late Archaic intruders who followed the herds from the southern Plains or central Texas. A short interlude of increasing moisture about 2,500 years ago permitted the grasslands to recolonize the region. The bison and their attendant hunters spread southward to the banks of the Rio Grande, where Bonfire Shelter again offered the optimal conditions for mass slaughter. Hurtling over the cliff, the beasts fell and were butchered; portions were dragged deeper into the shelter and stripped of meat, and the bones were broken and discarded. The remains of an estimated 800 animals form a massive bone layer three feet thick. The rotting meat scraps, bone, and grease apparently ignited spontaneously, like oily rags left in a pile, reducing much of the deposit to brittle fragments and ash and obscuring any possibility of detecting layers that might reflect different hunting episodes. Radiocarbon dates—derived from this burned bone and charcoal from small hearths used during the butchering process—indicate that these events took place about 500 B.C.

The dart points found in this bone bed (defined as *Montell, Castroville,* and *Marshall*) are more common at Late Archaic sites in central Texas. These specimens also resemble forms found at some Archaic bison kills in the Texas Panhandle. In the Lower Pecos, these styles were found

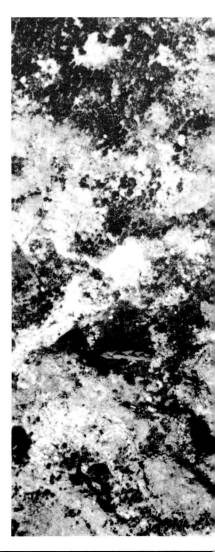

Aerial view of Bonfire Shelter, Rio Grande in background (Mexico).

in quantity at the Devils Mouth Site, Arenosa Shelter, and numerous other excavations and open sites. In all these contexts, they are considered time-markers for the Late Archaic period. Bonfire Shelter is the only site, however, where mass hunting techniques were clearly employed, indicating that for a brief time the bison of the Great Plains expanded their range to include the Lower Pecos. They were followed by their human predators, bearing their characteristic weapons. When the trend to aridity returned, the herds and their hunters retreated with the grasslands, leaving only this archaeological record of their intrusion.

A second change possibly coincides with the advent of the bison herds and hunters. In the miniature monochrome art style called Red Linear, scenes of combat, hunting, and ritual include one representation of a herd of bison racing toward a crack in the shelter wall. Although no concrete radiocarbon dates or associated cultural deposits can be related to this art style, the uncanny resemblance of this scene to the events at Bonfire Shelter seems more than coincidental.

Although separated in time by several thousand years, the lifeways of the Paleo-Indian and Late Archaic bison hunters of the Lower Pecos were probably similar in many respects to those of the prehorse Plains Indians. Big game hunting obviously played a major role in their economies, but this mobile food supply was undoubtedly supplemented by smaller game, fish, fowl, and plants. Predatory groups who follow migratory herds for a living must develop cooperative hunting techniques. Driving and mass slaughter of large untamed herd animals require a coordinated effort on the part of the hunters. Accounts of Plains Indian communal hunts prior to their acquisition of the horse describe methods by which they positioned the herds for stampede. In one approach, a *V*-shaped drive line was built of piled stones, arranged much like a funnel whose

Bones of extinct bison in bottom of excavation unit, 1964, Bonfire Shelter.

opening was the cliff or bluff selected for the jump. Hunters lay behind the piled stones hidden beneath brush or hides. A human decoy dressed in a bison costume wandered between the animals and the jump location. The curious bison would drift toward this runner until he had attracted them to the head of the drive line. At the appropriate moment, the hidden hunters would leap up waving brush or hides, starting the stampede. The decoy would jump into a hole dug for that purpose or dart out of the way as the herd began to run. If the lead animals saw the danger and tried to stop, the mass of panicked animals behind pushed them over the edge.

This technique reportedly required considerable coordination and timing so that the herd did not turn from the chosen path. Discipline was imposed so that an overanxious hunter did not prematurely start the stampede or frighten the animals before they were in the proper position. Shooting of individual bison was detrimental to the success of the mass kill and was discouraged. The jump technique thus required little use of weapons; this perhaps explains why so few projectile points are found in many kill sites. Another possible stampeding technique, known from Historic times, was the judicious use of grass fires to force the herds to run in the chosen direction. It is not known what methods were used to stampede the bison at Bonfire Shelter, but it is certain that they were successful.

Analogy to Historic Native Americans suggests that the bison was highly prized for a number of uses. The large quantities of meat obtained were dried on racks in the sun or over low fires. Powdered dried meat mixed with fat or bone marrow and various berries or fruits was a storable staple. Bones were made into tools or shattered to get to the nutritious marrow and boiled for bone grease. Bison hides were used for robes and made impermeable war shields. Bison horn headdresses transferred the strength of the beast to the wearer. Very few parts of the animal could not be used to advantage. However, in the upper bone bed of Bonfire Shelter, waste is apparent in the number of skeletal parts that were not dismembered and in the few butchering tools recovered. It seems the hunters were too successful, the overkill taxing the labor available to process all the carcasses fully. Both the bison periods at Bonfire Shelter were terminated by the onslaught of aridity, the retreat or demise of the herds, and acceptance on the part of the human population of a more foraging-oriented way of life.

1984 excavations at Bonfire Shelter. Hearth in far wall; right of unit is over 4,500 years old.

Deep in Bonfire Shelter, below the bison bone beds, ten feet beneath the current surface, are the traces of perhaps even earlier kills made by the most ancient of North American people. The scattered bones of mammals extinct on this continent for 10,000 years—elephants, camels, and horses— have been unearthed. No clear evidence of humans as the agent of death has yet been found with these bones, but the cut marks and breakage patterns on some skeletal parts suggest that these animals were trapped in the shelter and butchered. Bones from these and other extinct species at another site, Cueva Quebrada, were burned and broken, but there also, no hearths or flint tools confirm the presence of humans at this early date. Radiocarbon assays of charcoal at Cueva Quebrada range from 12,000 to 14,000 years ago, and the upper levels of the lowest bone deposit at Bonfire Shelter date to 10,000 to 12,000 years ago. Only additional excavation of Bonfire Shelter or a similar site will prove that humankind roved the Lower Pecos in company with elephants, camels, horses, sabertooths, and cave bears—all now long vanished, leaving only humans to consider their origins. ∎

LOWER PECOS LIFEWAYS
Housing and Daily Rounds

The first introduction to the prehistory of Texas that most visitors to the area receive is a display of artifacts (generally projectile points, sandals, bits of matting and netting, a bone awl, or a painted pebble) in some roadside museum or personal or public collection. These are all items that have been removed from places where the ancient hunters and gatherers left them— usually by amateur collectors unaware of the proper collection methods necessary for later scientific dating and interpretation.

This chapter deals with our best informed "guesses" about how these artifacts functioned in the daily lives of the lower canyon dwellers and about how these people related to their environment in general. Our reconstructions are based on five decades of archaeological excavation, combined with information from written accounts of Historic hunters and gatherers living adjacent to the lower canyons and from comparative studies of foraging groups from around the world.

Prehistoric Settlement Patterns

An archaeological site is any location that bears evidence of past human activity. A study of prehistoric sites across the lower canyon landscape, noting their characteristics, distribution, density, and configuration in time and space, provides us with data for an analysis of settlement patterns.

There are several kinds of archaeological sites in the region; although they appear distinctive in their

physical form, their functions were not always mutually exclusive. To complicate matters further, the same location may have been used in different ways at different times. Also, the entire landscape can be regarded in a broad sense as a site for mobile activities such as hunting, foraging, or plant collecting—the distribution of discarded harvesting tools and implements bears this out. There was a rain of artifacts and material by-products as each human group went about daily routines. The vast majority of this material waste is gone, leaving only a few puddles for us to deduce the total pattern of human activity that produced them.

Large hanging caves, created during the processes that formed the lower canyons, provided sheltered campsites for the hunters and gatherers from the time when they first entered the canyon country at the end of the Pleistocene. The sites were home base for hunting and gathering bands composed of men, women, and children. The caves were like any other home, providing shelter, security for the group, and a point from which members of the band could go about their daily chores. Daily tasks were determined mostly by the division of labor between the sexes.

The main river canyons contain the majority of the larger, occupied shelters. This was due not only to their spaciousness but also to the good foraging provided by adjacent uplands. Rockshelters, however, were not the only places selected for campsites. Outdoor camps along the riverbanks and low bluffs overlooking the rivers and around reliable waterholes were possibly even more common types of settlement.

The area extending some thirty miles upstream from the mouths of the Pecos and Devils rivers and

(PRECEDING SPREAD) *Evening scene in a cave shelter. The family is gathered around an earth oven, eating sotol cakes and cooked snails. A mother nurses her baby, and a boy looks over the canyon.*

View of Fate Bell Shelter in Seminole Canyon. A typical example of the kind of cave used by the Lower Pecos people.

the main Rio Grande canyon in between formed the residential core area of the lower canyon people. This region is bordered by a periphery zone that was exploited by trips from the main canyons. The fringing area included much of Terrell, Pecos, and Crockett counties, some of Sutton County, and the portion of Mexico that is drained by arroyos feeding into the Rio Grande.

Rockshelters and stream banks along the rivers in the residential core area were the preferred areas for camping. The availability of water was an obvious reason, but the aquatic animals, fish, and plants found there must have been equally important. From campsites along the main river canyons, the people could easily make their way to the canyon slopes and uplands where the edible desert plants were to be found. Generally, the frequency of rockshelter use drops off dramatically as one moves away from the main river canyons. Outdoor sites, too, tend to be more temporary in nature, the result of short stays or locations for specific short-term tasks.

The division of labor was one typical of other hunters and gatherers: men hunted; women gathered; and men, women, and children foraged. Men would set out singly or in small groups. From campsites along the rivers, they could easily walk along the canyons or to the uplands in search of the small game available. During such activities, the men would leave little in the way of refuse for archaeologists to identify. The remains of transient hunting campfires and lost or discarded projectile points are usually too insignificant to be found after hundreds or thousands of years.

The women would leave the base in the mornings in small groups to gather plant foods and to forage for wood, returning near the end of the day or when sufficient materials had been amassed. If small children were present, these were left in the care of other women or old men; nursing children would be taken along. Temporary overnight campsites were probably associated with gathering several miles away from the group's main shelter and then baking the accumulated bulbs of lechuguilla and sotol. The cooking process took several days and required the combined efforts of several men and women. Firewood was collected and, depending on the size of the band, one or several limestone-lined pits were prepared. Cooking locations tended to be traditional, resulting over time in the accumulation of sizable mounds of burned rock.

The use of limestone rocks in earth-oven baking occurs throughout much of the Lower Pecos cultural sequence. The earlier burned-rock accumulations tend to be either scatters or dome-shaped features. About A.D. 600, the midden forms change to a ring- or crescent-shaped deposit around the cooking pit itself. Such middens are usually mounded more on the west, northwest, or north side; the opposite sides may be open or free of burned rocks. Scattered midden debris in the form of chipped stone waste, stone artifacts, shell, and ashy soil often occurs south or southeast of the pit features. The finding of charred cut-leaf bases of lechuguilla and sotol in one such feature in Sanderson Canyon and the occurrence of hundreds of cut-leaf bases of sotol in the burned-rock portion of a midden under the overhang at Hinds Cave leave little doubt as to what was cooked in these features. Large quantities of land snails (*Rabdotus*) and frequent mussel shells even in middens several miles from the rivers suggest that the people would forage a few miles out from the pits while the food was baking.

In Val Verde County, the burned-rock midden accumulations become more common in the lower canyons of the larger tributaries as one moves away from the rivers. They also occur along the edge of the uplands near canyon heads. The crescent and ring middens constitute the most common archaeological site in the periphery zone of the core area— to the west, in Terrell County, and to the north, in Pecos and Crockett counties. A distribution study at Musk Hog Canyon, a small tributary of the Pecos River in Crockett County, revealed that burned-rock middens occur in literally every topographic and environmental situation in the canyon. The high frequency of crescent middens on the periphery of the lower canyons suggests that groups would leave the main canyons for short periods to hunt and to cook desert succulents in the peripheral zone, venturing as much as seventy miles from the Pecos and Rio Grande. At what time during the annual cycle this occurred is unknown, but winter is a good guess, since the aquatic fauna and fishing activities would be at a minimum during this time.

The same cooking process was conducted in rockshelters in both the lower canyons as well as in the peripheral zone. Archaeologists have found earth ovens in Fate Bell Shelter, Coontail Spin Shelter, and Hinds Cave as well as accumulations of burned rock at all rockshelters that were occupied for at least a moderate period of time.

The use of mortars and pestles to pulverize the cooked bulbs was a necessary sequence in earth-oven baking. Mortars were pounded out of the limestone bedrock at or near the cooking sites. These appear as symmetrical cone-shaped holes, usually occurring in clusters. Water was probably an important mixing ingredient in the recipe, because bedrock mortars tend to be clustered around water holes away from the main canyons. Mortars were also hollowed from tree trunks, and pestles were either elongated limestone cobbles or made from tree limbs.

Social groups were composed of families and single individuals banded together in a loosely structured unit. The size of bands is unknown, but if they were like the hunters and gatherers across the river in Mexico, they would number from about 25 to 150. A single band could have occupied several adjoining rockshelters or one large open-air campsite. Their preference was probably for a single open-air encampment, which provided some safety in numbers. Fishing drew

bands to settle along the rivers, and intensive foraging caused them to move periodically up, down, and across the river corridors to different locations. At times, the larger bands would break up, and family groups would range out from the residential core area to take advantage of limited seasonal resources.

Bands did not stay permanently in the rockshelters, although, judging from latrine deposits at Hinds Cave, they sometimes spent entire seasons in such locations. The use of shelters during the warm season, beginning in the early spring, is known from the kinds of plants brought into the sites. For example, at Hinds Cave, the dusty floor was sometimes covered with live oak leaves to keep down the dust; these leaves are shed in early spring just prior to pollination. Summer may have been a time when shelters were preferred for the shade provided against the heat. Shelters were occupied during periods of inclement weather and cold periods to escape the chilly winds. For most of the year, camps of artificial shelters were probably

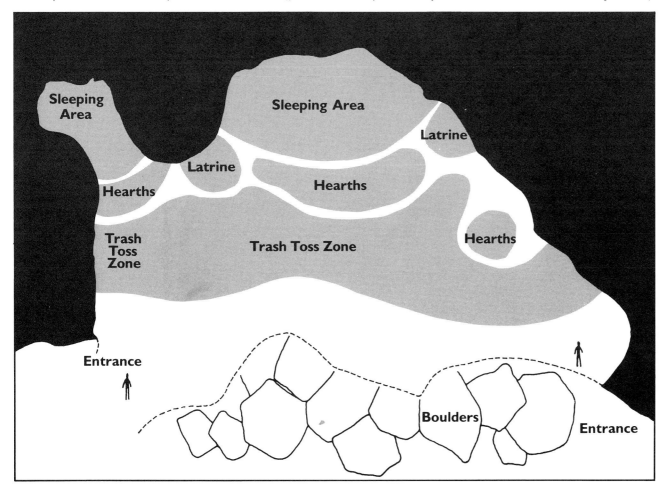

Floor plan of Hinds Cave. The shelter-caves in the deep limestone canyons were natural houses. Even without walls to delineate rooms as in modern homes, space in shelters such as Hinds Cave was segregated for various daily activities such as sleeping, cooking, latrine use, and trash disposal.

Three-thousand-year-old grass-lined bed in Hinds Cave provides the modern viewer an intimate look at ancient household habits.

built outdoors. Rockshelters would also be used for special tasks, such as earth-oven baking, during periods of wet weather, or by transient hunting or gathering parties for overnight or short stays.

Traces of painted figures and symbols occur in many of the sheltered overhangs in the lower canyon country. A number of these still stand as magnificent displays of ancient rock art despite their antiquity. These pictographs occur on the walls of many occupied shelters, but are also found on overhangs that were never occupied, possibly attesting to different social contexts for the painting and viewing of some of this art.

In general, isolated hearths, pit ovens, hunting camps, and gathering localities—that is, the single-purpose sites—are more easily distinguished as one moves away from the main camps in the canyons where the remains of specific activities have become masked and mixed with deposits from many periods of occupation. The overall picture that emerges is one of settlement along the river canyons, because of the constant availability of water and because every kind of environment could be visited with relative ease from there. Hunters ventured up the side canyons and into the uplands during the course of their hunting trips; overnight stays were necessary in order to be at good hunting grounds at opportune times of the day. Women and mixed foraging groups ranged out to gather foods, firewood, and other items such as grass, leaves, or whatever might be needed back at the base camps.

The Hunter-Gatherer Household

The security of a home has been pervasive in human psychological development throughout the course of history. It is the principal context where everyday fears and anxieties are relieved through social contact with those who are trusted and cared for. Personal views and beliefs are reinforced, and social attitudes are taught to the young. The function of an ancient household in a rockshelter or in a pole and brush dwelling on the banks of the Devils River was no different.

Space within the rockshelter or dwelling was divided into specific use areas. The flattest portion of the floor was the living room, where many day-to-day activities were carried out. Sometimes the dusty cave floor was covered with plant materials, such as leaves and twigs cut from various plants, including prickly pear. In the back portion of the living space near the rockshelter wall were sleeping areas, sometimes partitioned for privacy or warmth using poles and brush to form a semicircle out from the back wall. The segregated bedding areas may also have served to isolate women during menstruation or childbirth. The sleeping beds were shallow pits lined first with twigs and then with grass. These resilient beds were then lined with flat objects, such as discarded pieces of matting, leather, sandals, or prickly pear pads, and covered with checker-weave sleeping mats. The beds varied in size, probably depending on the size of the person or the number of people that used them.

In front of or beside the sleeping pits were the numerous hearths. Much food preparation was done in the shelters, as indicated by deposits of fire-cracked limestone, ash, food-processing tools (such as manos, metates, and mortars), charred food residue, and preserved plant materials. Remains from food preparation and hearth use were tossed out toward the front of the rockshelter. These trash or midden accumulations sometimes reached great depth, and their presence is a telltale sign that a rockshelter has been used as a living site.

Implements used in the course of daily life were made and often thrown away at the base camps. The residue from the manufacture of stone tools in the form of chert cobbles (from which flakes were struck), residual flakes, defective points and knives, the leftovers from basketry manufacture, and discarded items of wood, bone, and fiber all serve to indicate what the people were doing in the caves. Most of the discarded items were tossed toward the open side of the rockshelters, into other midden deposits.

The location of the latrines was specific. Latrine areas were situated at the far edge of the living space along the cave walls at either end of the rockshelters. Rarely are feces found away from the designated latrine areas.

Rockshelters were naturally designed houses, semicircular in plan with one closed side and one open side. While we do not have any specific data on the construction of outdoor dwellings, we would expect them to be like those described by Spanish chroniclers for the hunters and gatherers encountered across the Rio Grande in Chihuahua. If so, the shelters were semicicular, with one closed and one open side. The shape was conical, made of a pole framework (probably of sotol stalks) and covered with reeds, checkerweave mats, or skins. Space within the artificial dwellings was probably structured much like that within the rockshelters, only smaller in scale. Hearths would

have been located near the open side just as they were in the rockshelters.

Hearths were of two basic kinds, simple shallow basins to receive a wood fire or rock-lined basins constructed to radiate heat from the rocks after the fire had burned down. These fires may have had different functions. Some would serve as basic sources for light, heat, and quick open-flame cooking, while others would be used for oven baking and as heat radiators during cold nights. The stones lining the hearths probably served to keep the plant materials lining the floor from catching fire.

Accumulated personal or job-specific tools and implements had to be left behind when the group moved to another location. Because the region was shared with other bands, there was no guarantee that a particular group would be the first to return to a given site. Therefore, shallow pits were sometimes dug to hide objects that could be used again on returning. Obviously, there were times when the items were not retrieved, and such caches have been found by archaeologists. Digging sticks and baskets were found in one such cache at Hinds Cave by Fred Speck; a net bag with a mano was found at Fate Bell Shelter; one cache at Horseshoe Ranch Caves contained a net bag with a series of items representing a personal tool kit. Another basket at the same site contained a pair of sandals. Cached mortars and pestles have been found at Sorcerer's Cave and Pandale Crossing.

Child Care

The archaeological remains contain little to indicate how the ancient lower canyon people cared for their children. Cradles made of wooden frames and twilled or twined soft fiber body have been recovered. Cradles were necessary to carry infants safely during movements from camp to camp and during the women's gathering and foraging journeys. Pits lined with twigs and grass covered over with matting have been found that are virtually identical to ordinary sleeping beds, but are much too small for adults. Presumably these were beds for infants; one such "crib," found at the Perry Calk Site, was lined with a piece of buffalo skin. Infant burials indicate that children were treated with the same respect afforded adults in death. The Spanish often describe cruel and inhuman treatment of infants by northern Mexican Indians, including infant sacrifice during times of stress or to cure someone of sickness. Children were sometimes exchanged and sacrificed in cannibalistic rituals. To what extent these

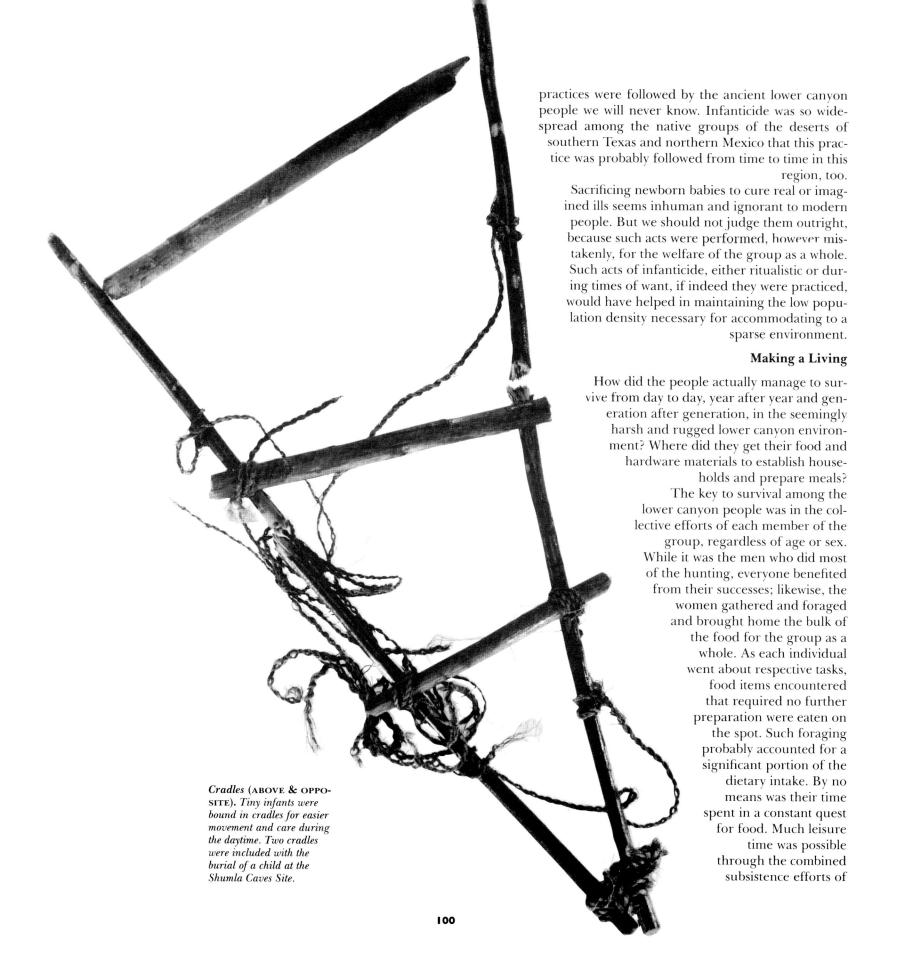

practices were followed by the ancient lower canyon people we will never know. Infanticide was so widespread among the native groups of the deserts of southern Texas and northern Mexico that this practice was probably followed from time to time in this region, too.

Sacrificing newborn babies to cure real or imagined ills seems inhuman and ignorant to modern people. But we should not judge them outright, because such acts were performed, however mistakenly, for the welfare of the group as a whole. Such acts of infanticide, either ritualistic or during times of want, if indeed they were practiced, would have helped in maintaining the low population density necessary for accommodating to a sparse environment.

Making a Living

How did the people actually manage to survive from day to day, year after year and generation after generation, in the seemingly harsh and rugged lower canyon environment? Where did they get their food and hardware materials to establish households and prepare meals?

The key to survival among the lower canyon people was in the collective efforts of each member of the group, regardless of age or sex. While it was the men who did most of the hunting, everyone benefited from their successes; likewise, the women gathered and foraged and brought home the bulk of the food for the group as a whole. As each individual went about respective tasks, food items encountered that required no further preparation were eaten on the spot. Such foraging probably accounted for a significant portion of the dietary intake. By no means was their time spent in a constant quest for food. Much leisure time was possible through the combined subsistence efforts of

Cradles (ABOVE & OPPO-SITE). *Tiny infants were bound in cradles for easier movement and care during the daytime. Two cradles were included with the burial of a child at the Shumla Caves Site.*

everyone. This time was devoted to socializing and to personal time, essential for psychological and educational development.

The canyon people's adaptive success was the result of several factors: the nondestructive way in which they used their environment, the relatively low population density (which never taxed the limits of the food resources), their ability to endure lean periods, their means of enculturation and education (which passed on successful traditions), and their balanced diet (which provided all the necessary vitamins, minerals, and calories).

Basic to their everyday life was the division of labor, largely based on sex and, to some extent, on age. Men performed the more demanding and dangerous chores, often at some distance from the camp. Women assumed those chores that kept them closer to the camp because of their role in child caring. The women's activities were often no less strenuous than those of the men, although less risky. Men were traditionally the hunters and women the gatherers; both men and women foraged. This division was probably not that straightforward, with men accompanying women on strenuous gathering and baking ventures and women going along on some of the more extended hunting forays.

Hunting Technology

By the time a boy went through his puberty ceremony, his rite of passage from childhood to manhood, he had learned most of the essentials that men needed to know. He had learned how to make the necessary weapons and to use them since childhood. He was taught how to identify the crucial signs required for tracking, where to expect game, how to make and set traps, how to select chert and chip stone tools, and what taboos he needed to observe so as not to anger the animal spirits. The boys learned to be men by direct instruction from kinsmen, by observation and mimicry, by listening to the stories told by successful hunters, and from examples set forth in myths and folklore.

For most of the time the ancient hunters lived in the lower canyons (from the end of the Pleistocene to

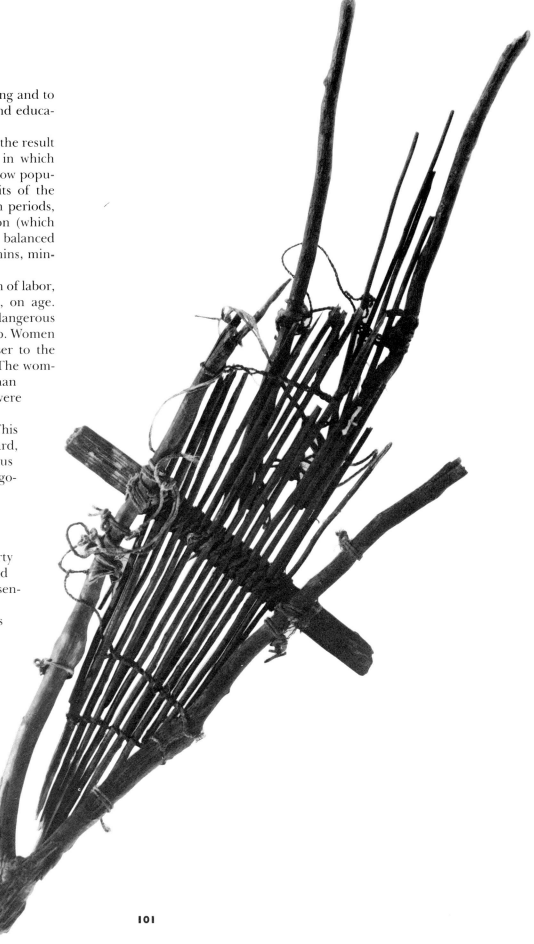

Atlatls. The principal weapon of the ancient hunters and gatherers throughout most of their history was the spear thrower (atlatl) and spear. The spear thrower was a device about eighteen inches long with a handle fashioned for holding at one end and a hook of some form at the opposite end. The hook fit into a cup carved in the butt end of the spear. The atlatl provided a substantial increase in thrust and gave the hunter the advantage of throwing the spear more accurately and for a greater distance than if it was thrown by hand (see illustration p. 16–17). Atlatls occur in various sizes and styles. Some of the styles may represent changes through time, while others may represent individual preference.

about A.D. 900), their principal weapon was a spear propelled with a spear thrower or atlatl. Spear shafts and fragments found in various rockshelters show that the spears were composite tools consisting of a main shaft and a foreshaft to which a stone projectile point was attached. The main shaft was either a slender hardwood sapling or a lechuguilla stalk. The butt or proximal end was cup-shaped to receive the small hook of the atlatl. Sinew was wrapped around the butt end to prevent splitting from the force of the thrust. The distal end of the main shaft was drilled to receive the foreshaft and also wrapped to prevent splitting from impact. The foreshaft had a notch cut into one end; the stone point was set into the notch and secured by a wrapping of sinew or plant fibers.

A small number of spear thrower fragments have been found in rockshelters, representing a considerable range in style, which may indicate individual preferences or possibly differences in time. One style is a flat board with a shallow groove at the distal end. The atlatl's hook is formed by a projection at the end of the groove. An example of this style came from a late period (about A.D. 400–700) deposit at Bonfire Shelter, and another from one of the Shumla Caves. Another atlatl style is a small, slightly curved limb with the hook carved at one end. This form was found at Coontail Spin Shelter in deposits that date to the latter portion of the Pandale Interval, about 3,500 years ago. A third style, found in the Shumla Caves, was carved with an oval cross-section; one edge was grooved and the hook was carved at the termination of the groove. This specimen also had a zigzag decoration incised along both sides, perhaps for personal identification. Atlatls can also be composite tools consisting of a wooden main shaft and a carved bone or antler hook.

One example of an atlatl carved from an antler tine was found at Shumla Caves. The end opposite the hook was socketed for attachment to the wooden shaft. A pin would have been inserted into the socket to secure the two pieces. No stratigraphic information is available on these last two specimens, but almost identical antler tine atlatl hooks have been found in central Texas that date about A.D. 400–700.

After about A.D. 900, hunters were armed with bows and arrows. Archaeologists have found no bows, but have found arrows of cane with wooden foreshafts tipped with small pressure-flaked stone points or with hardwood points. Arrows were fletched with two feathers. Personalized designs were often placed on

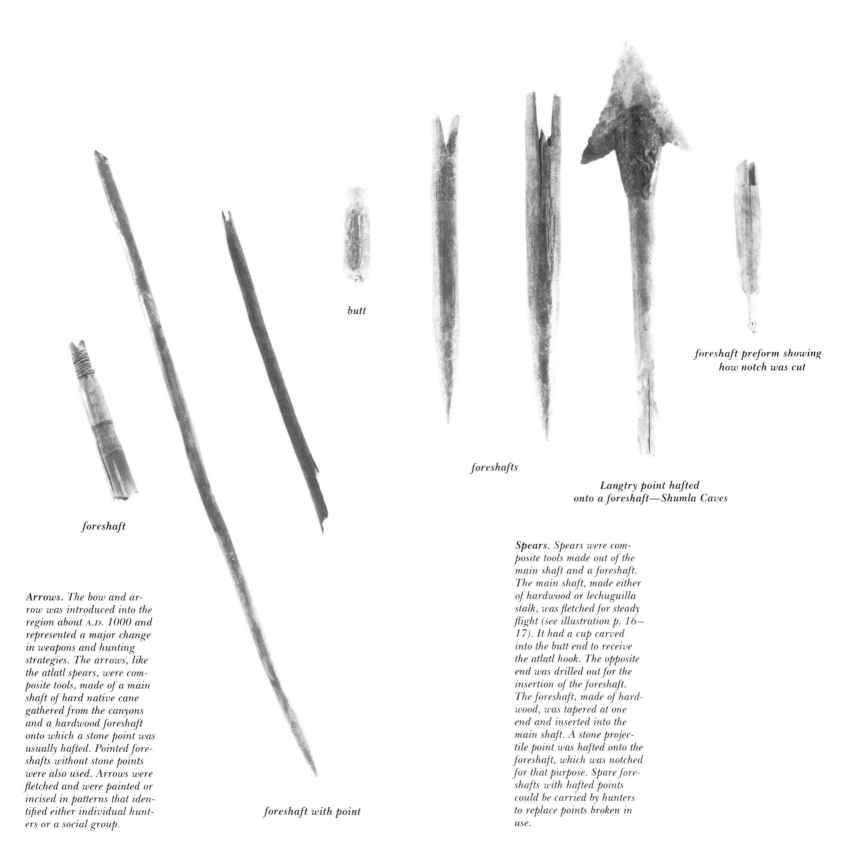

butt

foreshaft

foreshaft with point

foreshafts

foreshaft preform showing how notch was cut

Langtry point hafted onto a foreshaft—Shumla Caves

Arrows. The bow and arrow was introduced into the region about A.D. 1000 and represented a major change in weapons and hunting strategies. The arrows, like the atlatl spears, were composite tools, made of a main shaft of hard native cane gathered from the canyons and a hardwood foreshaft onto which a stone point was usually hafted. Pointed foreshafts without stone points were also used. Arrows were fletched and were painted or incised in patterns that identified either individual hunters or a social group.

Spears. Spears were composite tools made out of the main shaft and a foreshaft. The main shaft, made either of hardwood or lechuguilla stalk, was fletched for steady flight (see illustration p. 16–17). It had a cup carved into the butt end to receive the atlatl hook. The opposite end was drilled out for the insertion of the foreshaft. The foreshaft, made of hardwood, was tapered at one end and inserted into the main shaft. A stone projectile point was hafted onto the foreshaft, which was notched for that purpose. Spare foreshafts with hafted points could be carried by hunters to replace points broken in use.

the arrow shafts at the knock end. Painted decorations on the arrows identified the hunter and his group affiliation. This was important not so much to mark individual property as to make sure that the meat would be fairly distributed among the group to which the hunter belonged.

Men also carried clubs or rabbit sticks. These were carved out of solid wood and were shaped much like boomerangs. A handle was carved on one end and the flattened sides of the stick were incised with three parallel grooves. These sticks served many functions besides being weapons for clubbing rabbits. They could be used to scrape coals from a fire, or to fend away thorny brush, or as an anchor to twist fibers in repairing a net.

Men used nets and snares to catch fish, rabbits, and other game. Precisely how fish were netted is unknown, but most likely they simply placed a net across some chosen location in a river; fish swimming by would then become entangled in the net. Net fragments, commonly found in the collections, could be from such fishing nets. Seines may also have been used for smaller fish such as perch and minnows. Rabbits were probably taken by stretching a long net across an arroyo and then driving the rabbits into the barrier, where they could easily be clubbed or shot. This technique of hunting rabbits was widespread throughout the American Southwest and northern Mexico even in Historic times. Squirrels, rats, and other quarry were probably snared or trapped; snares

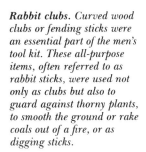

Rabbit clubs. Curved wood clubs or fending sticks were an essential part of the men's tool kit. These all-purpose items, often referred to as rabbit sticks, were used not only as clubs but also to guard against thorny plants, to smooth the ground or rake coals out of a fire, or as digging sticks.

and snare fragments have been found in many of the rockshelter sites.

Men on the move not only carried their weapons; they also took along a small net or fiber bag containing a basic tool kit from which they could make any tool they might need. One such bag was found cached intact in Horseshoe Ranch Caves. It contained such items as a spare sinew, rawhide strip, three deer antler pressure flaking tools, a limestone pebble hammerstone, four unfinished bifaces for future projectile points, uniface flake knives, pigment, rabbit mandibles, and mountain laurel seeds. The bag was first described as a "medicine bundle," but a more mundane function is suggested on the basis of the items represented. It is difficult to interpret the use of the rabbit mandibles and mountain laurel seeds. They may have been deemed essential to ward off evil or as offerings to animal spirits, or as hallucinogens and scarifiers during hunting rituals. The items needed for such rites were as important to the hunter as his spear and would therefore be an essential part of a basic tool kit.

Gathering Technology

Gathering for women was both work and a time for socializing with other women in the band. Because of the women's child-caring responsibilities, they probably ranged away from the campsite only for a few hours at a time. If overnight trips were necessary, men would go along. In the course of their gathering activities, women needed only a few basic items. Most important was the digging stick, a hardwood stick with a beveled, chisellike end, used to pry up lechuguilla and sotol bulbs from the ground, dig for certain root plants, knock fruit from cactus, and, if necessary, to club a snake or some other small animal.

Second only to the digging stick in importance was

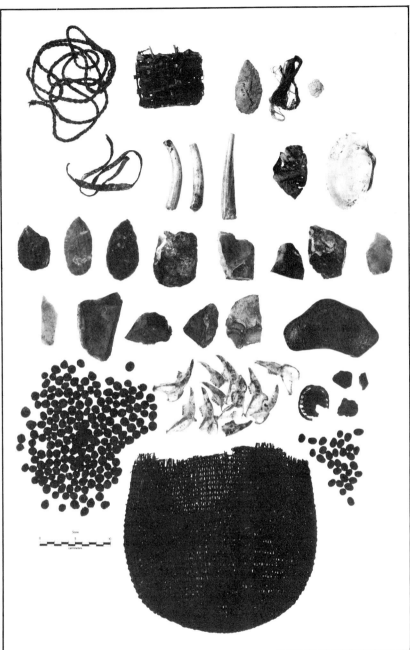

Horseshoe Ranch Caves medicine bundle. The contents of this net bag or medicine bundle indicate its purpose as a man's personal tool kit. It includes blanks for making projectile points, a hammerstone, spare sinew, cordage, jackrabbit mandible scarifiers, mountain laurel seeds for hallucinogenic use, and buckeye seeds, possibly for use as fish poison.

Example of a simple plaited basket. Such containers were almost box-shaped but were pliable and flexible.

Close-up section of three twilled mats. Twilling or plaiting was done in a variety of ways with techniques that changed with both the item being made and the time it was made. In twilling, both the warp and weft elements were flexible and interwoven. The simplest form is a one-over-one weave (LEFT). More complicated two-over-two (CENTER) or three-over-three (RIGHT) weaves were used for tightly woven mats and baskets.

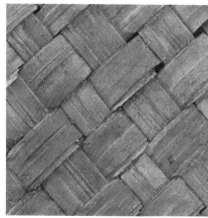

106

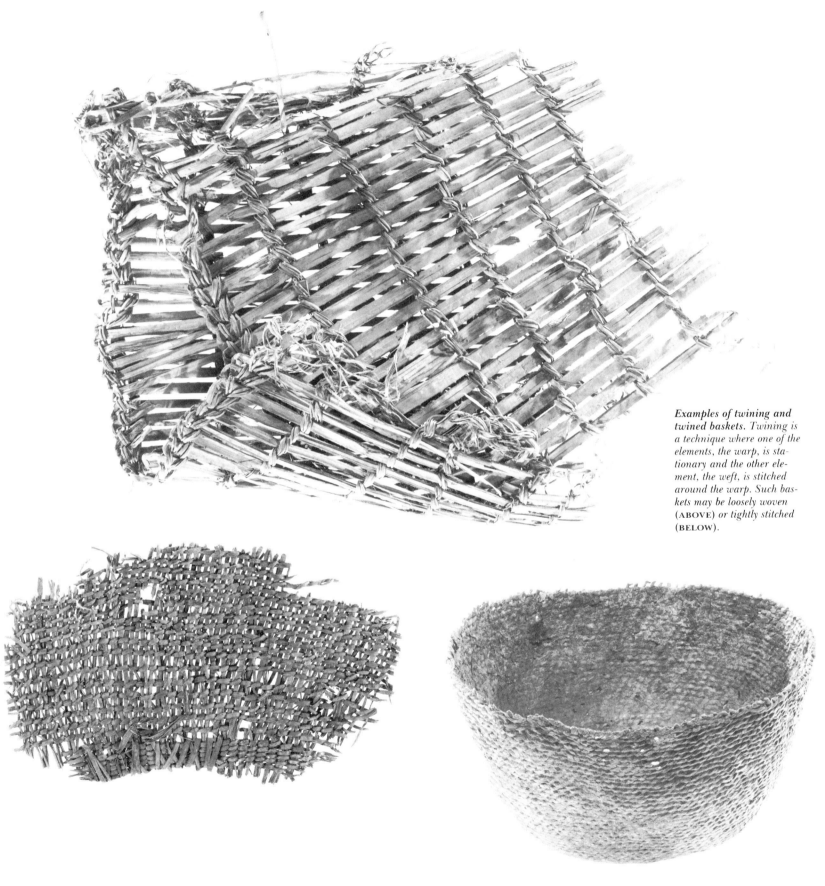

Examples of twining and twined baskets. Twining is a technique where one of the elements, the warp, is stationary and the other element, the weft, is stitched around the warp. Such baskets may be loosely woven (ABOVE) or tightly stitched (BELOW).

107

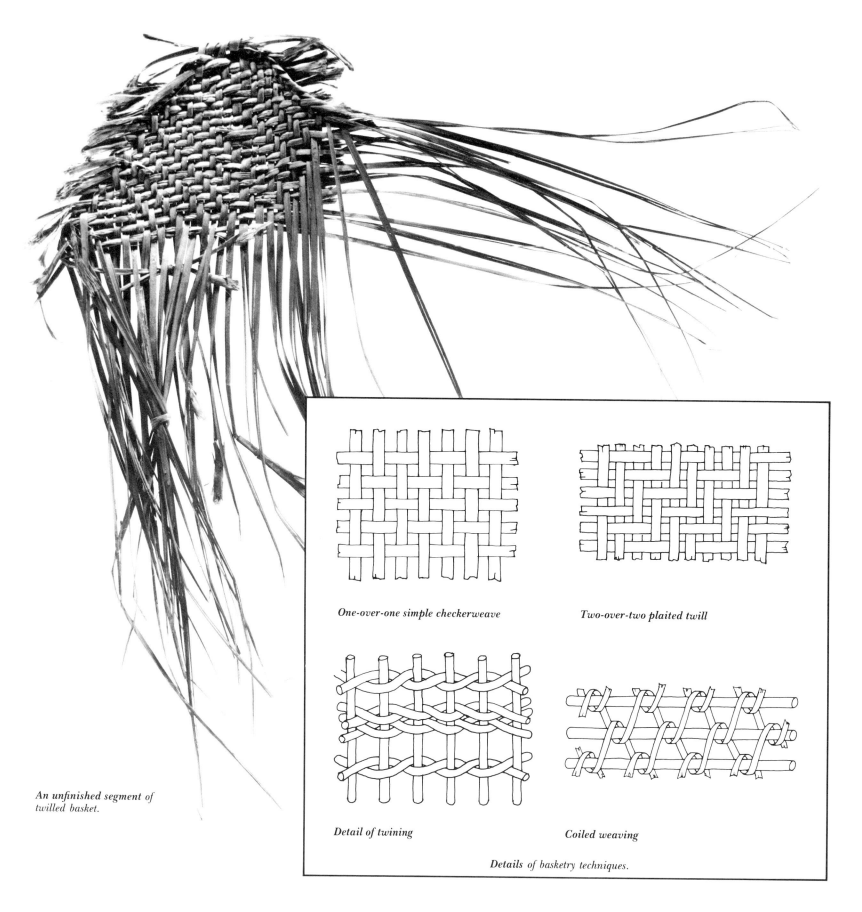

An unfinished segment of twilled basket.

One-over-one simple checkerweave

Two-over-two plaited twill

Detail of twining

Coiled weaving

Details of basketry techniques.

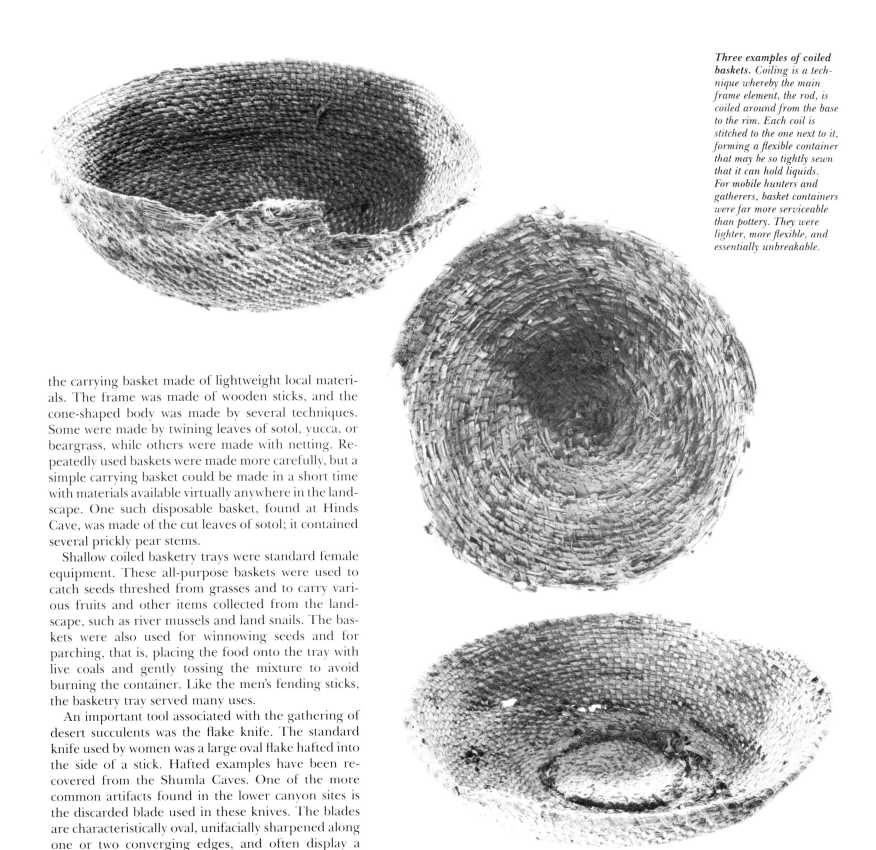

Three examples of coiled baskets. *Coiling is a technique whereby the main frame element, the rod, is coiled around from the base to the rim. Each coil is stitched to the one next to it, forming a flexible container that may be so tightly sewn that it can hold liquids. For mobile hunters and gatherers, basket containers were far more serviceable than pottery. They were lighter, more flexible, and essentially unbreakable.*

the carrying basket made of lightweight materials. The frame was made of wooden sticks, and the cone-shaped body was made by several techniques. Some were made by twining leaves of sotol, yucca, or beargrass, while others were made with netting. Repeatedly used baskets were made more carefully, but a simple carrying basket could be made in a short time with materials available virtually anywhere in the landscape. One such disposable basket, found at Hinds Cave, was made of the cut leaves of sotol; it contained several prickly pear stems.

Shallow coiled basketry trays were standard female equipment. These all-purpose baskets were used to catch seeds threshed from grasses and to carry various fruits and other items collected from the landscape, such as river mussels and land snails. The baskets were also used for winnowing seeds and for parching, that is, placing the food onto the tray with live coals and gently tossing the mixture to avoid burning the container. Like the men's fending sticks, the basketry tray served many uses.

An important tool associated with the gathering of desert succulents was the flake knife. The standard knife used by women was a large oval flake hafted into the side of a stick. Hafted examples have been recovered from the Shumla Caves. One of the more common artifacts found in the lower canyon sites is the discarded blade used in these knives. The blades are characteristically oval, unifacially sharpened along one or two converging edges, and often display a

Lower Pecos People: Division of Labor (projected, based on ethnographic studies of other hunters and gatherers)

Activity	Male	Female
Hunting	X	
Fishing	X	
Gathering	X	XF
Foraging	X	X
Infant care		X
Child care	X	XF
Hearth construction	XM	X
Fire making	X	X
House construction	X	XF
House features (beds, etc.)	X	XF
Weaving	X	X
Food preparation	X	XF
Cooking	X	XF
Flintknapping	XM	X
Woodworking	X	
Hide preparation	X	X
Healing	XM	X

XF or XM indicates that these activities are predominantly female (F) or|male (M)

prominent polish on the flat, unflaked side. Such tools from Hinds Cave still retain bits of sotol and lechuguilla residue, preserving a history of their use. Also, microscopic examination of edge-wear patterns revealed that these knives were used mostly to slice the soft plants, but a light chopping or hacking motion was sometimes used to cut more resistant materials. The knives were also used by women in everyday chores around the camp. Their maintenance and replacement made it necessary for the women to have some knowledge of flintknapping.

A number of activities were collectively performed by all members of the band physically capable of the task, including gathering firewood and grass for bedding and flooring or other materials needed for use around the camp by the group as a whole. Both women and men probably processed fibers and made textiles, depending on what was being made and how it was to be used. Cradles, sleeping mats, carrying baskets, coiled baskets, and other items generally associated with women's tasks were probably made by them.

While the men provided the raw material for bone awls, the women probably adapted and owned these devices for their textile making. Men made their weapons and other implements, and probably their own cordage, netting, and textiles. Sandals were most likely made by both sexes since the manufacture and repair of footwear would be necessary for both males and females during occasions away from the campsites.

Technological Efficiency

One of the more impressive aspects of the lower canyon people is their technological efficiency. Every bit of raw material needed to make the tools of their lifeway was readily at hand. The essential materials for hunting and gathering tools, clothing, food preparation, and other household needs were all available in the local environment. Excellent-quality chert for the manufacture of chipped stone tools can be found in outcrops in many of the lower canyons and along the canyon slopes. Chert is also abundant in the gravels of both major and minor canyons. Good chert becomes scarcer as one moves northward in the region, and these spotty outcrops were extensively used by mobile groups as they passed through the vicinity.

Likewise, fiber for cordage was abundantly available over the entire region; yucca and lechuguilla were the choice resources for fiber, although human hair was also used consistently. Fibers for baskets and mats were made of lechuguilla, yucca, and sotol; grasses and juniper bark were often incorporated into softer baskets, cradles, or mats. Stalks of the sotol and lechuguilla plants served a multitude of functions, for basket frames, spear shafts, fire hearth sticks, fire tongs, knife handles, painted sticks, digging sticks, and firewood, among other things. Perishable items recovered from the various rockshelters show evidence of repair, and reuse of discarded items was common. A torn or partly burned sleeping mat was no longer useful for that purpose, but the fragments could be used to line a pit or cover a cache, or be folded into a small container. Likewise, a worn-out sandal could be used to line a sleeping bed or be stitched to the sole of another worn sandal for quick repair.

The chance discovery of a source of firewood or a tree full of fruit was not passed up for lack of a ready-made carrying container. Yucca leaves were cut and split; the split segments were tied together to make long strips that could be wrapped around the firewood bundle and looped over the shoulder. This way the burden could be carried back to the campsite while keeping hands and arms free. Once at the campsite, the fiber strips were discarded. Such bits of knotted leaves constitute some of the more frequent perishable artifacts found in dry rockshelters. Similarly, yucca or beargrass leaves could be cut and quickly woven into a twined container to carry collected fruit. Such expedient technology was conditioned by the people's mobility and the availability of raw materials. The hunters, gatherers, and foragers did not need to load themselves down with a whole array of implements; impromptu containers, bundles, or tools could be made as the need arose during the course of their daily rounds and discarded when no longer required.

Sotol or agave knives. These two specimens from the Shumla Caves were made of large oval flakes hafted into the side of sticks. They were used for the daily tasks of cutting and slicing, especially for removing the barbed leaves from desert succulents. Once hafted, the chert blades were resharpened by removing chips from along the edge.

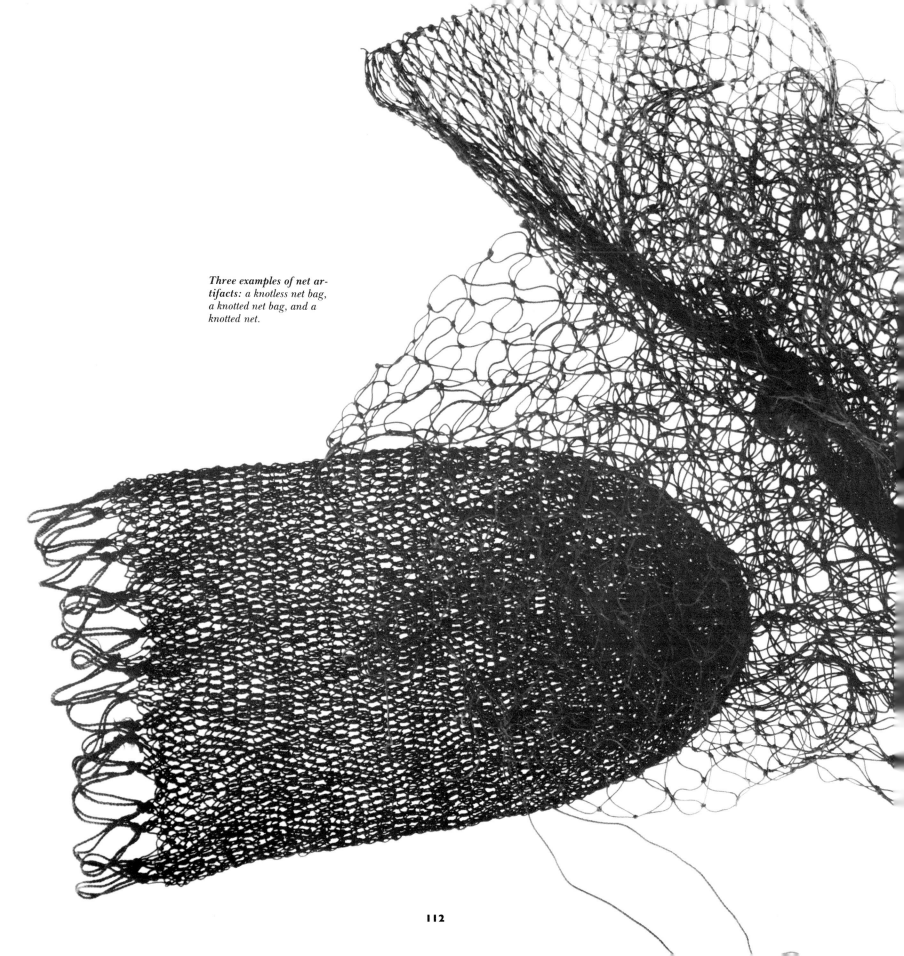

Three examples of net artifacts: a knotless net bag, a knotted net bag, and a knotted net.

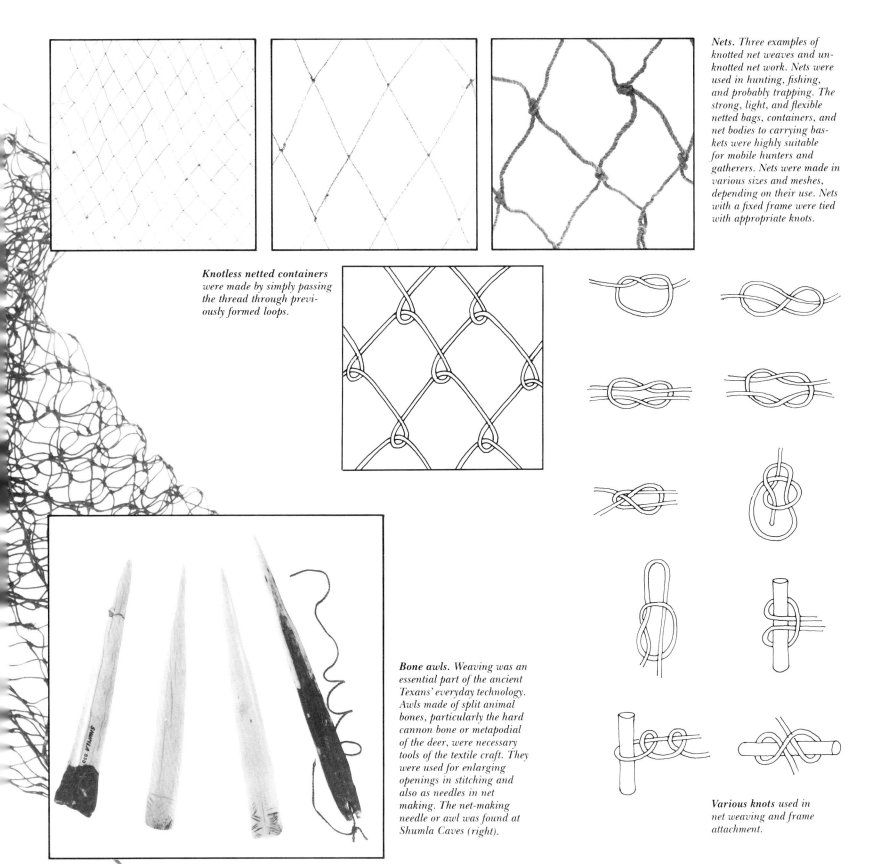

Nets. *Three examples of knotted net weaves and unknotted net work. Nets were used in hunting, fishing, and probably trapping. The strong, light, and flexible netted bags, containers, and net bodies to carrying baskets were highly suitable for mobile hunters and gatherers. Nets were made in various sizes and meshes, depending on their use. Nets with a fixed frame were tied with appropriate knots.*

Knotless netted containers *were made by simply passing the thread through previously formed loops.*

Bone awls. *Weaving was an essential part of the ancient Texans' everyday technology. Awls made of split animal bones, particularly the hard cannon bone or metapodial of the deer, were necessary tools of the textile craft. They were used for enlarging openings in stitching and also as needles in net making. The net-making needle or awl was found at Shumla Caves (right).*

Various knots *used in net weaving and frame attachment.*

113

Fire Making

Fire was an essential ingredient of any encampment, whether it was an itinerant hunters' camp or the band's base camp. To make a fire, all that was needed was a split, dry sotol stalk and another dry, pencil-sized stick of harder wood. Sotol stalks are relatively soft and fibrous and were used as the hearth portion of the fire-making apparatus. A notch was cut in the bottom near the edge of the split sotol stick. The cup formed to receive the fire drill was prepared on the flat surface of the stick. The fire drill was rotated by hand, although a bow-drill may have been used late in the archaeological sequence of the region. The notch on the underside of the hearth stick served as a space for smoldering embers to fall through onto a prepared batch of readily available tinder. Fire-making tools were kept for repeated use, since fire drills often show evidence of considerable wear and hearth sticks often exhibit several charred holes.

Knowledge of fire making was probably shared by both men and women. Like many other aspects of their technology, the raw materials for fire making could be found virtually anywhere in the environment. Other artifacts associated with fireplaces include fire tongs made of split sotol sticks bound together at the handle end, flat pieces of wood used to rake coals, and river pebbles that may have been used for stone boiling.

Subsistence and Diet

What would the grocery list be like for the ancient hunters and gatherers as they went "shopping"? It would depend upon the time of year and where they were hunting or foraging—but opportunism always ruled the day. No edible plant or animal was passed up, however unappetizing most of the food available to the lower canyon people would be to contemporary palates.

Combined studies of plant remains from dry rockshelter deposits (by Phil Dering, David Riskind, and Vaughn Bryant), of the contents of desiccated human feces from ancient latrines (by Vaughn Bryant, David Riskind, Glenna Williams-Dean, and Janet Stock), and of faunal remains from campsite middens (by Charles Douglas, Ernest Lundelius, and Kenneth Lord) have revealed the cuisine of the ancient canyon inhabitants. Also, studies on plant and animal ecology (by Phil Dering and David Schmidly) have shown where various species existed in habitats around the sites and what

Fire-making tools. Fire was essential to life in ancient Texas. Fire making was learned early in life by using available materials. A split dry sotol stalk (Dasylirion sp.) was used as a hearth stick. A small cup was carved into the split surface of the stalk to receive the fire drill. A notch was cut at the edge of the cup to allow the smoldering embers to drop onto the tinder placed beneath the hearth stick. The hardwood fire drill was rotated with the hands. Heat generated from the friction of the fire drill caused fine particles created at the same time to smolder. Blowing on the smoldering particles soon caused the tinder to flame.

Grinding slab and mano.
Prehistoric food processors
used in preparing hard-
cased seeds, such as grasses,
walnuts, or acorns, were
bedrock mortars (photo) or
grinding slabs together with
hand-held grinding stones,
or manos. These tools were
as essential to ancient Texans as the cutting boards
and food processors of modern kitchens.

people had to do in order to harvest various resources.

The riverine habitat was especially important for its available range of foods. Fishing played a major part in subsistence activities. Nets, poisons, hook and line, spears, and catching by hand were all techniques used to capture fish and turtles. Fish found in rockshelter and open campsite deposits along the river include longnose gar, blue sucker, river carp sucker, redhorse sucker, smallmouth buffalo, flathead catfish, and blue catfish. Turtles caught include the spiny softshell turtle and cooters. Among the mammals captured along the rivers were muskrats, raccoons, beavers, river otters, ringtails, Texas pocket gophers, and opossums. Other aquatic species found among the food remains were river mussels, leopard frogs, geese, ducks, and coots. Plant species used for foods were minimal along the rivers, but were exploited when encountered. Grasses and seeds of native cane were probably used, along with onions and the bulbs of the water lily; cattails and other aquatic plants probably served for greens, although no direct evidence of the use of aquatic plants has been identified in coprolites to date.

From tributary canyons and canyon bluffs and slopes, the hunters and foragers obtained ground squirrels, rock squirrels, gophers, several species of mice, kangaroo rats, woodrats, porcupines, badgers, coyotes, gray foxes, skunks, deer, mountain lions, bobcats, several species of birds, lizards, snakes (including rock rattlers and diamondback rattlers), and insects. Among the plants harvested were lechuguilla, sotol, yucca, prickly pear, persimmon, mesquite, wild grape, Mormon tea, hackberry, onion, acorns, walnuts, and, in some areas, pecans. Various grass seeds and weeds eaten as greens were probably also collected.

Uplands yielded many of the same animal and plant species as found in canyon slopes and bluffs. In addition, these were the primary habitat for certain species like cottontail rabbits and jackrabbits, antelope, and some mice, rats, snakes, and lizards. Deer were also hunted in the uplands. Snails were collected after rains during the warm season, and insects were gathered when encountered. Sotol communities occur at various localities in the uplands; lechuguilla, yucca, and prickly pear were also staple plants that could be collected easily in this habitat. Various grasses were collected, and many of the fruits of the canyons, such as persimmon, walnut, hackberry, and mesquite, were also present.

Staple plants available most or all of the year were the stems of prickly pear and the bulbs of sotol and le-

chuguilla. Prickly pear could be eaten raw or steamed, but sotol and lechuguilla had to be baked in earth ovens for several days. When ripe, from midsummer to late fall, prickly pear fruit was eaten in quantity. Precisely how it was prepared, other than being eaten raw, we do not know, although seeds recovered from coprolites often seem to be crushed as if ground on a metate or pounded in a mortar. Prickly pear seeds were recovered from the cracks of a wooden mortar cached in a crevice near Pandale.

The fruit of yucca, mesquite, persimmon, Texas walnut, pecan, native hackberry, and probably certain acorns were eaten when seasonally or geographically available in the eastern portion of the region along the Devils River drainage. Some acorns require leaching to remove the tannic acid before they can be consumed; this was probably done, since acorns are common seed casings found in the shelter fill.

The studies of human feces have all shown the degree to which these people depended upon the plant remains for their bulk food. Gathering activities by women and foraging by all members of a band provided the majority of the foods eaten. Hunting, although an important male function, contributed relatively little to the daily diet in terms of overall protein percentages. Most of the animal remains found in coprolites were those that were either caught by hand or snared or trapped.

Since meat is almost totally disintegrated in the human digestive tract, discrete kinds of meat consumed cannot be distinguished in fecal remains. However, the lower canyon people were not particular by current standards when eating the various kinds of animals they captured. Small animals were often eaten whole, without any form of preparation, and their skeletal remains appear in the preserved stools. Humans cannot digest hair, so any hair that is eaten along with the meat passes through the system. It is largely these undigested remains and discarded animal parts in trash deposits that permit identification of specific kinds of animals consumed.

Seasonal Movements and Scheduling

In regions where food resources are distributed over a wide area and the availability of various foods is determined partly on the basis of season, hunters and gatherers need to plan their movements carefully. In the lower canyons, strategies of seasonal movement were also determined by the availability of material resources such as firewood. Prolonged stays at one lo-

Digging sticks. The main tools for women's field labors were digging sticks and carrying baskets. Digging sticks were hardwood limbs cut and shaped with a pointed or beveled end. They were used to extract desert succulents and root plants from the ground or as fending sticks or clubs. Favored digging sticks were used for long periods of time, often causing them to become polished from the heat and oils of the users' hands.

cation diminished the chances of catching game and denuded the locality of firewood and critical plants, making a shift in settlement necessary.

The region encompassed by this study is only about 14,400 square miles in area (about 120 miles east to west and 120 miles north to south). However, the area is sufficiently large to display clinal weather effects and seasonal variation in the fruiting of certain plants. Since this is a marginal desert environment with a relatively long warm season, once flowering begins—in early or mid-spring—flowers and fruits become available until late fall. Three factors determine the flowering cycle of many of the desert plants in the region: temperature, amount of available sunlight, and moisture. Theoretically, these conditions can occur at any time during the warm season; botanists on the Hinds Cave project observed a second flowering for several plant species following a particularly heavy rainstorm in the summer of 1975.

The three lower canyon staples—prickly pear, sotol, and lechuguilla—could be harvested throughout the year; but with the onset of spring, additional plants became available and afforded a change in diet. Yucca flowers and onions were among the first to appear, and flowers from various cacti bloomed shortly thereafter. That flowers were eaten is shown by unusually high concentrations of pollen present in certain feces. Wild plums, occurring in the eastern portion of the region, were collected later in the spring or early summer.

Late summer was a time of plentitude for the hunters and gatherers. Mesquite beans, prickly pear fruit, persimmons, hackberries, and grapes were available in the canyons and uplands. Sotol, yucca, and lechuguilla seeds were also ripening. During late summer the people may have been concentrated in the deep canyons of the Pecos and Rio Grande, where they could take advantage of aquatic resources and forage throughout the resource-laden canyons and nearby uplands.

Fall foods included prickly pear fruit (which matures in a gradient from south to north), pecans along the Devils River drainage, mesquite beans, acorns, walnuts, and grass seeds. Heavy but spotty thunderstorms brought out onions and other greens and were probably carefully monitored to benefit from their effect on plant growth. Because a greater diversity of foods was available in the moister eastern portion of the region, populations probably shifted toward the Devils River drainage in the fall to take advantage of the acorns and nuts from the dense stands of oaks, walnuts, and pecans in this area.

Winter was the leanest period, when staples became the main plant foods. This was probably the season when hunting became most important and bands moved toward the northern fringes of the region. Many of the staple lower canyon plants occur here also, although aquatic resources are limited. Interest would have shifted toward upland species of plants and animals.

Details of earth-oven construction. Limestone, fuel, and a digging stick were all that was necessary to construct an efficient oven. A pit was dug and lined with limestone. A fire was made in the pit and allowed to burn down to coals. Bulbs of sotol and lechuguilla were placed on the hot rocks and covered with a layer of leaves and prickly pear stems. A mound of soil was used to seal the oven while the bulbs cooked for about two days.

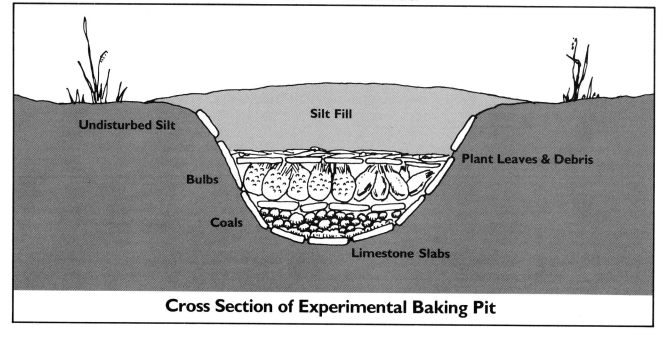

Cross Section of Experimental Baking Pit

Undisturbed Silt — Silt Fill — Plant Leaves & Debris — Bulbs — Coals — Limestone Slabs

There is no definite patterning discernible in archaeological remains to indicate whether or not the lower canyon people actually followed these seasonal movements within their territory. For them to have survived as successfully as they did, however, they must have known their environment sufficiently well that they always, somehow, came up with the necessities of life.

Childbirth, Sickness, and Death

Natural human events such as childbirth, sickness, and death are dealt with differently by various people. We know, of course, that the lower canyon dwellers had to handle these facts of life, but we do not know precisely how. Here we are left with some serious gaps in the archaeological record.

We know from ethnographic sources that it was common for mobile hunting and gathering peoples to isolate women during childbirth in a special hut. Women were treated similarly during their menstrual periods, the belief often being that some malevolent spirit was responsible. Practices associated with childbirth frequently included celebrating, particularly if the child was the firstborn son; the father may also have had to endure painful scarification or bloodletting rituals in efforts to ensure that the son grew to be strong. Rodent jaws, chert flakes, and pointed bone slivers all probably served as scarifiers.

Sick people were tended to by shamans or curers who used special powers and techniques to drive away what they believed to be the metaphysical causes of the illnesses. Some of these rituals were accompanied by medicinal teas, plants, and herbs. Generations of trial and error would have ensured that many of these methods were often effective. Psychological reassurance has its place in healing (especially if a patient has "faith"), and primitive though some of the techniques might seem in terms of modern medicine, we should never assume that they were just silly and ineffective. Several native plants do have medicinal qualities; the remains of these have been found archaeologically, although their presence in shelter deposits does not mean that they were used as medicines. All we can say is that they could have been.

Disposal of the Dead

Much can often be learned about a society by the way its members dispose of their dead. In cultures where social status is determined by birth or wealth, burials are ranked accordingly. Important people are given important funerals; the less significant are given little attention other than from their families. In the kind of egalitarian hunting and gathering society represented by the lower canyon people, one would not expect any distinctions or any degree of elaboration in burials. Indeed, for the first few thousand years, burials were not made in occupied sites, and we assume that simple outdoor disposal of some kind was the rule.

The placement of burials in occupied or sheltered locations did not occur until near the end of the long cultural sequence. Known occupied rockshelter burials occur along or near the back wall in what would generally have been the sleeping area. Burials were of two kinds: the most frequent was burial of the whole corpse, but cremations have also been found. Unoccupied sheltered locations such as Perpetual Care Shelter, Langtry Creek Burial Cave, and the Perry Calk Site were also used, and human remains have been found on the bottom of vertical shaft caves or sink holes, where they were either tossed or placed.

The burials were usually single interments with the body placed in a fetal or flexed position with the knees drawn up against or at right angles to the chest. Arms may be flexed against the chest or spread at right angles to the body. Where conditions are favorable for the preservation of textiles, simple-twilled or diagonal-twilled mats are usually found wrapping the corpse. Sometimes several such mats accompany a single individual. Most of the mats are plain, but some have been found with a diagonally woven diamond motif, often painted red. Rarely are other artifacts directly associated with the burials. Many of the bodies are found covered with limestone cobbles (which may include metates), sometimes painted red.

An infant at Horseshoe Ranch Caves represents one of the more elaborate burials professionally excavated in the region. The child had been placed on a large twilled mat of beargrass fibers, then covered with a large basket of sacahuisti fibers. The beargrass mat was then folded over, along the sides and ends, and placed in a large net bag. The child's body was found accompanied by four freshwater mussel shell pendants and twelve *Olivella* shells, all probably once strung on a cord. Two sets of cane tubes and a single unbound tube (perhaps some kind of musical instrument) were included in the burial. The child had a conical twilled basket placed on its head; a second and nearly identical basket was also recovered from the burial bundle.

View of three tightly woven twilled mats found with adult burial at Shumla Caves. Finely woven mats were often painted with simple geometric designs. Such mats were used to sit on, to line beds, or as bundles or basket liners.

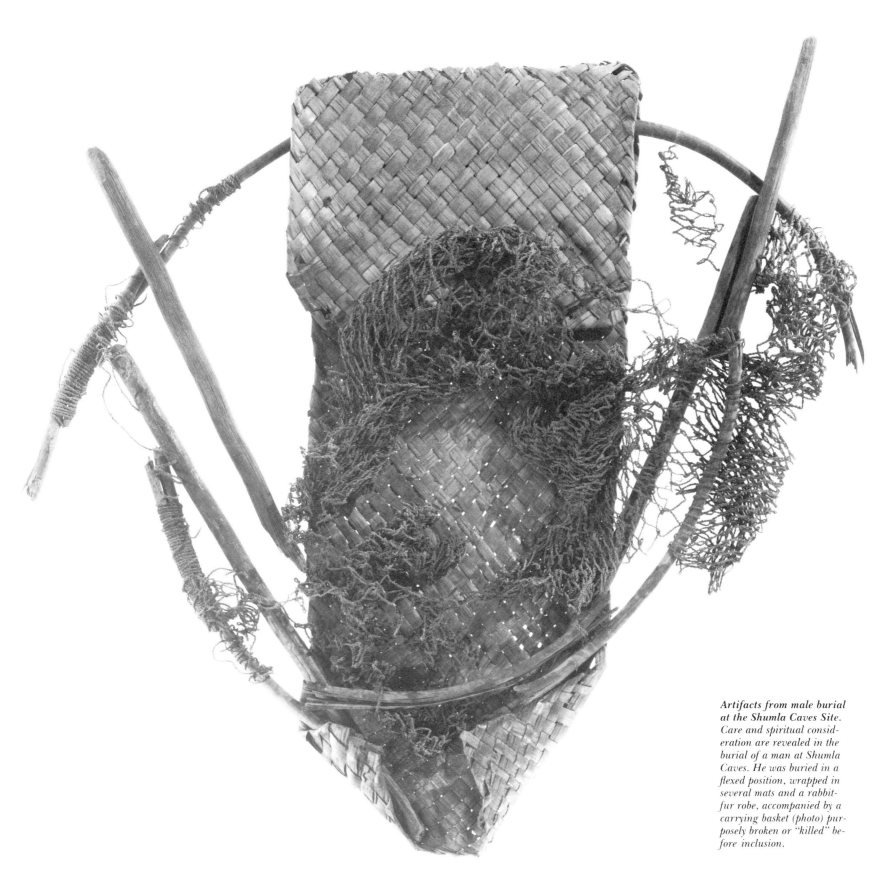

Artifacts from male burial at the Shumla Caves Site. Care and spiritual consideration are revealed in the burial of a man at Shumla Caves. He was buried in a flexed position, wrapped in several mats and a rabbit-fur robe, accompanied by a carrying basket (photo) purposely broken or "killed" before inclusion.

A male burial found beneath a layer of cactus and brush at Shumla Caves was accompanied by an interesting array of material remains: a carrying basket composed of a wooden frame and a broken net body containing a piece of checker-weave matting, two inverted coiled baskets, and a flat basket discovered beneath the carrying basket. The flat basket contained twenty-nine different articles. A rabbit-fur robe covered the body, which was wrapped in matting and tied with string. Cactus, fiber, and brush were also used to line the bottom of the burial pit.

Among the articles contained in the flat basket were two long necklaces made of snake vertebrae, fish hooks of cactus thorns, bone implements, a rawhide bag, a feather string, a manganese nodule, a joint of deer bone with a piece of manganese fitted into the small end, and a small checker-weave pouch holding a large, thin chert flake. This last item may have been a scarifier or simply a sleeve haft for a sharp-edged knife. A final interesting item was an assortment of buckeye seeds, possibly used for their mild narcotic effects or as fish poison.

The cremated remains of an adult were found in a fawn-skin pouch at Horseshoe Ranch Caves. At Moorehead Cave, Frank Setzler found a double burial of a male and a female. The woman had sandals on her feet and was wearing an apron made of fur strips attached to a twill-plaited belt around her waist. Her body was wrapped in fine twilled mats. Next to her were the charred remains of a man placed in a twilled mat decorated with a painted diamond pattern. A group burial consisting of five skeletons, four adults and a child, was found at Fate Bell Shelter by A. T. Jackson in the 1930s.

What did the people look like and what can we learn from the excavated burials? Studies conducted in the 1930s and 1940s showed that the people were of moderate stature, long-headed, with high vaults and moderately broad noses. Healed fractures were not uncommon; indeed, given the ruggedness of the terrain, one would expect to see limb fractures frequently. Teeth show extreme wear, attributable to the local diet of abrasive plant foods and the use of teeth as tools to shred and work fibers. The front teeth were often worn down past the enamel to the gum. Abscesses were unusually frequent compared to other Texas Indian skeletons. The lower molars especially tended to be lost relatively early in life, causing problems in occlusion and placing excessive stress on the remaining piece.

Artifacts with the Shumla Caves burial (RIGHT & OPPOSITE). Tools of a spiritual man? An unusual assemblage was found with the man buried at Shumla Caves, including a black mineral crayon inserted in the end of a bone, mountain laurel seeds (used for hallucinogens?), buckeye seeds, bundles of grass, fish-hook cactus spines (scarifiers?), a thin, sharp chert flake contained within a small woven envelope that served as its haft (bloodletting tool or scarifier?), a leather bundle, and two meticulously woven strings of snake vertebrae. While the snake vertebrae strings may appear to be a necklace, the unusual care and craftsmanship used in their manufacture suggest a more special function. Considering the strong hint of bloodletting tools in the assemblage, the woven strings of snake vertebrae may have been drawn through open flesh wounds in public bloodletting rituals.

Photo of skull (LEFT) showing unusual tooth wear. The combination of diet, chewing to extract nutrition from the fibrous leaf bases of sotol and lechuguilla, and use of teeth as tools in fiber shredding and softening wore them out at an early age. The unusual pattern of dental wear and premature loss of molars placed additional stress on the few teeth that remained.

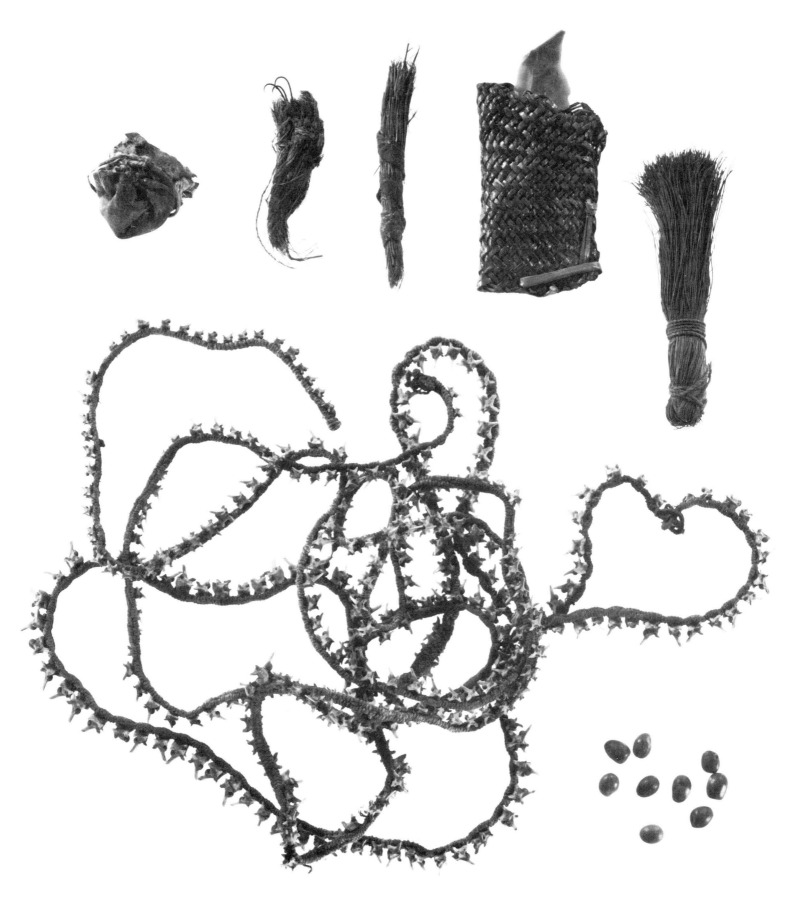

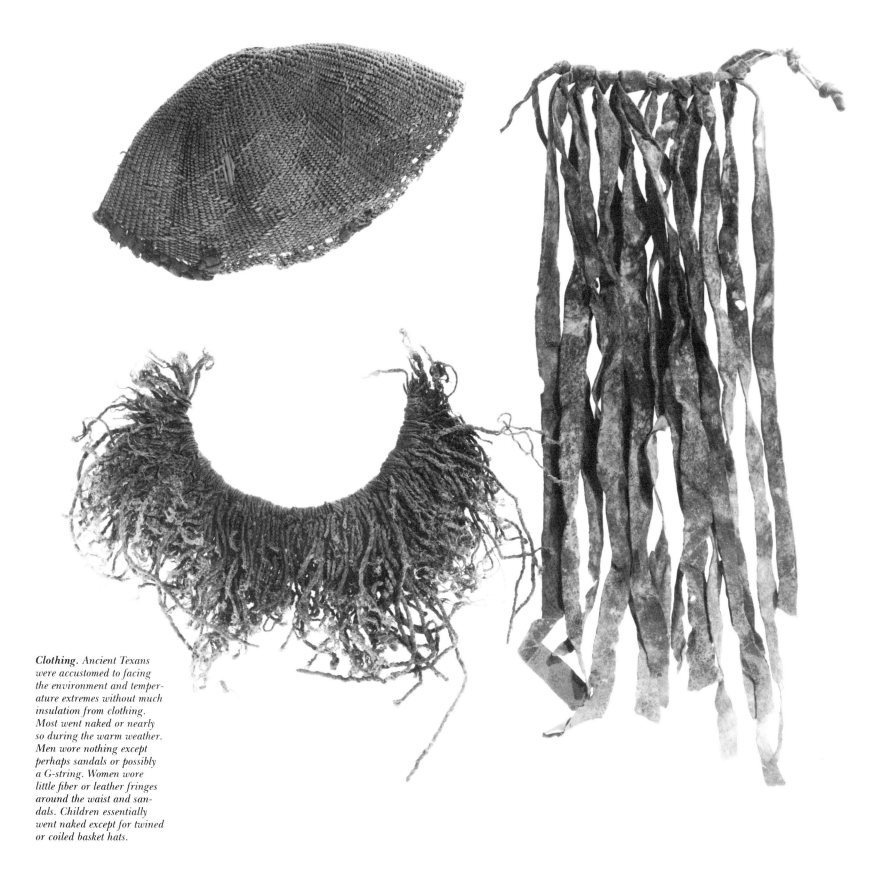

Clothing. Ancient Texans were accustomed to facing the environment and temperature extremes without much insulation from clothing. Most went naked or nearly so during the warm weather. Men wore nothing except perhaps sandals or possibly a G-string. Women wore little fiber or leather fringes around the waist and sandals. Children essentially went naked except for twined or coiled basket hats.

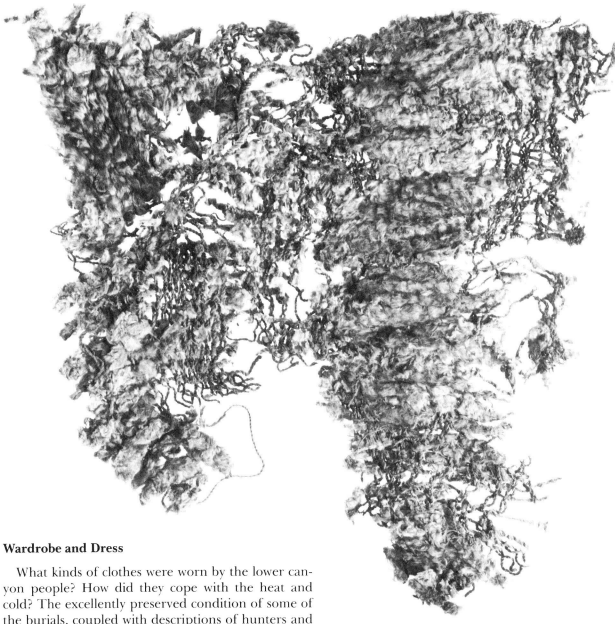

Wardrobe and Dress

What kinds of clothes were worn by the lower canyon people? How did they cope with the heat and cold? The excellently preserved condition of some of the burials, coupled with descriptions of hunters and gatherers from across the border in Mexico in early Historic times, has given us a glimpse of ancient wardrobes. Like all other elements in their material culture, clothes were made from plants and other resources available in the environment. Little clothing was actually worn by either sex during the warm weather. Cold periods, however, necessitated finding some sort of substantial body covering.

Women probably wore fiber or leather aprons made of strings or strips attached to a belt throughout the year. The Mexican Indians sometimes wore skirts of deerskin, but none of these have been reported in the lower canyons. Males may have gone naked during the warm seasons or worn only an apron or breech-clout. Rabbit-fur robes and bison skins were probably the main cold weather garments of men, women, and children, although only rabbit-fur robes have been found with burials in the lower canyons. The rabbit skins were cut into strips either placed parallel and woven together by cordage or twisted around an open cordage framework. A cloak of this kind was found

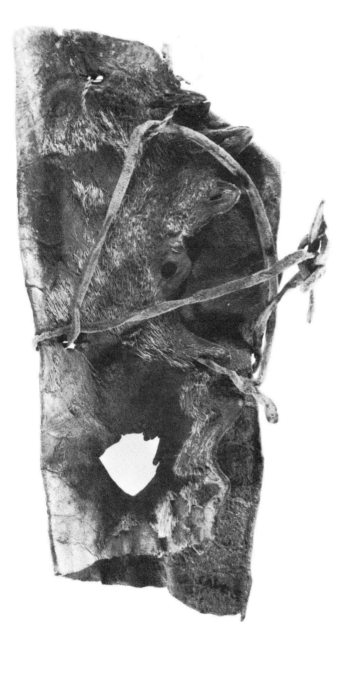

An assortment of sandals. Sturdy footgear was essential, considering the rough terrain. Woven sandals have been recovered in all sizes and styles. Many show signs of wear and were probably discards; others are sound enough to wear today.

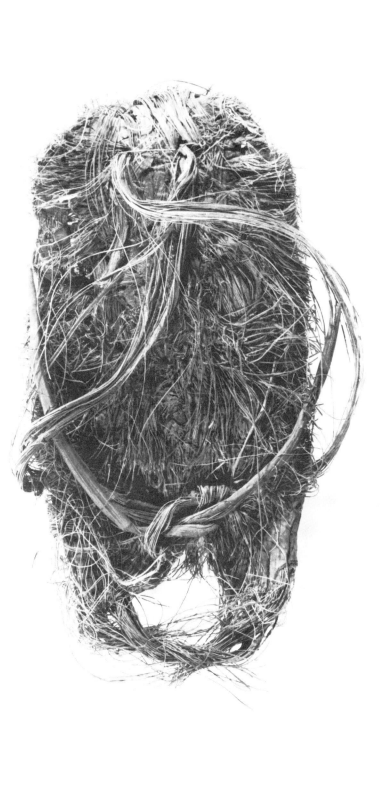

fastened by means of a cord of human hair to a corpse from Moorehead Cave.

Sandals of lechuguilla and yucca leaves, or rarely of animal skin, were the standard footwear. One child burial from Horseshoe Ranch Caves had a conical twined basket hat; such hats were commonly worn by women throughout the arid Southwest from west Texas to California.

Jewelry was not a common part of daily dress, judging from its near absence in the archaeological record and from historical accounts of neighborhood populations. Bone beads are the most common items of adornment found in lower canyon sites; small pendants of mussel shell or an occasional *Olivella* shell bead or stone pendant also occur, but none of these are numerous, and they are rarely observed in burials. Land snail shells (*Rabdotus*) strung on a cord have been found at Fate Bell Shelter. Necklaces of snail shells were described by the Spanish chroniclers for the hunters and gatherers who once lived south of the Big Bend region. The elaborate child's burial from Horseshoe Ranch Caves mentioned earlier is exceptional with regard to jewelry items.

Hairstyles are unknown from the archaeological record, although hair is sometimes preserved on desiccated corpses. A wooden comb was found at Hinds

Necklaces made of bone cylinders and shells (ABOVE) adorned the ancient Texans. Pendants (LEFT) also graced necks and perhaps served a symbolic purpose.

Cave that had red pigment adhering to the teeth and surface. Perhaps hair was sometimes embellished with ochre. To the south, in Mexico, Spanish explorers reported many hairstyles among both the men and the women. Men's hair varied from long, worn with a headband or braided, to cropped short about the ears. Women's styles were equally varied, from long and braided to short. Since human hair was consid-

ered a fiber resource, both long and short styles would be expected among the lower canyon people.

Body painting is only suggested from the archaeological record. Body painting and tattooing were common among the Historic Indians to the south, east, and west and most likely common among the lower canyon people as well. However, preservation of desiccated corpses has not been good enough to see this element of adornment. Some of the decoration seen on anthropomorphic figures painted in pictographs may signify distinguishing body painting. Incised and painted clay figurines may also represent attempts at illustrating body decoration. Indeed, such markings may have been the principal way of displaying group identity, since there was little opportunity to do so through color or design on the sparse or nonexistent wardrobe.

Ritual Music and Dance

Judging from the Historic groups of hunting and gathering peoples of the lower canyons, ritual behavior permeated their daily lives. They conceived the world as one filled with animated spirits; all things were viewed as having souls and life, from rocks, mountains, and springs to trees and animals. To cope with a world of spirit beings required a deep belief in the significance and efficacy of complex rituals. Births, deaths, the passage of boys and girls to adulthood, annual gatherings, and projected hunts and raids were all occasions for strictly prescribed ceremonies. Altered states of consciousness permitting a special rapport with the spirit world brought about through music and dance—and possibly through the use of hallucinogens—were common on these occasions.

Instruments of various kinds, including log drums, rasps for rhythmic chants, rattles, and bone or cane flutes or whistles were used by Historic desert Indians of northern Mexico and south and southwest Texas. Although only notched sticks (for use as rasps) have been recovered from the lower canyons, the ancient inhabitants probably employed all of these same sorts of musical devices.

The archaeological remains of ritualistic practices are probably more apparent in the lower canyon area than in any other region of the state. Pictographs, petroglyphs, clay figurines, and painted pebbles all attest to a culture rich in ceremonial behavior. These mysterious products of the spirit and imagination of a long-gone people are treated in detail in the following chapter. ∎

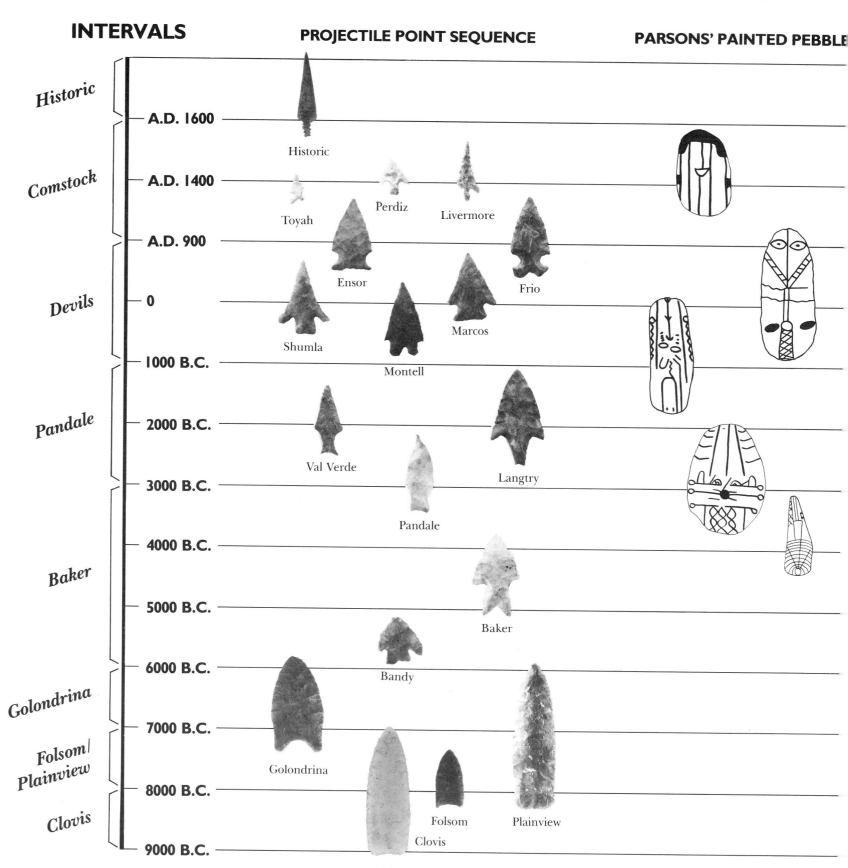

INTERVALS

PROJECTILE POINT SEQUENCE

PARSONS' PAINTED PEBBLE

Historic

A.D. 1600

Historic

Comstock

A.D. 1400

Toyah

Perdiz

Livermore

A.D. 900

Ensor

Frio

Devils

0

Shumla

Marcos

Montell

1000 B.C.

Pandale

2000 B.C.

Val Verde

Langtry

3000 B.C.

Pandale

4000 B.C.

Baker

5000 B.C.

Baker

Bandy

6000 B.C.

Golondrina

7000 B.C.

Folsom/
Plainview

Golondrina

8000 B.C.

Folsom

Plainview

Clovis

Clovis

9000 B.C.

SEQUENCE CHART

SEQUENCE   PICTOGRAPH SEQUENCE   SANDAL SEQUENCE

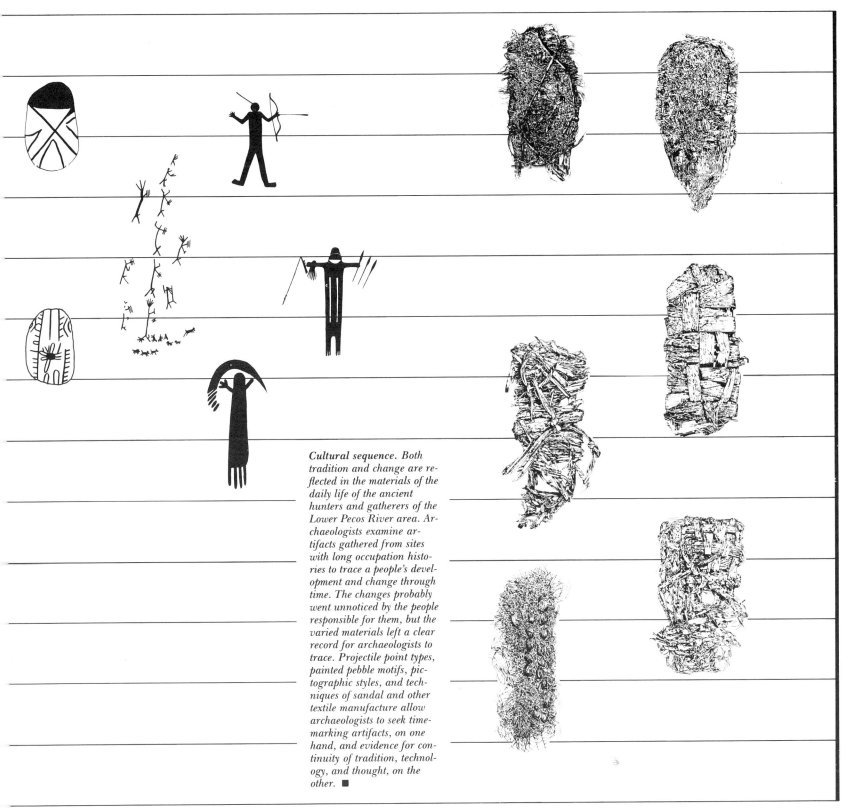

Cultural sequence. Both tradition and change are reflected in the materials of the daily life of the ancient hunters and gatherers of the Lower Pecos River area. Archaeologists examine artifacts gathered from sites with long occupation histories to trace a people's development and change through time. The changes probably went unnoticed by the people responsible for them, but the varied materials left a clear record for archaeologists to trace. Projectile point types, painted pebble motifs, pictographic styles, and techniques of sandal and other textile manufacture allow archaeologists to seek time-marking artifacts, on one hand, and evidence for continuity of tradition, technology, and thought, on the other. ■

PREHISTORIC DIET
A Case for Coprolite Analysis

by Vaughn M. Bryant, Jr.
TEXAS A & M UNIVERSITY

Modern archaeology is a sophisticated science. Yet in the past the archaeologist's primary concern was excavating sites, recovering items that would look nice on museum display shelves, and trying to understand the material contents of prehistoric cultures. Today, aided by a wide range of new techniques developed by specialists in fields such as botany, geology, medicine, physics, and zoology, the archaeologist can gain a clearer image of the health, diet, and material culture of groups who left their records at the many sites we now excavate. One of these relatively new research areas is the study of prehistoric diets through the analysis of human coprolites (fecal remains).

Ever since the 1700s, archaeologists have been actively excavating sites and making guesses about ancient human diets. However, it was not until 1896 that Harshberger first suggested that the undigested seeds and bones found in prehistoric human coprolites might offer clues concerning the precise kinds and quantities of foods actually eaten by ancient cultures. Unfortunately, his original observations and suggestions were generally ignored for the next sixty years, and during that period few archaeologists made any attempt to recover coprolites or to conduct even a cursory examination of the few dried samples they saved.

In the early 1960s, this lack of interest began to change when a Canadian plant pathologist named Eric O. Callen began his study of ancient Peruvian human coprolites during his search for the origin of cereal plant pathogens in South America. Callen's early techniques were simplistic by our current standards, yet his work focused attention on the recovery and study of human coprolites. After his initial success and the attention it drew from archaeologists, Callen continued his studies and worked to improve his techniques of coprolite analysis until his untimely death in 1970. By then, coprolite analysis had become accepted as an important aspect of archaeological analysis.

When conducting a coprolite analysis, the first task is to determine the biological origin of each specimen. The determination of whether a coprolite is of human or nonhuman origin often can be made prior to actual analysis. Fecal pellets from small rodents and the feces of many herbivores such as llamas, deer, antelope, sheep, cows, bison, and horses can be recognized easily by their shape, size, and predominantly plant fiber contents. Other coprolites, such as those from car-

nivores, can be identified by their hard coating of dried intestinal lubricant secreted as protection against intestinal wall puncture by sharp bone fragments. The fecal remains of other types of animals are more difficult to distinguish from human coprolites, especially when the specimen has been crushed or fragmented. Another factor that makes coprolite identification difficult is that all human feces do not conform to a single size or shape. Depending upon the diet and the interval between bowel movements, human feces can appear in a variety of shapes ranging from segmented pellets to flattened masses resembling the dung of cows.

Human and nonhuman coprolites also can be separated based on their contents. When a coprolite is placed into a solution of trisodium phosphate, the liquid generally becomes tinted within seventy-two hours. The resulting color and translucency of the fluid are fairly reliable indicators as to the coprolite's origin. Carnivore coprolites usually color the solution white, pale brown, or yellow-brown, whereas herbivore coprolites produce a pale yellow or light brown color. Human coprolites, on the other hand, emit a dark brown or black color and make the solution opaque. In addition, nonhuman

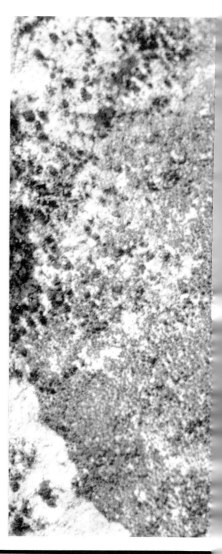

coprolites generally produce a musty odor when in the solution, whereas human coprolites emit a foul odor. The intense smell is common in human coprolites whether they were produced fairly recently or are thousands of years old and comes mainly from the gaseous by-products of protein digestion. Those volatile compounds include methyl mercaptan, hydrogen sulfide, and methane, which are produced from the normal bacterial putrefaction that begins inside the intestinal track and continues when a coprolite is processed for analysis. Perhaps this aspect is one reason why coprolite research was so late in developing and why even today there are few research centers or scientists who specialize in this type of analysis.

After the chemical processing has been completed, the actual contents of a coprolite offer additional clues to its probable origin. Humans tend to eat an omnivorous diet and to cook their foods. Thus, human coprolites from ancient cultures often contain a wide assortment of diverse materials that might include items such as bark, charcoal, cracked and ground seeds, pollen grains, snail shell fragments, bits of egg or clam shells, feathers, insect parts, bone fragments, mammal hair, a variety of plant fibers, or plant crystals.

Some of these items are also found in nonhuman coprolites, yet it is rare to find as wide a diversity in specimens that are not of human origin.

One of the most frequently asked questions concerning coprolite analysis pertains to the kinds of information that they can tell us about the cultures that produced them. The answer is entirely dependent upon the specific human coprolite sample that is being examined and the procedures used to analyze that specimen. Under ideal circumstances, a human coprolite, or a group of them, could yield pertinent information regarding seasonality, paleoenvironmental conditions, food preparation techniques, actual diet preferences, and the general health of an ancient population. Some of this information, such as the presence of intestinal parasites, could be obtained from the analysis of a single coprolite. In other cases, such as determining diet patterns, many coprolites must be examined and their combined data are then used as a basis for making dietary assumptions.

Pollen grains are often found in coprolites, since the grains are made out of a very durable substance that is unaffected by the human digestive system. During certain seasons of the year, pollen is dispersed into the air

in great numbers, is inhaled, settles in drinking water sources, or falls on prepared foods about to be eaten. In coprolites, certain pollen types can provide an indication of the season during which a specific meal was eaten. Different plants flower in each season of the year, and their pollen is most abundant in the atmosphere during their blooming period. By applying that information to the types of pollen found in coprolites, we can predict when prehistoric humans occupied specific archaeological sites. For example, coprolite studies from Pueblo sites in the American Southwest show that those sites were used throughout the year. On the other hand, studies of coprolites from rockshelter sites in the Lower Pecos region show that many sites were occupied seasonally rather than serving as permanent year-long residences.

Another dietary practice confirmed by the analysis of human coprolites was the little known, yet

An **Opuntia** *(prickly pear) phytolith, or plant crystal, recovered from a 2,700-year-old human coprolite found in the Lower Pecos region. Crystals of various sizes and shapes occur in great numbers in the fruits and pads of prickly pear cactus. Based upon morphological comparisons, the specific crystal illustrated is believed to have come from the pad portion of a prickly pear cactus and serves as evidence that prehistoric peoples in the Lower Pecos region relied upon this cactus as one of their important food sources (1,000x).*

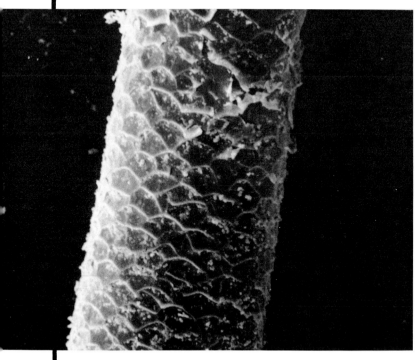

A hair from **Odocoileus virginianus** *(white-tail deer) recovered from a 4,600-year-old human coprolite found in the Lower Pecos region. Although meat is generally completely digested and thus is not found in human remains, hairs that may accidentally have been eaten with the meat are not digested and thus remain as evidence of meat eating (1,200x).*

widespread, practice of eating flowers. In the Lower Pecos region, flowers seem to have been an important human food resource. Studies of Lower Pecos coprolites from about 6,000–0 B.C. reveal that some of the most popular food sources were flowers from yucca, sotol, agave, cactus, and sunflower plants. Why these early people ate so many of these flowers is still a mystery, but recent evidence indicates that many of these flowers and their pollen grains contain a wide variety of essential minerals and vitamins, especially high amounts of many B vitamins. Perhaps those ancient people in the Lower Pecos region felt better if they ate flowers, or perhaps flower eating was associated with some type of important ritual in their culture. Even today many health-food stores sell fresh pollen in powder or tablet form to people who use it as a valuable daily vitamin and mineral source.

Clues about ancient climates and the plants that used to live in the Lower Pecos area also can be reconstructed from the analysis of coprolites. For example, coprolites containing pollen or seeds from plants that no longer live in a region can serve as an indicator that the temperatures, rainfall, or soil conditions were different in the past. In a similar manner, parts of animals in coprolites such as bones, hair, feathers, scales, or insect fragments are good indications of the environments in which those animals once lived. If those remains, like pollen and seeds, represent past types that are different from those of today, one can conclude that environmental changes have probably occurred. In the Lower Pecos region, for example, many researchers generally believed that the semidesert environment of today did not exist until recently. However, coprolites as old as 6,000 B.C. contain the remains of plants and animals generally found in that region today. Thus, this new information suggests a much earlier establishment of the present semidesert habitat in the Lower Pecos region than most thought possible.

Perhaps the most valuable information gained from coprolite studies is our understanding of what foods were eaten and how those foods were prepared. This type of information is especially useful for a number of reasons. First, archaeological evidence from the Lower Pecos region and elsewhere suggests that most prehistoric people lived short lives compared to those of modern people. Their average life span tended to be about one-half as long as ours; thus, people in their thirties were already considered old and nearing the end of their lives. Why did they die so young? Some have speculated that their diets were at fault, yet the coprolite evidence suggests just the opposite. If anything, their diets were healthier than the ones most people eat today.

Second, the animal bones, seeds, and other remains of food products found in the deposits of archaeological sites are always suspect, since some or all of them could have been carried to the site by rodents and carnivores that may have used the rockshelters during periods when they were unoccupied by people. However, the undigested items found in human coprolites offer precise records of what was eaten. Since the ancient Lower Pecos cultures did not eat the types of processed foods used today, their diets were filled with coarse fibers from cactus pads; the broken bones of small mice, woodrats, lizards, fish, and birds; the hair and feathers of game; whole or ground seeds of fruits and nuts; and undigested outer shells of insects such as grubs and grasshoppers, which they apparently ate during certain seasons of the year.

Third, through analysis of coprolites we now have a better understanding of how the Lower Pecos peoples prepared some of their foods. From the presence of cactus fibers in almost every coprolite ever examined from the Lower Pecos region and from the finding of numerous singed spine bases, we have concluded that cactus pads were one of their main food items. We suspect that pads were first held over an open fire or placed on hot coals to burn off the spines. Next they were probably boiled in deer skin sacks filled with boiling water or steamed in grass-lined pits to soften the tough fibers and to remove bitter alkaloids.

Various types of seeds were another important food resource for the Lower Pecos cultures. Seeds and nuts are especially useful foods because they are rich in carbohydrates, and nuts are also a valuable source of fats and oils. In addition, both can be collected and eaten or stored for later use. The coprolites of the

Lower Pecos peoples are filled with the remains of seeds as well as nuts, suggesting that both were frequently used as food. Millet, sunflower, and cactus seeds were some of the more common types; they were generally ground or pounded into coarse flour before they were eaten. Judging from the presence of both charred and uncharred seed fragments, the lower canyon people probably mixed flour with water to form a gruel in some cases, while in other instances they made flour dough and baked it on hot coals or hot rocks to form unleavened bread.

Mouse-sized rodents, lizards, and small birds were sometimes skinned and then steamed or boiled before being eaten. However, based upon the high frequency of charcoal fragments in coprolites and the presence of some pieces of burned bone, the more common preparation procedure was probably to roast small game whole on hot coals. Once the feathers or hair were burned off, the small animal was then eaten whole. This may seem difficult to believe, yet it is well documented by coprolites containing almost the complete skeleton of some small animal or the types of seeds and insect parts one would commonly expect to find in the digestive system of small birds and rodents.

Coprolite evidence has told us a lot about the Lower Pecos peoples that we previously did not know or only suspected. We now know that they obtained most of their meat protein primarily from small game that was probably caught by the women and small children rather than by the men. It was much more common for them to have a mouse, lizard, small bird, or woodrat for dinner than it was for them to eat the meat of larger game such as rabbits, deer, antelope, or bison. Therefore, if the men of the Lower Pecos culture spent most their time hunting larger game, as is common among most hunting and gathering societies, they probably expended more calories searching for game than they obtained from its meat when they were successful.

We also know that the Lower Pecos groups ate a diverse diet that consisted mainly of foods from plant sources. The meat protein they did eat was minor, perhaps no more than twenty percent of their overall diet. They were opportunists who were skilled in recognizing what food resources were available and then finding ways to exploit those resources to the fullest. Also, it seems highly unlikely that they had any problems of obesity. The evidence from their coprolites shows that they ate mainly complex carbohydrates with a high fiber content, that they ate small, lean animals that lacked much fat content, and that the only source of sugar in their diet was the fruits of cactus, persimmons, grapes, and hackberries. Salt deposits are not known from the Lower Pecos region, and thus most of their salt intake came from the natural foods they ate. In addition, the evidence suggests that their healthful diets gave them all the minerals and vitamins they needed and that their foods were free of high-calorie fat sources—except for nuts, which were not abundant in the Lower Pecos region and were only available during certain seasons of the year. When one also realizes that they often lived in rockshelters located high on the sides of canyons, a picture emerges that suggests these individuals had to be trim and lean to maintain their lifestyle.

There is a lesson to be learned from the ancient dwellers of the Lower Pecos region. By accident, or by intention, they ate a varied diet filled with high fiber and a balance of high amounts of complex carbohydrates, moderate amounts of lean meat protein, and low levels of fat, sugar, and salt. Their skeletal evidence suggests that most had shorter life spans than we do today, but their early deaths were not the fault of their diets. Instead, we suspect that disease and the rigors of their lifestyle took the heaviest toll. The absence of intestinal parasites in their coprolites tells us that they did not suffer from that type of affliction yet; unfortunately, neither their coprolites nor their skeletons give us accurate clues about other aspects of their health. For example, did many of them suffer from heart attacks, high blood pressure, cancer, and some of the other major health problems that afflict us today? We think not, since modern hunting and gathering societies tend to be almost entirely free of those types of ailments.

The wealth of information that we have gathered from an examination of the coprolites left by the peoples of the Lower Pecos region has given us new insights about their lifestyles, their diet preferences, their probable health, and even the climates in which they lived. The coprolite information also has helped archaeologists understand the remains of the material culture that have been recovered from the many sites of the Lower Pecos region. ∎

*Opuntia (**prickly pear cactus**) seeds recovered from a 3,500-year-old human coprolite from Hinds Cave. These cactus seeds were ground and slightly charred, suggesting that they may have been collected and ground into a coarse flour, which was then baked on hot stones or on hot coals (20x).*

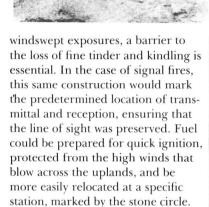

SMOKE SIGNALS
An Early Warning System

by Solveig A. Turpin
TEXAS ARCHAEOLOGICAL RESEARCH LABORATORY

Communication takes many forms, depending upon the nature of the information being conveyed, the technological skills of the communicant, and the commonality of the signals used, whether visual, vocal, or symbolic. The pictographs of the Lower Pecos, for example, passively embody the mythology, religion, social order, world view, and history of past cultures. In response to more immediate needs, many North American Indian groups shared an elaborate sign language that transcended the many different languages and dialects they spoke. Their use of smoke and fire to transmit messages over long distances has captured the imagination of frontier folk writers, as all youthful fans of the Lone Ranger and Tonto well know.

The Lower Pecos River region is ideally suited to the development of a visual means of communication, such as smoke or fire signaling. The vast expanses of flat plains that border the canyons are dotted with high domed outcrops. The deeply entrenched canyons present a unique set of acoustical conditions. From some locations along the rims, every spoken word is audible in the shelters below; from others, wind, echoing rock faces, and buffering vegetation deaden all sound. Some

evidence that the later peoples of the Lower Pecos used the visual power of fire and smoke to transcend these difficulties is found in series of small hearths rimming some deep canyons and in isolated features atop high domed outcrops on the plain.

Morphologically, all these hearths are similarly constructed of native limestone blocks arranged in a circle 70 to 150 cm in diameter. In most, a large flat slab is placed to one side. The hearths on the canyon rims are situated on flat benches that either project out over the canyon or rise slightly above the rim. In some cases, the hearths are so close to the precipitous canyon wall that the exterior blocks are sliding over the edge.

These features differ from the typical cooking hearth found on the large campsites of the caliche flats bordering the canyons. There flat or slightly mounded rock pavements were apparently built to support the fire. These cooking and heating platforms are usually constructed of Buda Limestone gathered from the remnant outcrops that fringe the flats. This highly fossilized limestone turns a distinctive bright red when heated and apparently retained warmth for a significant period of time. The circular hearths of the rim and atop the hills would fulfill a different function. Here, on the barren

windswept exposures, a barrier to the loss of fine tinder and kindling is essential. In the case of signal fires, this same construction would mark the predetermined location of transmittal and reception, ensuring that the line of sight was preserved. Fuel could be prepared for quick ignition, protected from the high winds that blow across the uplands, and be more easily relocated at a specific station, marked by the stone circle.

The hilltop hearths are similarly constructed of limestone blocks placed in a circle on the crest of high domed outcrops. Advantageous settings, for example, are overlooking former fords of the major rivers or on the most prominent hills rising above the flat and featureless upland plain. Although fewer hilltop hearths have been recorded, one pictograph in a shelter adjacent to the Pecos River may illustrate how the system worked. In this panel, a series of four black domes, rays radiating from their crest, are the background for a red-outlined human figure who stands with arms upraised. Only three of the hills are now visible, the fourth having been erased by natural rock decay. By overlapping the series of arcs and flattening the peaks farthest from the human figure, the artist has used a form of perspective to create the illusion of distance. The lines emanating from the peaks simulate rays or columns of smoke blown by a prevailing wind. Although portraying human figures with arms upraised is a common device in two of the Lower Pecos art styles, it could, in this context, imply alarm or surprise at the content of the message. This pictograph also provides some clues as to the age of the smoke signaling practice. The red and black line drawing is superimposed upon a complex panel painted in the Pecos River Style, the oldest of the Lower Pecos art forms. Its relative brightness and clarity contrast with the faded and eroded underlying pictograph, indicating its comparatively later age. Stylistically, the signaling scene most resembles the representational styles of late prehistory and early history, an age placement consistent with the most current reconstructions of Lower Pecos prehistory.

Smoke signaling by the native peoples at the time of contact is reported for central and coastal Texas, the San Antonio area, and northern Mexico. The efficiency of fire as a signaling device in the Lower Pecos is first demonstrated in Historic times by the earliest Spanish expedition, Gaspar Castaño de Sosa's ill-fated trek from Monclovas, Mexico, to the Pecos pueblos in 1590. His caravan apparently crossed the Rio Grande near Del Rio, intending to follow the Pecos River north to the pueblo country. Impeded by the rough terrain and lack of water, the wagon train wandered between the Pecos and Devils rivers for almost a month before it succeeded in finding a way down to the waters of the Pecos. Castaño's journal later mentions the lighting of luminaries (small fires) to guide the lost leader back to the camp in the dark of night.

This historical use of signal fires can be eliminated as an explanation for the hearths along the deep canyons. No wagon train could be maneuvered to the high flats above the Rio Grande, and it would seem extraordinarily perilous to draw a mounted and lost scout toward the precipitous rims. However, that the Indians of this time used similar methods of communication is shown by Castano's scouts sighting smoke signals near the Texas/New Mexico border. By the time European colonization came to the Lower Pecos, more effective means of communication had been developed, and the use of fire and smoke as a signaling device probably became obsolete.

Other factors lead to an estimate of Late Prehistoric and Protohistoric age for these features. Long-distance communication between related groups is a defense strategy, especially against intruders who are not as familiar with the terrain. Their approach can be quickly conveyed to fellow members of the social group or alliance, allowing them time to prepare for a confrontation or to disperse into hiding. Smoke and fire would be a persistent alarm, continuing to transmit while the senders went on with their mobilization or retreat. The need to warn the inhabitants of rockshelters would be a priority, given that the potential for ambush or capture is much greater in the restricted canyon bottoms than on the open plain, where there is room to maneuver or take a stance. All the rim-lined hearths are along canyons noted for their densely occupied shelters.

In the current interpretations of Lower Pecos prehistory, the times of greatest social mobility and unrest are the Late Prehistoric and Protohistoric periods, from A.D. 600 to the mid-eighteenth century. In fact, the Late Prehistoric period is defined on the basis of the introduction of traits that differ radically from the Archaic practices. The bow and arrow replaces the atlatl; in art, the Red Monochrome Style portrays a new world view; burials and living sites shift from shelters to upland locations— all indicating the intrusion of population from the north and west.

Somewhat later, pressures from the south appear in the form of migrations by the desert tribes of northern Mexico and the upper Rio Grande to the mouth of the Pecos River to hunt bison and trade for furs. Spanish slaving expeditions to capture laborers for the mines of northern Mexico probably penetrated the Lower Pecos, although such illegal *entradas* are rarely documented. By the 1800s, the times of the marauding Apaches and later Comanches, the indigenous people of the Lower Pecos had vanished, either exterminated or displaced. Protected by the harsh terrain of their desert refuge, the new population of mounted and armed guerrillas would have had different defensive needs than their more sedentary predecessors. If ever the inhabitants of the Lower Pecos had dire need of an early warning system, it was during the upheavals of late prehistory and earliest history, prior to the acquisition of the horse and firearms.

The vocabulary of smoke and fire is limited to a set number of prearranged messages, understood by the sender and receiver but not comprehensible to outsiders. This shared recognition of the meaning of signals implies a social cohesiveness or affiliation not often attributed to small bands of nomadic hunters and gatherers. Just as the widespread distribution of the Pecos River Style pictographs reflects a unified belief system that transcended local politics, these hearths suggest that, under the pressures of alien population movements, a measure of social unity was achieved. ∎

THE ARTISTIC RECORD
Rock Paintings, Pebbles, and Figurines

An outstanding display of pictographic art, virtually unknown outside of Texas and surprisingly obscure within the state, embellishes the walls of shelters and overhangs that line the lower canyons near the mouth of the Pecos River. These archaeological sites represent some of the most impressive ancient rock art galleries in North America. There are not only pictographs, but other media used for symbolic expression: painted and incised pebbles with abstract linear designs; small, unfired clay figurines depicting humanlike forms; designs painstakingly pecked into solid rock surfaces (petroglyphs); painted sticks; pebbles "dressed" in leaves; and fiber bundles representing anthropomorphic figures.

The Murals

There are several distinctive styles of pictographs recognizable in the lower canyon area: the Pecos River Style, characterized by massive polychrome anthropomorphic and abstract figures; the Red Monochrome Style, featuring large, more realistic human and zoomorphic motifs; the Red Linear Style, identified on the basis of tiny, dark red stick figures; and the Historic Style, similar in technique to the Red Monochrome, but exhibiting themes indicative of European contact.

Three of the styles can be chronologically placed. The Pecos River Style belongs to the Archaic period, based on the use of the atlatl as a common motif. The Red Monochrome Style is post-Archaic, showing anthropomorphic figures using the bow and arrow. The Red Linear Style is disputed by some archaeologists, some of whom see only atlatls, while others seem to recognize bows and arrows in the paintings. Historic painting is quickly identified because it depicts scenes and figures indicative of European culture (horses, guns, churches, and costumes).

Pecos River Style The earliest and most numerous pictographs are of the distinctive Pecos River Style. They often consist of more than one color, and the panels are dominated by humanlike figures. These forms are sometimes accompanied by abstract symbols and animallike figures, principally mountain lions and deer. Equally impressive are abstract polychrome designs, covering large sections of a shelter wall, which incorporate long wavy lines in red, yellow, and black.

The caves were occupied as shelters for 9,000 years, but it seems unlikely that the earliest paintings are that old. Some of the pictographs are covered by as much as four feet of cultural deposits, which would certainly suggest an antiquity that extends several thousand years.

The Pecos River Style paintings incorporate several colors in interesting combinations. Dark red predominates, followed by black, light red, yellow, orange, and white. Red, orange, and yellow were obtained from ochre. White was derived from clay and was used least often. Black was produced from manganese oxides and carbon. Some pictures include as many as five colors, but most are tricolored. Liquid colors were applied with a brush. Crayons molded from dry pigment were also used. Two pieces of yellow crayon (triangular blocks of limonite) were found in the Fate Bell Shelter. The ochre had been ground to a powder,

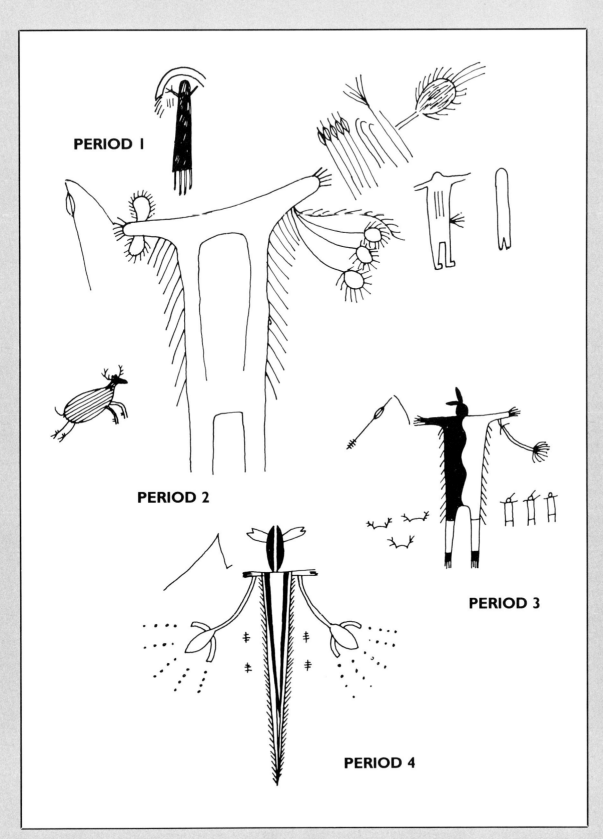

PERIOD 1

PERIOD 2

PERIOD 3

PERIOD 4

Pecos River Style shaman figure sequence suggested by W. W. Newcomb (taken from Rock Art of Texas Indians, by Forrest Kirkland and W. W. Newcomb, Jr.). Newcomb recognized a direction of development for the anthropomorphic figures from crude images (Period 1) to more realistic styles (Period 2), which became conventionalized (Period 3) and finally emerged as abstract forms (Period 4).

mixed with water, molded, and dried. Other crayons have also been found, as have the manos and metates on which the pigments were ground. Grease or fat was sometimes used as a binder. Paint brushes were sotol leaves, folded lengthwise, wrapped, and shredded at the ends.

W. W. Newcomb has established a tentative chronology for the Pecos River Style pictographs based on distinct substyles that are sometimes found superimposed over one another. A few monochromatic anthropomorphic figures found at some sites have been assigned to a tentative Period 1. They are dim, cigar-shaped or vertically elongated rectangular figures, usually with arms but mostly lacking heads and legs.

Distinctive humanlike forms with associated accoutrements emerge during the next period (Period 2). These figures are large, many over six feet tall, some over ten. They are elongated with parallel sides or with broad shoulders, outlined in dark red or red-orange. The bodies may be filled in with lines or may be a solid color. The majority are illustrated in front view, but a few are shown in profile. Heads are not shown, but headdresses may be, with horns projecting upward.

Costuming appears in this period. Some of the dominant figures are depicted with a cluster of feathers about the waist. Strange accoutrements are often attached to the arms. The atlatl with a feathered dart is linked to the right hand. At the left hand are curved stafflike objects that may be rabbit clubs and oval objects shown with fringed lines. The left arm embellishments vary considerably and may represent a robe carried across the arm, a hunting net, or perhaps net bags filled with personal possessions. These figures all appear to be hunters and warriors.

Naturalistic animals also appear in the second period. White-tail deer are most common and are painted in red, usually running in a herd. Their bodies are oval, the legs straight lines. Horns, tails, toes, and ears are all pictured. Some are shown pierced with spears. All are diminutive (about the size of a terrier) compared to the humanlike figures. The mountain lion is also a frequent subject. Unlike the deer, it may be quite large, dominating the panel. It is outlined in ticked lines, sometimes filled in with solid red or with red and black, and has a long body and a graceful tail. Other recognizable zoomorphic figures are birds, possibly buzzards or eagles.

During Period 3, anthropomorphic figures are painted in two or three colors, and black is used more

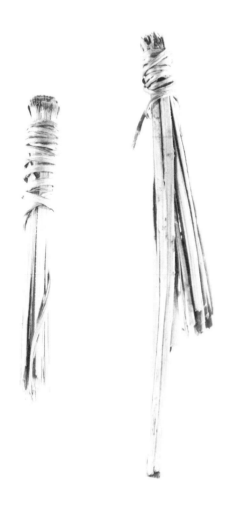

Small fiber bundles such as these were most likely used to apply paint during production of the cave murals.

White shaman. Majestic costumed ghostly human figures accompanied by abstract symbols painted in red, yellow, orange, black, and sometimes white pigments are characteristic of the Pecos River area.

often. They are smaller than those of the previous period, and heads are shown on most. Fingers, feet, and toes are also frequently depicted. Headdresses suggest that feathers became part of the costume at this time. Deer-antler headdresses are exclusive to this period and provide a convenient tie to Historic Indians who were living in the marginal desert of this region. Accoutrements are more stylized than in the second period. The atlatl and spear, for example, are not as common, and the mysterious pouches dangling from the arms have become long wavy or straight lines.

The only animals associated with Period 3 are deer. These are much more stylized, represented only by their antlers. The colorful human figures vary in size, form, and pattern. Nevertheless, they are easily distinguished by their simple outlines and stylistic detail.

The most stylized humanlike figures appear in Period 4. They are painted in three colors, and circles and dots appear as body ornamentation. None were overpainted, but, unfortunately, none were painted over earlier figures either. Therefore, while these figures represent a stylistic development, their relative position in time is unproven.

The geographic range of the Pecos River Style is surprisingly limited, despite the common occurrence of these murals in the area near the mouth of the Pecos River. It is confined to that well-watered region encompassing all but the southeast corner of Val Verde County and includes the Pecos, Devils, and Rio Grande canyons and their tributary systems. The western limit is Meyers Springs in Terrell County. Northern limits are Geddis Canyon in Terrell County and the Crockett and Sutton county lines. The Edwards county line marks the eastern limit. The Pecos River Style occurs in Mexico along the lower reaches of the canyons of the Rio Grande.

Human and animal symbols lead some archaeologists to assume that the paintings represent the rituals of a hunting cult, but this view may be too narrow. A broader interpretation is that the pictographs were painted for several kinds of rituals: boys' initiation rites, the recording of significant historical events, or the group's annual renewal ceremonies.

The artists were hunters and gatherers who lived in this marginal desert since about 7000 B.C. We do not know how they were related to the many loosely organized tribal groups that occupied the region of northern Mexico and southern and southwestern Texas when the Europeans arrived. We do know that Coahuiltecans, Tobosos, Coahuilenos, Chi-

sos, and Conchos shared a common lifestyle and drew their needs from the resources in the arid, thorny landscape. Interactions, sometimes hostile, took place between these people, and their social and political structure was similar.

Attitudes toward the natural and supernatural world were deeply rooted in tradition and shared a common base in antiquity. The general function of a specific act or ritual changed little from one linguistic or political group to another, due to the historical ties and conservative nature of religions in culturally stable environments. Some of the earlier pictograph styles are thought to date as far back as 2000 B.C., and we can assume that the first people who chose to settle in the lower canyons had their own forms of art, which, unfortunately, have not survived.

Why people chose to express themselves through the various media they did, we can only guess. We can be certain, however, that the art is not a form of hieroglyphics, nor, would we think, "art for art's sake." It was a form of communication for several kinds of information. If the information related to the supernatural, then surely many of the artists were shamans, recognized authorities on the human soul and the forces controlling human destiny. They acquired their knowledge through apprenticeships, instruction, and direct experience.

As Joan Halifax says in her book *Shamanic Voices*: "They are in communication with the world of gods and spirits. Their bodies can be left behind while they fly to unearthly realms. They are poets and singers. They dance and create works of art. They are not only spiritual leaders, but also judges and politicians, the repositories of knowledge of the culture's history, both sacred and secular. They are familiar with cosmic as well as physical geography. The ways of plants, animals, and the elements are known to them. They are psychologists, entertainers and food finders. Above all, however, shamans are technicians of the sacred and masters of ecstasy."

W. W. Newcomb, in *The Rock Art of Texas Indians*, suggests that the anthropomorphic figures were the focal points of most paintings. He favors the interpretation that these figures depict shamans, ordinary humans dressed as gods or mythical characters. He bases his view on the fact that the paintings occur in occupational localities rather than in special shrines. The overpainting suggests that the paintings themselves were not sacred. Newcomb feels that the importance was in the ritual and associated narrative rather

Like a giant overlay, a centipedelike motif was painted over earlier anthropomorphic or shaman figures by Pecos River Style artists in a Pecos canyon shelter. Overpainting such as this has allowed anthropologist W. W. Newcomb to recognize an evolutionary sequence within the Pecos River Style.

An unusually well preserved panorama of Pecos River Style pictographs at Panther Cave at the mouth of Seminole Canyon provides important clues to the role the art may have played in the ancient society that produced it. This mural is composed of many separate sets of motifs, each representing an individual event, indicating that this shelter was repeatedly used for the rituals during which paintings were produced.

than in the work of art itself.

The paintings cannot be interpreted or understood from a modern perspective. Contemporary values are so far removed from those of the ancient artists that any attempt at an interpretation can only be speculative. The use of metaphors in the conversation of hunters and gatherers is well known and represents a rich body of colorful oral literature that underscores the sophistication of their reasoning and intelligence. What appears to be a natural symbol, such as a person, a serpent, a prickly pear leaf, or a negative handprint may be a metaphor that carries an entirely different message. The meanings are lost when the culture comes to an end.

The Pecos River Style was produced by many different artists working within a relatively narrow set of rules, which had to be followed for the audience to receive the message. The rock art is a visual expression of their cognitive world, a world filled with animistic beings and spirits. It brought them into close communication with other living and nonliving beings.

As Robin Ridington observes in his study of the Beaver Indians of Canada, material possessions that must be carried from place to place were a burden. Such portable artifacts competed with infants, food, and essential tools for the finite carrying capacity of the forager. Ridington notes that for such people techniques that can be carried in the mind and put to

The combined symbolism of color and form (as seen in these two views of a black and red shaman figure from Panther Cave) may have communicated specific meanings, perhaps a certain deity or the band affiliation of the costumed actor. Unfortunately, the original meanings are forever lost in time. The rounded, turtlelike shape to the right also defies interpretation.

The famous panther from Panther Cave is an outstanding example of an animal motif found at several sites. The panther must have occupied an important place in the symbolic universe of the Lower Pecos people. Two shaman figures from Panther Cave (OPPOSITE) that look as though they are wearing feather decorations.

use by incorporating local resources were more cost-effective than artifacts.

In human groups with no written language, people rely on their capacity to store, recall, synthesize, correlate, and communicate information. The memory capacity of the human mind is estimated at over a trillion bits, not enough to retain all of the experiences of a lifetime. We retain a selective amount with peculiar biases, but there are patterns. The ordinary things that happen on a daily basis seldom get imprinted. It is the extraordinary, the sensational, the unusual events that are remembered. Experienced teachers, or shamans, were very much aware of this. They used repetition and visual effects to startle, to invoke fear, to induce pain as a means of indelibly imprinting specific information.

Richard Gould states that among western Aborigines in Australia, patterns of circles and connecting lines depicting tracks of a mythical ancestor, or the novice himself visiting localities, are painted or scarified onto the novices' bodies. These designs are maps of waterholes, soaks, or other vital resource locations across a broad, barren landscape.

These are some of the techniques that we assume constituted the instruction of the lower canyon people. Individuals were able to obtain from the wilderness of the lower canyon environment any item necessary for hunting, gathering, making clothing, or household maintenance. Memory was used to convert these various raw materials into food, tools, fire, and shelter. Equally important were the sources of power to overcome malevolent spirits that could bring harm to people or drive their game away.

Group identity is maintained through a common belief system that communicates the particulars of the natural and supernatural worlds and the people. Traditions identified the people with the land. Myths set the people apart from others. The land and rivers were sacred dwelling places of supernaturals from which they traced their origins. The myths carried geographical details that served not only as historical ties, but as legal ties as well. The rock art could be seen as posted signs claiming ancestral rights to the land.

Red Monochrome Style One Late Prehistoric rock art style has been identified on the basis of the depiction of the bow and arrow. These murals are painted in light red, reddish-orange, or yellow and usually show boldly painted solid human and animal figures.

Shamans with antler headdresses, *Pecos River Style,
Fate Bell Shelter in Seminole Canyon* (**LEFT AND
ABOVE**). *Ghosts, gods, and demons assume the shapes of
humans, animals, or combinations of the two in the primitive world. Deer played an important role in the lives of
the ancient Texans; although they were hunted as food,
their significance was much greater. They were an important symbol in the people's concept of their world and in
maintaining harmony with the universe. Deer heads with
antlers attached were believed to have had special power.
Deer were semidivine celestial animals in many American
Indian religions and were connected with sun, fire, sky
beings, and especially shamans. W. W. Newcomb suggests
that the "shaman" figures depict costumed dancers. The
winged figures with deer's head and antlers may represent
an important spirit being or a costumed shaman acting
out a ritual scene.*

Human figures are shown full-face, while animals are illustrated in profile. One is impressed with the naturalism of the animals: deer, rabbits, turkeys, mountain lions, and catfish are identifiable. Less detail is shown in the humans. Heads are distinguished, as are hands and fingers, but rarely feet. Male genitals are shown on some figures, but not on others. Most, if not all, of the figures are male and are illustrated with bows and arrows. Tassels and pouches are sometimes suspended from uplifted arms. Some human figures are pierced with arrows, but the animals are not. One scene, from a shelter in Seminole Canyon, shows a hunter shooting his bow and arrow at rabbits. A fence or a rabbit net is also illustrated. Communal rabbit drives, in which the animals were herded against nets, were widely used in the deserts of northern Mexico and North America.

There are two large Red Monochrome sites in the lower canyons. One is in Seminole Canyon, the other in nearby Painted Rock Canyon. Both shelters are low and periodically flooded. Another flooded shelter is west of the Pecos River in Meyers Canyon. There are a wide variety of paintings, including Pecos River, Red Monochrome, and Historic Indian styles.

Red Monochrome paintings, in addition to humans and animals, contain positive and negative handprints. The abstract, occasionally complex patterns seen in the Pecos River Style are absent. Red Monochrome sites are numerous as one goes north from the mouth of the Pecos River, although most sites are small. However, the farther away from the lower canyon one goes, the simpler the motifs.

Red Linear Style Six sites with paintings in this style are currently known to exist in the lower canyon area. These diminutive paintings in dark red represent humans and animals. The humans are drawn as stick figures. Their small size and the suggested action of the scene set them apart from the other styles. The Red Linear is unfortunately undated, because of the difficulty of distinguishing weapons due to the abstraction. Certainly the theme of these murals is decidedly different from any of the others.

Males are clearly indicated by genitals and females by a painted loop in the pelvic area. One pictograph includes males and females in what some see as sexual positions. This assumption has led to an interpretation of these paintings as part of some fertility rite. Some of the Red Linear pictographs may have been depictions of historical events, such as a successful

hunt, raid, or macroband gathering.

The painters of the Red Linear and Red Monochrome styles may have been recording witnessed events. They could have been ordinary people, rather than shamans. The ritual significance of these pictographs is not as obvious as that of the Pecos River Style.

Miscellaneous Paintings Not all examples of rock art in the lower canyons can be grouped under the previously discussed styles. The existence of a painting inspires others to leave their mark or record some significant event in their lives. Many marks left by people lacking an alphabet appear as random symbols, surrounded by free space. When bold red or orange, they are grouped under the Red Monochrome Style and are considered to be quite late in the archaeological sequence.

Some are clearly even later works illustrating non-Indians. These paintings undoubtedly represent actual historical events or observations. Buildings with crosses denote Spanish missions; horses, riders with hats, lassos, and guns chronicle the Indians' encounters with Europeans. Four such sites are known in the lower canyon area. Vaquero Shelter shows mounted vaqueros, or cowboys, lassoing longhorn cattle. Also shown in this mural, but possibly painted by a different artist, is a symbol with three crosses representing a Spanish mission and an individual wearing a buttoned coat and a hat, holding a pipe. A positive handprint can be seen on this panel, the whole of which is superimposed over a much-faded Pecos River Style painting.

Another Historic mural was found in Castle Canyon on a small tributary of the Devils River. This contains what appear to be Red Linear images in addition to figures wearing hats and dresses. A shelter in Rattlesnake Canyon shows positive hand prints in red, a horse, and a human figure bearing crosses. Certainly the most complicated mural containing Historic motifs by several artists is in the shelter at Meyers Springs, west of the Pecos River. Churches, priests, riders on horseback, figures with guns, wheeled carts, tipis, crucifixes (one of which was almost certainly drawn by a Spaniard), and positive and negative hand prints are among the various design elements.

While the symbols of the Pecos River and Red Monochrome styles seem to depict male-connected things (animals, men with atlatls) and may relate much of their folklore regarding hunting, animal behavior, and the forces that control the universe, we

Pecos River (OPPOSITE) *and Rattlesnake Canyon* (pp. 155–157). *The myriad complex Pecos River Style murals depicting separate scenes, in a mixture of styles and motifs, painted at different times in Rattlesnake Canyon may one day provide archaeologists with a code for recognizing places or points in time. Small canyons leading from or to the Rio Grande, such as Seminole and Rattlesnake, are notable for their Pecos River Style rock art. These canyons may have been much-traveled prehistoric north–south corridors across the Rio Grande, leading to their popularity as sites for visual symbols.*

Separate scenes from Black Cave, Pressa Canyon (**THIS PAGE AND OPPOSITE**), *suggest three entirely different Pecos River Style artists and painting events. Note the similarity of the upper boxlike figure* (**LEFT**) *to the "TV set" at Fate Bell Shelter. This odd shape is depicted beneath a multicolored "cloud" here and a serpentinelike figure at Fate Bell. The "locomotive" (**UPPER RIGHT**) is an equally mysterious symbol. All these bold visual motifs must have evoked immediate understanding and response on the part of their contemporary audience, but stretch the imagination of the modern viewer. The rare profile view of two "shaman figures" (**LOWER RIGHT**) may be a symbolic representation of a historic meeting between two bands. The simplified shaman figure wearing a deer antler headdress is part of a separate Pecos River Style mural.*

should not assume that they relate to men's activities alone. The function of the art could fall within several realms. Initiation, prewar ceremonies, victories, continuance and weather rites, and curing rituals for individuals and the group as a whole are all distinct possibilities.

Judging from the size, color combinations, complexity, and time and paint resources consumed, the paintings themselves constituted a major part of the rituals. Pictographic art was created to display certain symbols of specific myths, legends, deeds, or events. Paintings may have been produced to entice the supernatural or to appease it, but the act itself was the essential ritual, in that it provided examples and instructions to the audience. It was a display of power—that is, knowledge—by some person in possession of the proper formula for instruction. The art was a means of enhancing the memorization of detail through visual stimulation.

Influences Were the lower canyon artists influenced by neighbors or is their style unique? Unfortunately, our knowledge of the rock art in the surrounding areas is very poor. Two prerequisites for rock art to be preserved are available rockshelters and an arid environment. Not all the adjacent regions have such localities—the two that come closest are the Edwards Plateau and the Big Bend area. Pictographs have been recorded in the Edwards Plateau, east of the lower canyon area, but these are few and consist of abstract linear designs in red, black, or yellow that are stylistically separate from the lower canyon styles of any age. To the west, in the Big Bend area, art styles are varied and do not show any recognizable relationship to the Pecos River Style, but parallels can be seen with the Red Monochrome and Red Linear styles. Mostly, however, the rock art in the Big Bend region has a stylistic flavoring all its own. The rock art outside the Rio Grande drainage, to the south in Mexico, is largely unstudied. What is known strongly suggests that the Pecos River Style is essentially confined to those canyons that drain into the Rio Grande. If the lower canyon people took the idea of illustrating visual symbols on protected rock faces from others, they quickly adopted their own style of expression.

Deer, panthers, and serpents are zoomorphic beings that acquired powerful supernatural positions in the religions and myths of many Mesoamerican cultures. These symbols are also pervasive in the Pecos River Style rock art. Were these symbols the result of

Pecos River Style, Rio Grande Canyon (Mystic Shelter). Human, animal, and abstract forms together depict relationships in the minds of the artists who painted this Devils River canyon shelter (ABOVE) and Pecos River canyon site (BELOW). The imagined spirits were as real to the ancient Texans as the animals themselves. The rockshelters in the Lower Pecos River area were formed by natural weathering (exfoliation or spalling of the softer limestone strata). These natural processes together with water seeping through tiny fissures and cracks as seen here continue to deepen the shelters and threaten the preservation of the ancient pictographs.

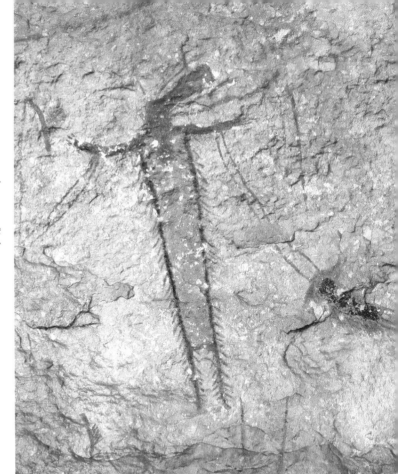

Pecos River Style, several views (**LEFT, RIGHT, & BE-LOW LEFT**), *showing variability within the style. Combinations of anthropomorphic figures and abstract symbols communicated to the ancient Texans the values and beliefs essential to coping with their world.*

Period 4 Pecos River Style shaman figure (**RIGHT**). *This is a conventionalized form of shaman figure, dated late in the Pecos River Style by W. W. Newcomb, based on superposition and stylistic evolution.*

Panthers from Pecos River and Seminole canyon shelters. Panther images, usually painted in red, are predominant figures in the Pecos River Style. They are usually shown high above anthropomorphic figures on the shelter walls. This positioning, possibly indicating dominance, may mean that the panther assumed the form of a major deity in the world of the ancient artists. Natural weathering and spalling of painted surfaces has greatly deteriorated many of the Pecos River Style paintings.

These Pecos River Style murals illustrate both simplicity (OPPOSITE, ABOVE) and complexity (BELOW) of motifs and motif arrangement.

cultural diffusion—that is, borrowing—by the lower canyon people from higher cultures? Or were these themes common to the basic hunter-gatherer groups that gave rise to Mexican civilizations and continued essentially intact in the lower canyon culture? The implied antiquity of the Pecos River Style would indicate that the art form was indigenous to the lower canyon area and was part of a broader general pattern that was widespread over northern Mexico and adjacent regions north of the Rio Grande prior to the rise of the great Mesoamerican centers. If the art was produced as part of a ritual to ensure continuation of the people and to reinforce those beliefs that served to provide social and group identity, the distribution of the symbols could provide some information on the geographic range of the artists. The limited geographic distribution of the Pecos River Style pictographs could signify the approximate extent of the artists' territorial range.

The Pebbles

One curious artifact frequently found in the protected deposits in lower canyon rockshelters is elongated limestone pebbles, painted in abstract linear designs. These represent the longest continuous art form known in North America, dating from about 6500 B.C. to about A.D. 1400. Surprisingly, despite the frequency with which they are found in lower canyon sites, painted pebbles constitute one of the least studied forms of prehistoric art.

The designs are usually in black, but are sometimes in red. Painted pebble designs appear to be part of a different symbolic complex than that depicted on the shelter walls. Some linear motifs seen in pictographs have been compared to those on painted pebbles, but the relationship is not convincing.

The occurrence of painted pebbles in the cave deposits of the lower canyons was noted by J. E. Pearce and A. T. Jackson, Frank Setzler, and E. B. Sayles in the 1930s. It was A. T. Jackson who provided the first documentation on the geographical occurrence of these artifacts in central and southwest Texas in his *Picture Writing of Texas Indians*.

The first effort to synthesize information was by Walker Davenport and Carl Chelf, who studied specimens unearthed during several expeditions in the lower canyons in the 1930s, including the Witte Museum excavations in Eagle Cave and Shumla Caves. Their work was a brief descriptive study with line drawings. Although their data lacked chronological

Red Monochrome Style. The stationary realistic human and animal figures of the Red Monochrome Style in this shelter recess in a small tributary of the Rio Grande show general similarities to the Pecos River Style and may have evolved from it. The bow and arrow depicted in the hands of certain Red Monochrome figures separate them in time from the earlier Pecos River Style, which shows the use of the atlatl and spear. Knowing the date of arrival of the bow and arrow in the region allows archaeologists to place a maximum date of about 1,000 years on the Red Monochrome Style.

control, they did suggest that the pebbles represented a long cultural trend. This observation was based on recovery of painted pebbles as deep as nine feet in some cave deposits. Their illustration of specimens served as a guide in later chronological studies.

The most informative study conducted was an unpublished work in the 1960s by Mark Parsons, who had the advantage of working with an additional collection from Eagle Cave and a smaller sample from Fate Bell Shelter. These new collections were not only from a more precise archaeological context, but were found in deposits that had been dated by the radiocarbon method. Parsons observed that the painted pebbles possess three basic attributes, which combine to form the core motif. One component is a median line that bisects the upper two-thirds of the pebble. Usually a single line, it may be flanked on either side by an additional line that parallels the median or the edges of the stone. The second component is a motif drawn at the wider or lower end of the pebble in a triangular, circular, or lenticular form, often made complex with the addition of radiating lines, loops, or other embellishments. Third is a pair of elements placed on either side of the median line at the opposite end of the pebble from the second component. In later styles, this takes on the appearance of eyes.

Parsons describes six styles of painted pebbles. When these are compared to trends and known chronology, he is able to provide a continuum that spans the time from about 6500 B.C. to A.D. 1400. The six styles range from an abstract, fine line at the beginning of the sequence to a bold-line representation of the features of a human face at the late end of the sequence. The shift from abstract to representational figures could signify conceptual changes.

Painted pebbles are usually found in midden deposits after being discarded. Many show signs of having been reused as hammerstones. Often they have been broken by heavy blows that may have been intentional. There has only been one recorded instance of painted pebbles found in a deliberately placed circumstance. This find was made in an upper (Devils Interval) deposit of Bonfire Shelter, dated 1,400–1,600 years old. It consisted of three painted pebbles placed side by side on the floor of the shelter. One was painted in a highly conventionalized anthropomorphic design, and a second was a more abstract symbol. The third was too faded to determine its design.

The finding of the three pebbles at Bonfire Shelter raises a number of questions regarding their function.

Bold zoomorphic figures, (LEFT) *a serpent motif, and a negative handprint made by blowing pigment around the hand illustrate variations in the Red Monochrome tradition. These paintings are preserved in a shallow recess above the Pecos River canyon.*

Pecos River Style handprints (RIGHT) *provide a contrast in technique to the Red Monochrome prints. The artists painted a design on the hand and stamped it against this shelter wall in Seminole Canyon.*

Red Monochrome Style. *The Red Monochrome handprints* (LEFT) *in this Devils River shelter may represent the symbolic signatures of passing hunters who dipped their hands into paint to leave hand impressions.*

Red Monochrome Style (RIGHT). *The ancient artists' conception of spirits may seem strange to the modern viewer. Perhaps our imagery would be no less strange if we attempted to paint pictures of our guiding spirits.*

Red Linear Style (LEFT & RIGHT). *The vivid action scenes and tiny stick figures of the Red Linear Style painted in this recess in a tributary of Pressa Canyon provide a marked contrast to the bold, stationary multicolored figures of the Pecos River Style.*

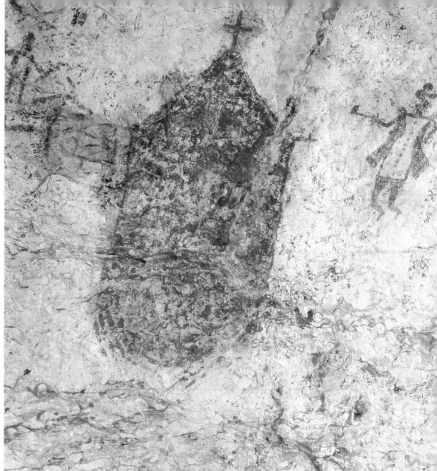

Historic pictographs. *Two scenes from the Historic pictographs at Vaquero Shelter.* (**LEFT**) *A horse and rider are crudely depicted in a Pecos River canyon shelter. Extraordinary historical events motivated some of the ancient artists to record their experiences on rock surfaces. The arrival of the equestrian Spaniards and their vast herds of livestock left an indelible impression on the native Texans who witnessed such events. The scene at the right (***ABOVE***) depicts a mission and a Spanish officer.*

That the three were found together and display different motifs may suggest that they were used in rituals to narrate myths or as part of a divination associated with a curing ceremony. The mobility of this art form would allow the event to take place virtually anywhere.

Parsons suggests that the pebbles represent female figures. There are instances in which the second design component was covered with a bound leaf of grass, possibly indicating menstrual pads. The pebbles may be associated with menstrual taboo, common in Native American cultures. The painted pebbles could have been used as figurines or icons in religious ceremonies, as items possessing supernatural power or magical qualities used in curing rituals, or even in sets during initiation or other communal activities where specific information was communicated. They might well have been produced as sacred items that, once used, reentered the secular world.

Engraved Pebbles Small pebbles bearing engraved designs are sometimes found, although not as commonly as those that are painted. The designs are usually linear scratches placed in accordance with the orientation of the pebble. Examples have been found with designs that parallel the painted pebbles. There is no reason to consider the engraved pebbles as a separate functional class from the painted ones. Indeed, because of close similarities in style, they are considered a subset of the painted pebbles. Perhaps the engraved pebbles were made in situations where pigments were unavailable.

The Figurines

Clay Figurines Small unfired clay figurines are occasionally found in cultural deposits of lower canyon rockshelters. These are generally crude and simplified in form. They are usually cigar-shaped, often embellished with conelike appendages and incised or, rarely, painted designs. We do not know when the figurines were first made because only a few specimens are datable. Figurines have been found in deposits that date within the Pandale Interval (about 3,400–4,000 years ago) and in more recent deposits in the Devils Interval.

Like the painted pebbles, the figurines are usually found singly in midden deposits. Many are broken. Often the head is detached. The head of an incised figurine was found in a rockshelter on the Mexican

side of the border. A group of four figurines was found lying side by side in an ashy deposit in Hinds Cave. This is the only instance of figurines found in deliberate placement. Two of the four Hinds Cave figures are females.

Most figurines emphasize the head and torso. The bodies may be decorated with incised or punctuated lines. Heads may be distinguished by a tapering at the shoulders, or simply as a somewhat pointed end on a

Painted pebbles. Stream-worn limestone pebbles were painted in bold black (or rarely red) lines in abstract designs. Such painted stones constitute the earliest art recovered from the lower canyons and may have been figurines symbolic of spirits or forces and used in healing, divining, or storytelling.

cigar-shaped form. One small figurine from Coontail Spin Shelter emphasizes the face. This is the only instance where the nose is indicated. Female figurines have breasts and, in one instance, a painted vulva. Figurines lacking breasts may represent males. There is great variation in form among the figurines. This may be due to the range in time. The similarity in some of the cigar-shaped figures to earliest Pecos River pictography is interesting, although it may be fortuitous.

The figurines are made by forming a small mass of clay between the hands into an elongated shape, or by rolling a rod of clay and folding or breaking it into two or three pieces and welding the pieces together. Some are very fine and indicate the execution of a deliberate pattern. One painted fragment from Muertos Cave near Shumla shows a design very similar to those seen on painted pebbles.

Figurines may have had special group significance. Scarification and body painting were widely reported among the people of northern Mexico and southern and western Texas by Spanish explorers. There were several reasons for body painting. Certainly it was associated with warfare, but shamans and dancers also painted themselves during rituals and ceremonies. Where people have little diagnostic clothing to display identifying marks, they often use their bodies as a medium for embellishment. Hairstyles denoting the marital status of women and scars or tattoos showing the age of men or signifying group identity are traits widely found among peoples who lived in warm climates and used few clothes.

Why are some of the figurines decorated and others plain? Probably the decorations were there to communicate some important information, such as marital status or group identity. In many mobile societies, the ultimate gesture of friendship between two bands was the gift of a member of one's own band. The individual being traded was often a child, but unmarried women were exchanged as well. If these women were decorated during initiation rites, their birth and kinship affiliation would be apparent wherever they went thereafter. Perhaps the decorated figurines were ways in which the kinship affinity of certain women could be symbolically indicated. Or the figurines might represent the myth of certain bands who became permanently affiliated.

Fiber Figurines Several artifacts, each of which consists of a bundle of yucca leaves folded in half and wrapped with a single untwisted leaf, were found at Hinds Cave, side by side in an ash heap. These curious figures are so simply constructed that their function cannot be confidently ascertained, but they could easily symbolize human figures. Their construction follows a specific pattern, and the deliberate placement in the shelter deposit would suggest that they represent some form of cognitive symbol. All came from deposits that date about 4,000 years ago.

Figurines were used in the American Southwest and in Mesoamerica in a variety of ways. The small collection of clay figurines known from the lower canyon area indicates that they either were not frequently used or were made of materials not easily recogniz-

Clay figurines. Symbols of witchcraft or spirits, or perhaps just toys, these small figurines of unfired clay depict crude anthropomorphic forms (both male and female) and represent an art style unique to southwest Texas. Clay figurines have been found in 3,000-year-old shelter deposits.

able. The few examples known do not bear similarities to those of the American Southwest or Mesoamerica.

Several major functions could have been served by the figurines, such as in human or natural resource increase ceremonies, in curing, as religious icons, or as symbols for sacrificial victims. Certainly one of the more common explanations is their use in fertility rites. A study by Noel Morse suggests that figurines were used among the Pueblo Indians of the American Southwest in efforts to bring about fertility.

The shamans were the medicine men and the sorcerers. They used herbal treatments as well as magic in their efforts to cure the sick and depressed. The use of figurines as dolls in curing ceremonies is worldwide among nonliterate peoples. Anthropologists have noted the frequency of dolls around homes of Indians in Colombia that were used in curing ceremonies. Once the ceremonies are over, the dolls are discarded. Thomas Lee of the New World Archaeological Foundation has speculated that the number of clay figurines around some of the ancient households in Chiapas may have been due to a similar cause.

The use of figurines in witchcraft in order to produce sickness or death is also widespread in nonliterate societies. Lee has observed that the number of figurines in such instances is limited, because they are usually hidden before or after use. The cache of figurines at Hinds Cave could indicate such a circumstance.

Most of the figurines are found in midden deposits, however, and are fragmentary. Some have been found burned. While their use in magic rites might explain their overall infrequency and the Hinds Cave cache, it does not seem to explain the context in which the remainder of the specimens have been found. Could they have been used as substitute sacrificial victims— as offerings to the high deities in the absence of human sacrifices? Thomas Lee has noted that figurines made of wood, cloth, clay, and metal, for example, were used in sacrificial ceremonies among the Otomies and Huastecans. These rituals were conducted during fiestas on the edge of a lake, and the figurines were sacrificed to the female water deity to ensure a balanced rainfall. Perhaps the figurines in the lower canyon sites were used in substitute for human sacrifices. This might explain the decapitation and burning of some of the figurines.

Might the figurines simply have been used as dolls by children? We can be sure that toys were used by children of the lower canyon, because child play and toys are universal. The fiber figurines found cached at

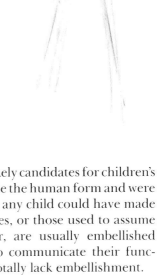

Fiber figurines. Dolls of ancient Texas children may have been made simply by bending and wrapping bundles of leaves from desert plants into crude human shapes. The function of these intriguing 4,000-year-old artifacts is unknown, but they probably symbolized the human form.

Hinds Cave are the most likely candidates for children's toys. They vaguely resemble the human form and were so simply constructed that any child could have made one. Iconographic figurines, or those used to assume some supernatural power, are usually embellished with features necessary to communicate their function. The fiber figurines totally lack embellishment.

Petroglyphs

Petroglyphs are designs cut, ground, or pecked into a rock's surface. This form of rock art is much more permanent than pictographs, but equally difficult to date. Two major petroglyph sites are known in the region. One is on a smooth, flat limestone surface near the mouth of Lewis Canyon, overlooking the Pecos River in Crockett County. This site covers about two acres. The other site is on a similar surface in Sutton County east of Ozona, Texas.

At Lewis Canyon, the symbols are pecked into the

rock and appear in many forms, predominantly circles and lines, which occur in great variety. The symbols are conventionalized and bear no resemblance to other forms, except for three human hand designs and one male stick figure. The Sutton County Site does not cover as large an area as the Lewis Canyon Site, but it is similar in many respects. Dome-shaped Archaic burned-rock middens cover some of the rock surface that bears the pecked symbols. The middens are unexcavated and could provide a means of obtaining a relative age for the petroglyphs.

Several small petroglyphs are known, in addition to the two large sites. Some, such as at Fate Bell Shelter, occur in boulders in, or next to, occupied rockshelter sites. The occurrence of petroglyphs increases significantly as one goes west from the Pecos River. They are particularly common in the Trans-Pecos area of Texas, west of the Big Bend region. The antiquity of the petroglyph sites in the lower canyon area is unknown, but, as suggested by the presence of burned-rock middens overlying the rock art in Sutton County, these could be among the more ancient rock art forms in the region.

Parallels in Northern Mexico

We cannot recreate the cognitive world of the ancient lower canyon people, but we can come closer to understanding their art by examining the ways in which other nonliterate peoples create their art.

An ethnographic account of Indians living across the Rio Grande in Mexico, compiled by William Griffen, indicates a petroglyphic site used as a shrine

Modern ranch traffic and vandalism threaten this petroglyph site, which has withstood the effects of natural weathering for perhaps thousands of years.

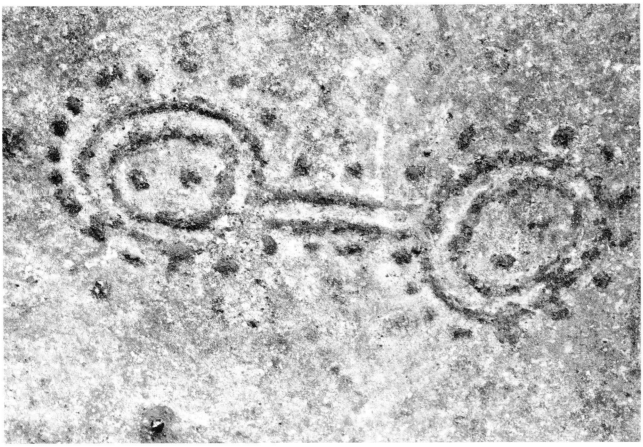

and visited by a shaman. In another instance, a missionary mentions that Indians recorded the success of a battle on a rock surface. Griffen provides a rich list of ritual activities among the northern Mexico desert Indians that is useful when considering the art of the lower canyon. His observations were made among hunters and gatherers whose culture was similar. Indeed, it is likely that descendants of the lower canyon people were among those he describes.

The ceremonial behavior of the northern Mexico people was associated with various activities that included warfare, hunting, curing, alliance pacts, and initiations. The Tobosos who lived in the basins and ranges south of the lower canyon region held dances during conferences. These dances were described as lasting throughout the night, sometimes up to eight days. Peyote was commonly used on these occasions. The people would paint their bodies and perform bloodletting rituals. Dancers were adorned with brilliant feathers and carried whips, arrows, and fans in their hands. Prewar and prehunting dances were also held. These were all-night circle dances performed

around a deer skull with antlers intact. The association of adornments on many of the Pecos River Style anthropomorphs would seem to support Newcomb's claim that they depict dancers.

Archaeologists are less equipped to deal with the cognitive aspect of the ancient way of life than with the technological or subsistence aspects; but the mental world was as important as the physical. The pictographs, painted pebbles, clay figurines, and other objects found in the lower canyon sites are tangible products of expression of their cognitive world. Archaeologists also tend to disregard the activities of everyday living: family, interactions between spouses or between children, evening visits around the campfire. Much too often we interpret a concentration of burned rocks as a hearth on which meat was cooked, but hearths were also the focal points of social interaction. Treatments for sickness and injury were associated with certain tools, just as hunting or gathering had necessary hardware. The artifacts considered here are symbolic and should be viewed as art objects, not as technology. ■

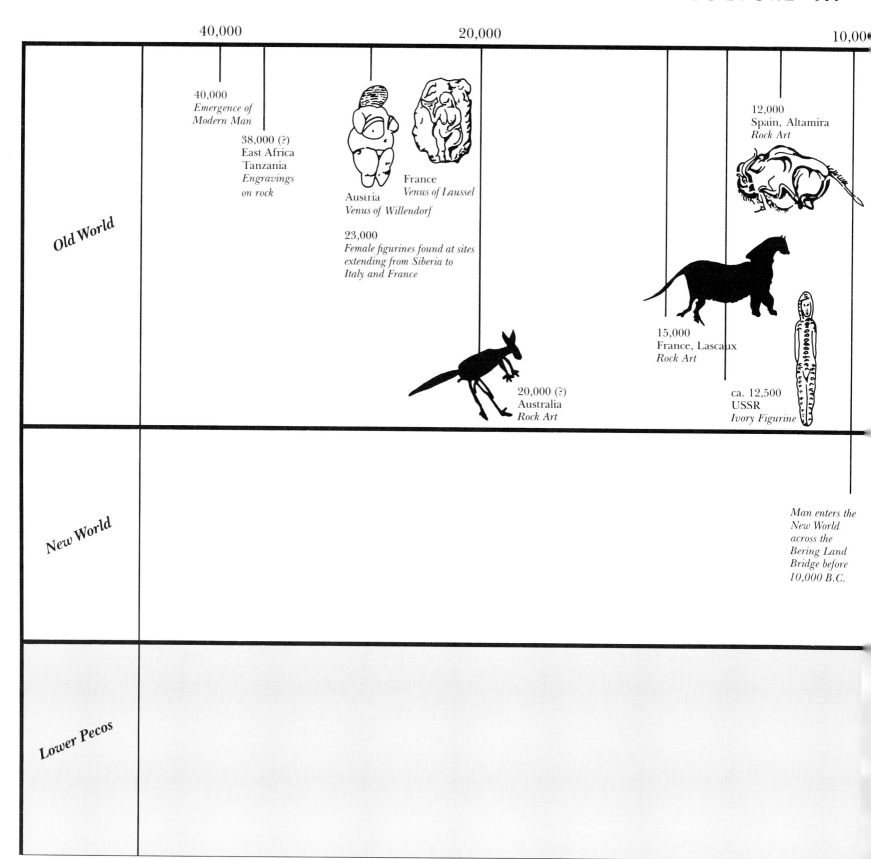

Old World

40,000

20,000

10,000

40,000
*Emergence of
Modern Man*

38,000 (?)
East Africa
Tanzania
*Engravings
on rock*

Austria
Venus of Willendorf

France
Venus of Laussel

23,000
*Female figurines found at sites
extending from Siberia to
Italy and France*

12,000
Spain, Altamira
Rock Art

15,000
France, Lascaux
Rock Art

ca. 12,500
USSR
Ivory Figurine

20,000 (?)
Australia
Rock Art

New World

*Man enters the
New World
across the
Bering Land
Bridge before
10,000 B.C.*

Lower Pecos

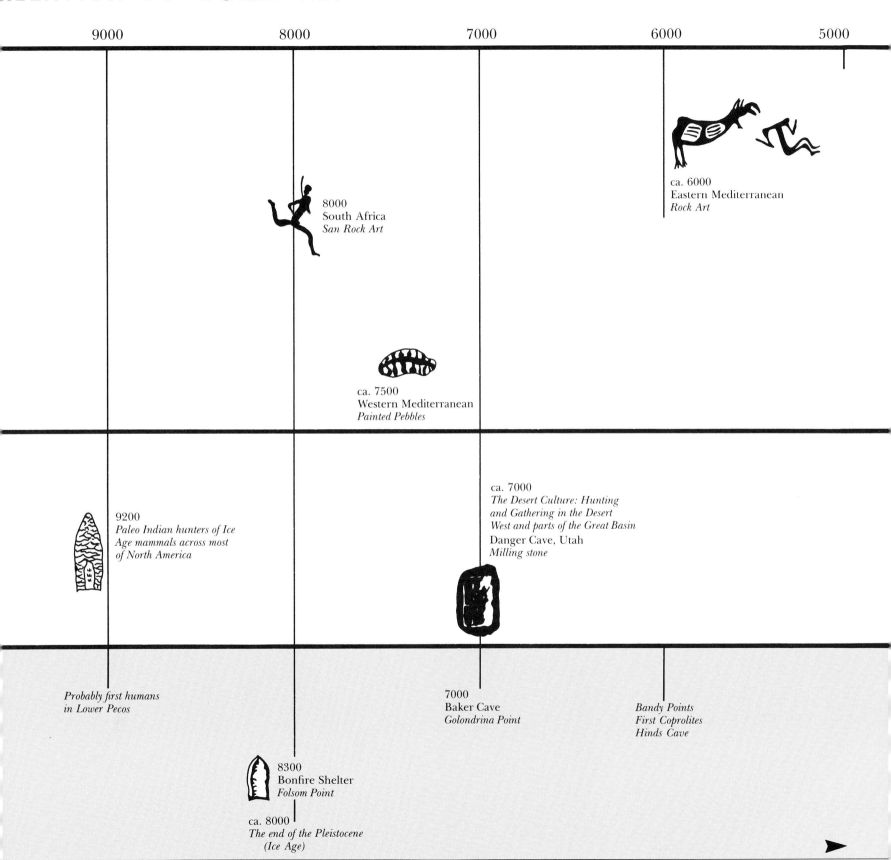

9000   8000   7000   6000   5000

8000
South Africa
San Rock Art

ca. 6000
Eastern Mediterranean
Rock Art

ca. 7500
Western Mediterranean
Painted Pebbles

ca. 7000
*The Desert Culture: Hunting
and Gathering in the Desert
West and parts of the Great Basin*
Danger Cave, Utah
Milling stone

9200
*Paleo Indian hunters of Ice
Age mammals across most
of North America*

*Probably first humans
in Lower Pecos*

7000
Baker Cave
Golondrina Point

*Bandy Points
First Coprolites
Hinds Cave*

8300
Bonfire Shelter
Folsom Point

ca. 8000
*The end of the Pleistocene
(Ice Age)*

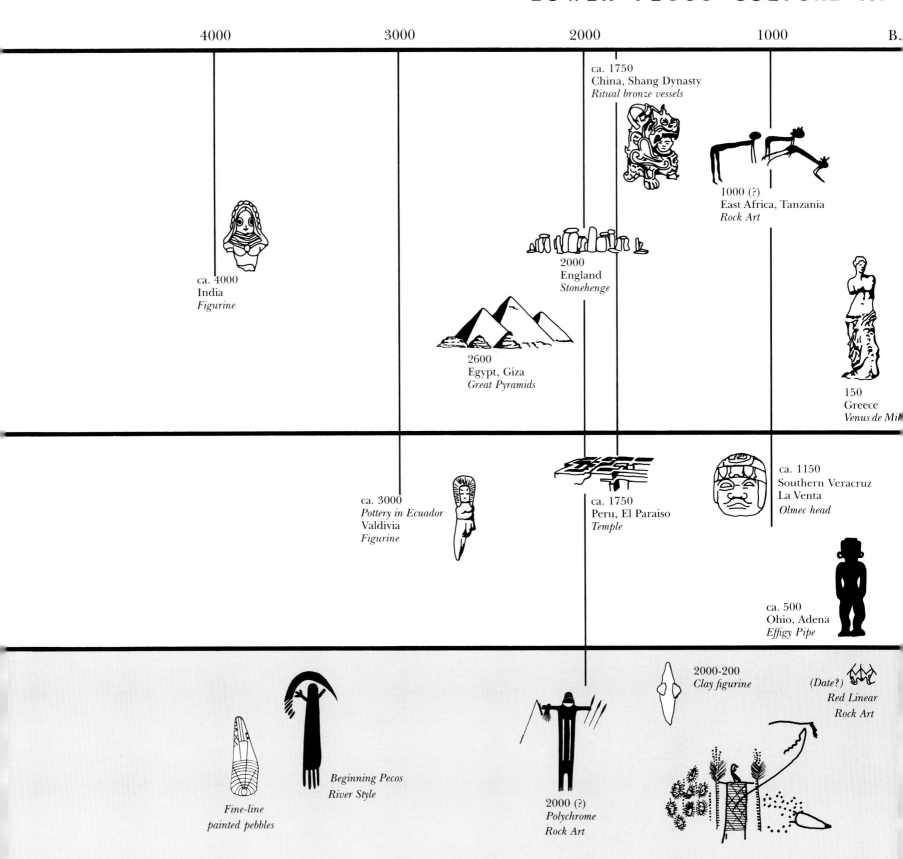

4000   3000   2000   1000   B.

ca. 1750
China, Shang Dynasty
Ritual bronze vessels

1000 (?)
East Africa, Tanzania
Rock Art

ca. 4000
India
Figurine

2000
England
Stonehenge

2600
Egypt, Giza
Great Pyramids

150
Greece
Venus de Mil

ca. 3000
Pottery in Ecuador
Valdivia
Figurine

ca. 1750
Peru, El Paraiso
Temple

ca. 1150
Southern Veracruz
La Venta
Olmec head

ca. 500
Ohio, Adena
Effigy Pipe

2000-200
Clay figurine

(Date?)
*Red Linear
Rock Art*

*Beginning Pecos
River Style*

*Fine-line
painted pebbles*

2000 (?)
*Polychrome
Rock Art*

RELATION TO WORLD ART

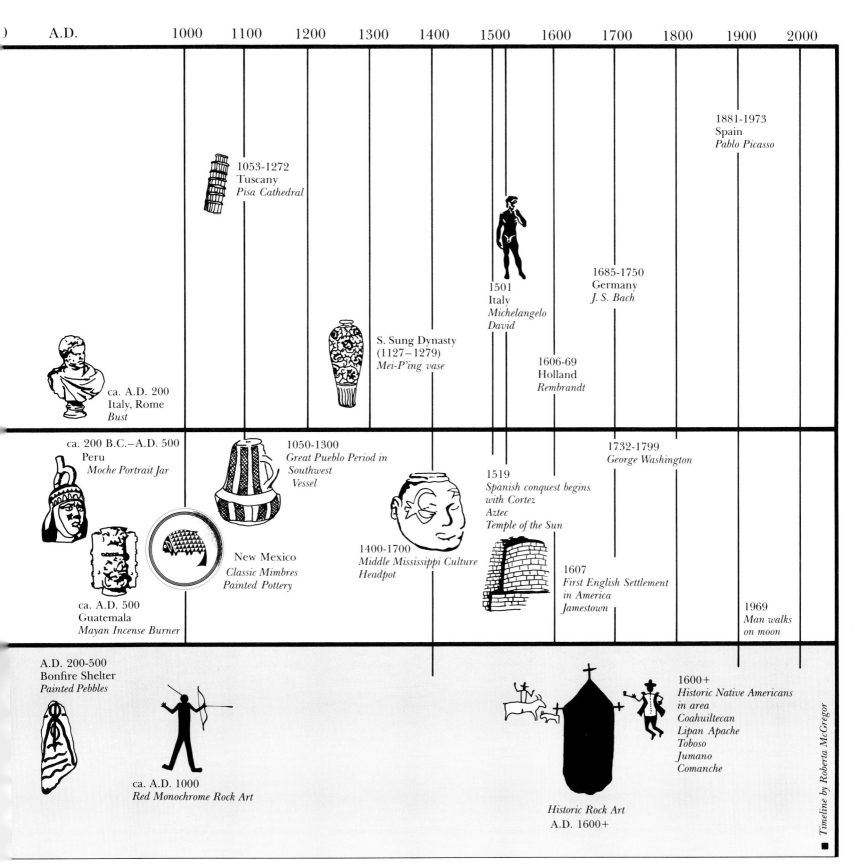

A.D.   1000   1100   1200   1300   1400   1500   1600   1700   1800   1900   2000

1881-1973
Spain
Pablo Picasso

1053-1272
Tuscany
Pisa Cathedral

1501
Italy
*Michelangelo
David*

1685-1750
Germany
J. S. Bach

S. Sung Dynasty
(1127–1279)
Mei-P'ing vase

1606-69
Holland
Rembrandt

ca. A.D. 200
Italy, Rome
Bust

ca. 200 B.C.–A.D. 500
Peru
Moche Portrait Jar

1050-1300
Great Pueblo Period in
Southwest
Vessel

1732-1799
George Washington

1519
Spanish conquest begins
with Cortez
Aztec
Temple of the Sun

New Mexico
*Classic Mimbres
Painted Pottery*

1400-1700
Middle Mississippi Culture
Headpot

1607
First English Settlement
in America
Jamestown

ca. A.D. 500
Guatemala
Mayan Incense Burner

1969
*Man walks
on moon*

A.D. 200-500
Bonfire Shelter
Painted Pebbles

1600+
Historic Native Americans
in area
*Coahuiltecan
Lipan Apache
Toboso
Jumano
Comanche*

ca. A.D. 1000
Red Monochrome Rock Art

Historic Rock Art
A.D. 1600+

■ *Timeline by Roberta McGregor*

RECORDING AND INTERPRETING LOWER PECOS PICTOGRAPHS
Methods and Problems

by Terence Grieder
THE UNIVERSITY OF TEXAS AT AUSTIN

Two separate problems face the student of rock art. The first is to get an accurate record of the art, or what remains of it, so that it can be examined at leisure and compared with other examples. The second is to find an interpretation of the art, so that its meaning for the original audience can be understood, at least in a general way. Although these problems are easy to state, no really satisfactory solution to either one has been found in more than fifty years of study. The history of modern study of rock art can be encapsulated in the attempts to solve these two problems.

Methods for Recording the Rock Art

There are three methods for recording rock art: to make a hand-painted or drawn copy of it, to trace it from the wall onto a transparent surface, and to photograph it. Each has its advantages and disadvantages, and recent serious attempts to record the art have made use of more than one method. Documentation of the geographical situation and archaeological levels and mineralogical specimens of pigments contribute to making a complete record of the paintings. Our attention here focuses on the basic problem: to produce an accurate record of individual designs and of their relationships.

The oldest recording method is drawing and painting copies of the designs on the rock onto sheets of paper. By far the best and most complete painted records are those of Forrest and Lula Kirkland made between 1934 and 1941. An expert professional watercolorist and a serious student of rock art, Forrest Kirkland made detailed scale copies of most of the rock art known in Texas. His copies are still the basic record for most of this art.

Having myself done watercolor copies of some of the same shelters copied by Kirkland, I am especially aware of the advantages of having more than one artist's copy. Not only does each artist have a personal way of handling the brush and ordering experience, but each one also sees things the other missed. For example, in 1964 some art students and I again copied the canoes painted in one of the rockshelters that Kirkland had copied in 1940. Erosion over twenty-four years may account for some of the things we did not see in 1964, such as the abundance of marks between the black posts, but how can one explain things we saw that Kirkland did not see, such as the rudderlike element

and, most notably, the lower part of one of the black posts? Color photographs for comparison should resolve the conflicts; but given the extreme faintness of many of the marks, they do not so much resolve disputes as permit the viewer to create new versions. The notorious subjectivity of historical records generally is demonstrated very graphically in the records of rock art. There was, of course, an original work independent of all observers, but the closest we can come to discovering it is by examining the versions of many different witnesses using a variety of recording methods.

Tracing of the designs has been done on rice paper dampened and pressed to the walls and by drawing with grease pencils on transparent acetate taped above the painted areas. Max Winkler and I used this method for the reconstruction of the long wall of a large shelter high above the Devils River. These paintings were of particular interest because their eroded condition suggested that they were among the older examples. Despite their location in the middle of a deep, protected shelter high above the canyon floor, only spots of color remained. The wall had also been painted repeatedly. Every color spot was re-

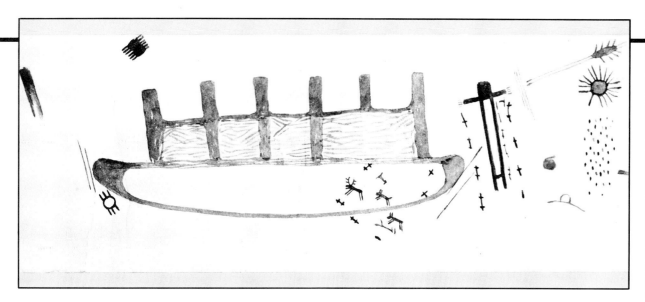

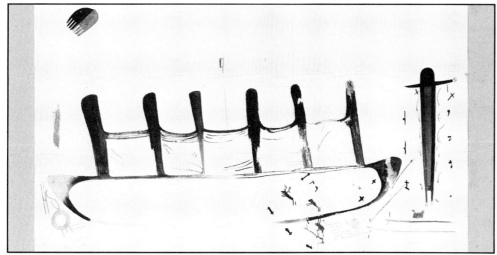

corded on the acetate, despite the fact that few motifs could be distinguished. Later, when the acetate sheets were hung in order against the white wall of a studio, the colors could be selected one by one and the larger configurations could be more easily identified. This permitted partial recovery of a set of paintings we at first gave up for lost.

Photography has the advantage of objectivity, and it has been used to record everything that could be caught on the film. The Kirklands and other early recorders used the camera mainly for general views of the sites, since the lack of color film made photographs of the paintings of minor use. The limits of simple black-and-white photography were reached by about 1960 in the photographs of the paintings published by David Gebhard. Black-and-white photographs, along with drawings, continue to provide the basic pictorial record in recent publications, such as those of Solveig Turpin. For designs in red or black that are not too faded, black-and-white film can provide a good record, but the film does not adequately record the lighter values, especially the yellows.

In the 1940s, when color film became widely available, it became possible to record the paintings more fully, but no photographic record in color was attempted before the Amistad Reservoir project of the early 1960s. Photographic methods are still improving. The outstanding work of Jim Zintgraff is an example of how far photographic technique has progressed. Solveig Turpin and others have perfected the technique of stereophotogrammetry, in which stereoscopic color and black-and-white pictures are made from fixed points along a line parallel to the painted walls. With maps of the photo stations, the combined coverage of Zintgraff and Turpin is about as thorough a photographic record as can be obtained with current technology.

Two copies of the same "canoe" from a Val Verde County rockshelter. The older (1940) copy (ABOVE) is by Forrest Kirkland. The more recent (1964) copy was made by Terence Grieder. Note the discrepancies, not attributable to erosion, such as the rudderlike element and the lower part of one of the black posts not recorded by Kirkland.

Copy by Solveig Turpin of small Red Linear Style painting of what appears to be a bison driven toward a geometric design possibly symbolizing a barrier or cliff face.

The conclusion one reaches after examining the methods for recording rock art is that there is no substitute for seeing the original art. But for comparative study, copies are indispensable, with all their limitations. The flooding of a large portion of the painted shelters has given the copies special importance as the only surviving record.

One of the factors that none of the methods can satisfactorily record is the relative chronology evident on the painted surfaces. Seven objective criteria help put the paintings in sequential order: (1) more recent paintings overlap older ones; (2) older paintings are more faded than younger ones; (3) those located in the center or deepest part of the shelter were ordinarily painted be-fore those in the outer parts; (4) larger paintings are commonly overlapped by less faded smaller paintings, so large scale is a sign of age; (5) a polychrome style is older than monochrome, based on these other criteria; (6) the size or type of shelter is significant, since the Pecos River Style is ordinarily found in the larger shelters with smooth walls and the later styles more frequently appear in smaller shelters and in more open locations; and (7) a more geometric or conventional nonobjective style is found in the older art and a more naturalistic representational style in the more recent. The last three help differentiate large style groups, but the first four give indications of the relative age of paintings within particular styles. They do not, unfortunately, give us any indication of absolute chronological age or even of the lapse of time between overlapping paintings.

Expert observers have considered these criteria and come to quite different conclusions about the amount of time the Pecos Style represents. David Gebhard noted the homogeneity of the style and suggested "perhaps less than two hundred years," while W. W. Newcomb thought "several millennia." The studies made since Gebhard's estimate have so enriched our knowl-edge of the style that a long span of time is accepted now by most authorities.

Problems of Interpreting the Rock Art

Even with a perfect record of the paintings, there remains the problem of interpreting them. At first thought, it seems like a simple matter. Solveig Turpin's discussion of a small red painting demonstrates both the problem and the value of even a tentative solution. She tells us that "a large humped animal strongly resembling a bison" is being "driven toward a geometric design" that might be a net, except that "netting bison is a somewhat ineffective mode of hunting." The geometric design could be "a corral, barrier or cliff face, or could be simply symbolic of capturing the animal." It is painted in the Red Linear Style, which is so rare it must represent a fairly brief period. Thomas Dillehay's research showed the expansion of the bison's range into the Lower Pecos region about 600 B.C.–A.D. 600. Assignment of the Red Linear Style to a group who followed the bison into the region during that period is plausible and serves as a foundation for deeper interpretation of other paintings in that style. Since the Red Linear Style overlaps the Pecos River Style, it also gives a terminal date for the Pecos River Style.

The nonobjective appearance of the Pecos River Style has suggested a different line of interpretation, one in which the crucial features are ceremonial and mental. First proposed by Thomas Campbell and developed by W. W. Newcomb, it takes the tall, frontal human figure as the basic motif and suggests it represents a shaman, or member of a society of shamans, perhaps using mescal beans to induce visionary experiences. These human figures usually carry spear throwers (often called by the Aztec name *atlatl*) and darts or spears.

It is tempting to call these figures hunters (or fishermen where shown with a fish on a line), but in the Pecos River Style they are rarely shown actually killing deer or catching fish. Just as often they are shown with cougars, which are not being hunted but seem to join the human figure in ritual. To modern southwestern Indians, cougars are the patron animal of deer hunting and war. The stiff human figure with weapons accompanied by a cougar can be interpreted as a deity or shaman in a war or hunting ritual.

That such a ritual may have had peaceful significance is suggested by

the Plains and Woodland calumet ceremony in which the spear thrower or its dart (or, later, the arrow) was the sacred symbol of peace and life, becoming the stem of the peace pipe. The ritual exchange of weapons, which lies behind the calumet ceremony, is a worldwide token of peaceful intentions, and the "shaman" figures with their spear throwers may represent force held in restraint by a social compact. Peoples as far apart as the Zuni and the Hidatsa have myths of divine twins who are hunters, warriors, related to the sun, fertility, and increase, and naturally to weapons. In Historic times, male aggressiveness was controlled by rituals with such associations, and it is hard to imagine that such socializing rituals were absent in earlier times.

It is clear that the interpretation of Lower Pecos petroglyphs rests on ethnology. To improve our understanding of the rock art, it will be of

only limited use to identify particular objects in the paintings. We make greater progress by detailed studies of the practices and ideas of living peoples as they were witnessed in earlier times and as they survive today. Interpretations grow by the clustering of information from many different fields and many different regions: climatology, botany and zoology, archaeology, history, and so forth. Interpretation of these obscure designs has often seemed hopeless, but progress is being made by casting a much wider net for a much greater variety of information. This alerts us to the richness of associated meanings that we can be sure the rock art had; we must be wary of short statements that try to interpret their meanings. When we have a full sequence of well-understood art styles in the Lower Pecos region, we will know that at last we really understand that part of the world and its ancient inhabitants. ■

Copy of a very early (to judge from overpainting) and badly eroded example of Lower Pecos art from a shelter high above the Pecos River. Terence Grieder and Max Winkler made this copy by drawing with grease pencils on transparent acetate taped above the painted area.

PAINTED PEBBLES
Styles and Chronology

by Mark L. Parsons
TEXAS DEPARTMENT OF PARKS AND WILDLIFE

My fascination with painted pebbles began in 1960 or 1961, when I was fortunate enough to sign on as a shovel hand with the Texas Archeological Salvage Project, which had begun excavating archaeological sites to be inundated by what is now Amistad Reservoir. Ed Jelks, the director of the project, showed me Late Prehistoric pebbles he had found at the Kyle Site in Hill County, and we speculated about what they represented. Then, as I worked in the field at rockshelters like Coontail Spin, Arenosa, Fate Bell, and Eagle Cave, I saw a number of pebbles as they came out of the ground. Some of these, at Fate Bell and Eagle Cave, were from very early archaeological contexts, and my excitement grew as I realized that this was an artistic tradition that had persisted for thousands of years.

I began to collect information and drawings. I noted (as Davenport and Chelf had before me) that the more complex and organized designs from painted pebbles fell into groups that shared certain attributes. Eventually six such groups emerged. I assumed each of these represented a *style*, by which I meant a "way of doing things" shared by a particular group of people at a given time. I noted that these styles shared certain elements that were present throughout

the series, though expressed somewhat differently in each. This fact increased my excitement. Not only had the pebbles been painted for thousands of years, but there was a continuous thread, a *core motif* that ran throughout that span! Here, surely, was an unparalleled opportunity to study the evolution of an artistic tradition over a great length of time.

To attempt such a study, however, would require something we did not have: a chronological placement of the styles. At that time, a chronology of projectile point styles was emerging from carbon-14 dates obtained in archaeological excavations at Amistad Reservoir. Unfortunately, because well-preserved painted pebbles are relatively rare, no such chronology had been established for painted pebble styles. We had early dates (about 6500 B.C. at Eagle Cave) and late dates (A.D.1300 at the Kyle Site in central Texas), but very little in between.

Along about 1965, I took a course in art history and got permission to use painted pebbles as a term paper topic. I determined to attempt to order my series of styles chronologically and reasoned that, in a chronological series, like should be adjacent to like. I looked at the styles to see how the core motif was expressed in

each and was able to arrange them in a series that fit the chronological information we already possessed and that also placed like next to like. I added some speculative (but not wild, I hope) ideas about possible functions for the pebbles, and about how changes in design between styles might have taken place, and turned the paper in.

At the time, I expected that I would soon publish a paper incorporating the stylistic and chronological scheme I had advanced. As the vagaries of life would have it, that has yet to happen. Also, I optimistically expected that archaeological excavations would soon confirm or refute my sequence. However, little archaeological excavation has taken place in the region since the reservoir was filled, and few additional painted pebbles have been recovered. What is more, the information preserved in the dry caves of the region is rapidly being destroyed by indiscriminate diggers. It now appears that we may never obtain a complete sequence from excavation. It is with this in mind that I seize this opportunity to present an outline of my chronology, and perhaps some further speculations as well.

To understand the styles, and the reasons for my chronological arrangement, we must first discuss

Style 1

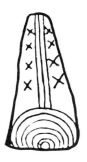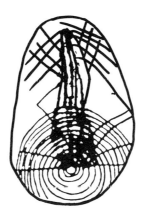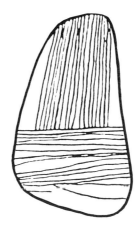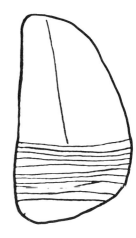

what I have called the *core motif*. This consists of three elements that are expressed in all the pebble styles. I gave each of these elements a simple descriptive name to facilitate discussion. Frequent reference to the illustrations will prove very useful to the reader.

In the lower canyon region (the only area in Texas where large numbers of painted pebbles have been found), selection of the "proper" kind of pebble was an important part of the manufacturing process. The artists almost always chose flat limestone river pebbles, ovate or triangular in outline, with one end wider than the other. The design painted on the pebble was nearly always consistent in its orientation to this shape. Since I believe that these objects represent human beings, the narrow end of the pebble nearly always corresponds to the "head" portion and the wide end corresponds to the lower part of the body.

The three elements of the core motif are defined by their relative positions on the pebble. One, which I call the *bisecting element*, is expressed as one or more vertical lines that bisect the upper portion of the pebble. At the lower end of the bisecting element is what I call the *central element*, because many secondary elements, including the bisecting

element, radiate from it. It may actually be positioned anywhere from the center of the pebble to the center of its base, depending in part upon the style. Finally, the bisecting element is flanked by additional symbols that together are called the *flanking element*. These three elements are expressed and combined differently in each of the styles, and each style may have additional attributes peculiar to it. With the help of the accompanying illustrations, these styles are briefly described below.

Style 1

Style 1 is the earliest known in the sequence, dating from perhaps 6500 B.C. in the lower canyon region. It is distinct technologically as well as stylistically, being painted with very fine lines. The central element is expressed as a group of concentric circles centered at the middle of the bottom edge of the pebble. The bisecting element is usually three parallel lines. The flanking element is often a series of *X*s or oblique lines on either side of the flanking element.

Painted pebbles often have distinct designs on their reverse faces, but Style 1 seems to be the only type in which some specimens possess de-

signs that are continuous from one face to another (an exception is the "cap" of Style 6). One illustrated example has a large portion of its design painted on its sides (roughly rectangular in cross-section; the shaded area represents the upper surface).

Style 2

In Style 2, the central element is usually placed near the center of the lower half of the pebble. It is expressed as a rectangular or circular shape with linear and spatulate forms radiating from it, sometimes extending to the edge of the pebble. The bisecting element most commonly occurs as three parallel lines, or the outer two lines may diverge in accord with the outline of the pebble. In a few examples, the bisecting element becomes only a single vertical line, a trait that dominates in later pebble styles. The flanking element has become a series of horizontal crescent-shaped lines, probably evolving from the oblique lines seen on some Style 1 examples.

Style 3

Style 3 is very similar to Style 2, differing primarily in that the flanking element is expressed for the first

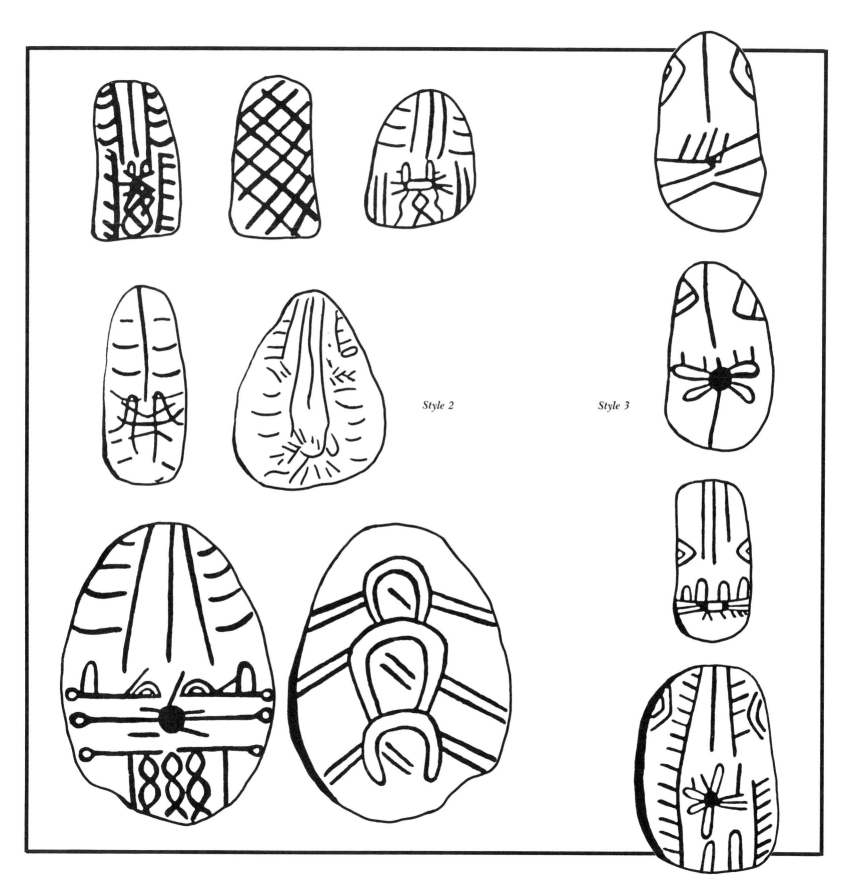

Style 2

Style 3

182

time as a single chevron-shaped form on each side of the bisecting element. The latter is still most often three lines, but several examples with single bisecting lines are known.

Style 4

Style 4 is unfortunately represented by only three specimens. It is presented as a style only because of the remarkable internal consistency of the designs. As in earlier styles, the bisecting element is expressed as three lines. In this case, however, the central line is altered by the addition of two or more *V*-shaped forms, giving it the appearance of a simplified drawing of an arrow. The flanking element is radially changed, shifting from Style 3's chevrons to lenticular or circular elements with a central dot and pendant zigzag lines.

Style 5

Style 5 pebbles are the most numerous type found in the lower canyon region. A number of pebbles of this style have been carbon-dated to just before and after the beginning of the Christian era. In this form, the bisecting element is almost always expressed as a single line. The central element is most often an open bracket or parenthesis-shaped form, though closed lenticular and circular versions are also seen. It is sometimes decorated by dots or short lines that give the element a fringed appearance. The flanking element remains a horizontal lenticular shape with dots or short dashes at the center. The pendant zigzag line seen in Style 4 is now absent, though vestigial marks may remain in that position.

Style 5 can, on the basis of at least two linked variables, be divided into two substyles. Some pebbles, in addition to the traits described above, have two prominent linear forms running obliquely upward from the area of the central element. Pebbles

of this type are consistently larger than Style 5 pebbles that do not have this characteristic. Since both variants have been found together in the same stratum, it may be that this difference reflects the presence of distinct groups of people rather than separation in time.

Style 6

Style 6 pebbles differ from the previously described types in several ways, probably because the local cultural stasis that seems to have persisted for several thousand years was in some way disrupted. This style has not, to my knowledge, been found in a good datable context in the lower canyon region, but pebbles from a Late Prehistoric layer at the Kyle Site in central Texas share some diagnostic traits with Style 6 pebbles. If this late date holds true, Style 6 pebbles were painted after the bow and arrow had supplanted the spear thrower in the area. A radical change in pictograph styles at the time suggests that a new population was present.

For the first time, the primary distinguishing characteristic of a pebble is not one of the three elements that make up the core motif. Instead it is a solid black area at the upper end of the pebble that represents the human hairline. The entire design seems clearly to depict a head and face. The core motif is present, but its elements are extremely variable, possibly because the artists were borrowing ideas from pebbles they picked up on the surfaces of the sites they occupied. The bisecting element is most commonly expressed by a single line, but there are many exceptions, some with as many as two supplementary lines on either side. The central element has become horizontal, in keeping with its interpretation as the mouth of the face. It may be rectangular, lenticular, or linear. The flanking element now obviously depicts eyes, but

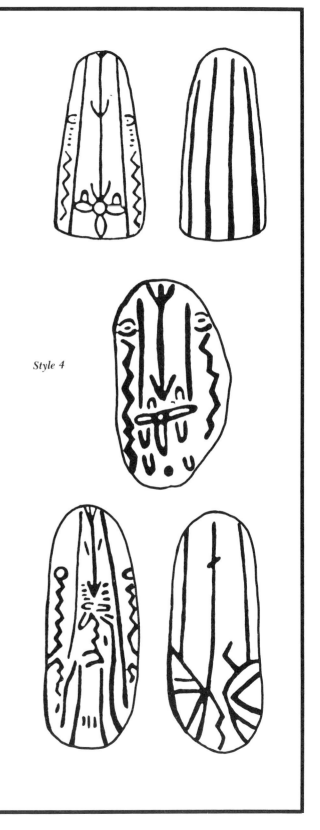

Style 4

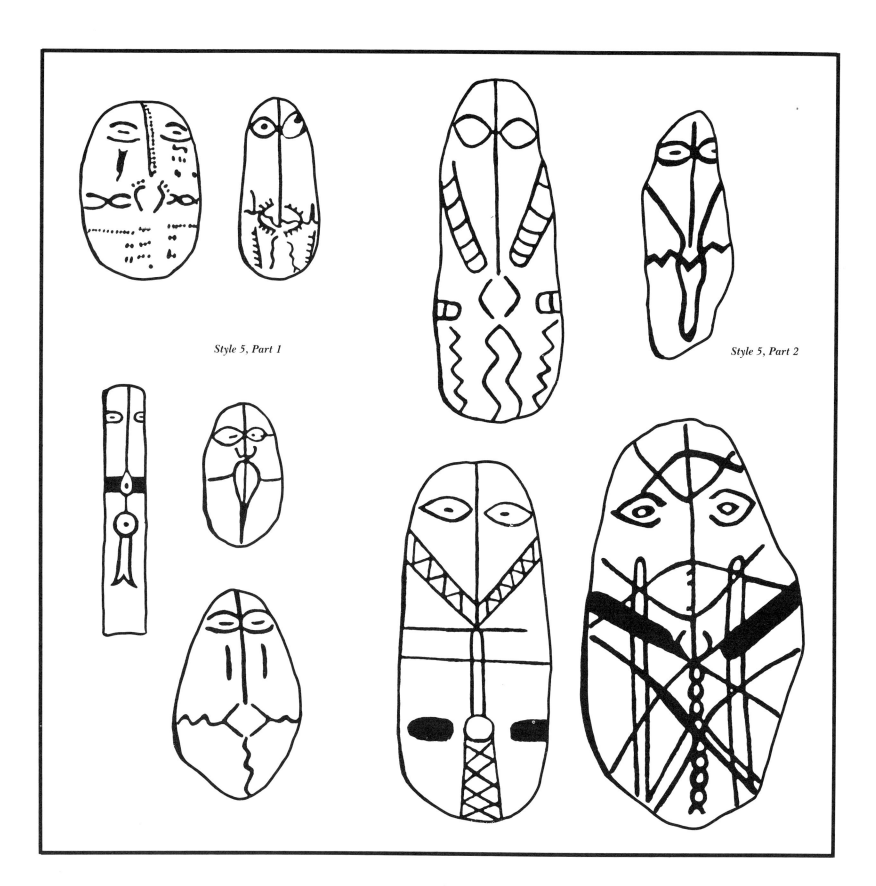

Style 5, Part 1

Style 5, Part 2

its specific expression may be borrowed from almost any previous pebble style.

Conclusion

As noted, the logical basis of my chronological arrangement of this series of painted pebble styles was the idea that like will fall next to like. Specifically, in this series Styles 1 and 2 express the flanking element as multiple units; 1 through 4 express the bisecting element as three lines; 2 through 4 have very similar expressions of the central element; 4 and 5 have the same sorts of flanking elements; and 5 and 6 share the expression of the bisecting element as a single line. It is likely that similar patterns exist in the secondary elements of painted pebble styles, with perhaps some breakdown in Style 6 due to the apparent borrowing from earlier specimens. In conclusion, it should be noted that many pebbles exist whose designs appear very haphazard; the ones I have classified are just the best-organized designs. Designs typical of painted pebbles (and unlike the cave art) have been found painted on other objects of similar size, such as mussel shells, bones, split plant stalks, and clay figurines.

The significance of pebble designs is open to speculation. However, I feel that painted pebbles represent the human figure and demonstrate a tradition involving at least three or four reinterpretations of specific body parts depicted. Most of all, I would like to stress again that painted pebbles represent a unique opportunity to study how art changes over an immense span of time and how we must preserve the archaeological context, the deposits in the dry caves of western Texas, from random destruction and vandalism if we are to find more pebbles in proper archaeological context for future study. ∎

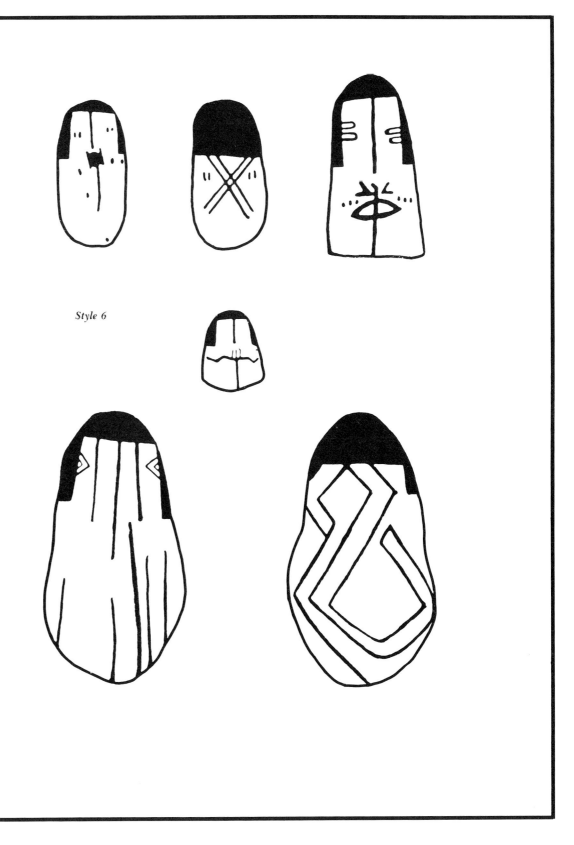

Style 6

THE RED MONOCHROME STYLE AND LATER PICTOGRAPHS
The Art of Newcomers to the Lower Pecos

by Solveig A. Turpin
TEXAS ARCHAEOLOGICAL RESEARCH LABORATORY

Following the decline of the Pecos River Style, the tradition of wall painting in the Lower Pecos continued in a stylistically and conceptually different form, the Red Monochrome Style. A hallmark of the Late Prehistoric period, the Red Monochrome pictographs reflect the overlay of a new cultural system with its characteristic world view.

Perhaps prompted by imitation of the Archaic paintings, the Late Prehistoric artists portrayed their monochromatic concept of the universe on the barren white exposures of native limestone along the major water courses. The central character is once again human but, unlike the Pecos River Style mystical shaman, the Red Monochrome figures are crude but realistic portraits. At the larger sites, frontally posed, life-size and lifelike men and women stand with legs apart and hands upraised, much like victims of a holdup. A seeming preoccupation with fingers and toes results in exaggerated detail of the hands and feet. This emphasis is reinforced by the large number of negative and positive handprints characteristic of the style. Although facial features are never shown, many of the people have curious bumps on the sides of their heads. These protrusions have been variously interpreted as ears, caps,

or hairstyles. Male genitals are occasionally shown, but some figures are apparently dressed in tunics or long skirts. Adornments include single feather headdresses and tassels hanging from the elbow. The frequent illustration of the bow and arrow clearly places these pictographs in the Late Prehistoric period or post– A.D. 600.

Interspersed among the human figures are naturalistic animals of many species—dogs, deer, turkeys, rabbits, catfish, and mountain lions. All these animals have been identified in Archaic rockshelter deposits and all are still native to the region. The mammals and birds are invariably drawn in profile, but the aquatic species are portrayed as they would have appeared to the artist looking into the water. Rarely are any animals shown as hunted or wounded. In the two cases where a hunter has leveled his arrow at an animal, the target is a rabbit, hardly a symbol of hunting prowess. In one scene, five dogs are pursuing a deer, perhaps illustrating the role of man's best friend in prehistory. The dogs are always shown as short and stubby, with ears perked, tail up, and mouth open, as though yapping. These dogs and another favored topic, turkeys, are so similar from site to site that they are virtually interchangeable.

The Red Monochrome style has long been recognized as intrusive. The internal consistency in themes and attributes indicates a mature art form but one that lacks antecedents in the Pecos River Style. The strong resemblance between the Lower Pecos examples and certain figures in the Big Bend region suggests its introduction by nomads of the margins of the southern Plains. The Big Bend figures are all frontally posed human figures with the same protuberances around the ears so notable in the Lower Pecos pictographs. In her studies of the Brewster County examples, Miriam Lowrance of Sul Ross University draws parallels between the two regions, citing descriptions of the Jumano Indians written by early Spanish explorers that matched these characteristics. The Jumanos apparently wore their hair cut short and curled about the ears, resembling a cap, a possible interpretation of the Red Monochrome lumps. In addition, some members of the Jumano tribe were known to have led a nomadic life at the time of contact, traveling between La Junta on the Rio Grande and the Caddo trade fairs in east Texas. The first Spanish expedition through the Lower Pecos apparently encountered a group of

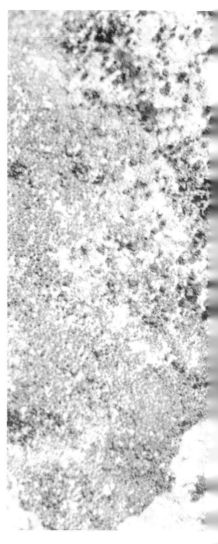

Jumanos near modern-day Sheffield, on the middle Pecos River. So little else is known of the Jumanos that attributing the Red Monochrome pictographs to them does little to enlarge the cultural context of the art.

The pictographs themselves provide support for their introduction by groups foreign to the Lower Pecos. Hostility is a major theme, expressed by a large number of human figures riddled with lances or arrows. Unfortunately, the wounded are not distinguished by any other unusual characteristic that might point to them as enemies or identify them with another tribe. The Red Monochrome artists preferred to paint on light surfaces under slight overhangs, high on cliff faces or around permanent waterholes. They seemingly avoided the deep rock-shelters favored by the artists of the Pecos River Style, perhaps because they had been too recently occupied.

Other traits that differentiate the Late Prehistoric from the Archaic—such as a move toward upland camps, cairn burials on exposed rims, and new artifact types—are also more prevalent to the north, suggesting that new populations were entering the Lower Pecos, carrying their own customs with them. Thus, the late phases of pre-

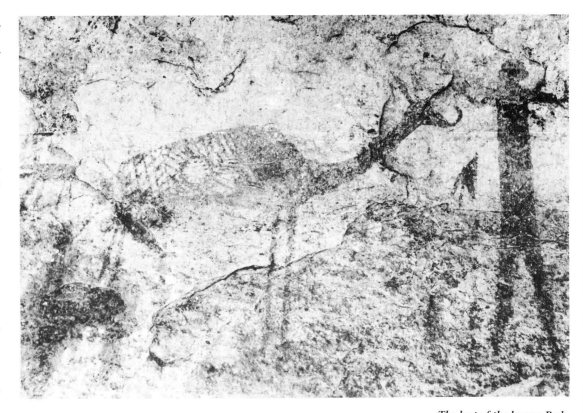

The best of the known Red Monochrome panels. The X-ray style deer with outstretched tongue is believed borrowed or influenced by Athapascan art styles. Note the protrusions from the side of the human figure's head, a common characteristic of this style.

Vaquero Shelter: church, costumed officer, and hand-print—one of the more famous Historic pictographs.

history are apparently a time of considerable flux, precipitated by the movement of people rather than ideas.

Closely aligned with the Red Monochrome pictographs are a series of geometric designs consisting of intersecting straight lines, blanket patterns, and globular animals or insects. These geometrics have been placed in a separate category, the Bold Line Geometric Style, but they may well be coeval with the Red Monochrome. Although these styles, too, disappeared from the region, the continuity of wall painting was carried on by the renegade Apaches and Comanches until their extermination in the late 1800s.

Under pressures from Spanish and then U.S. expansion, the Historic Indian groups, mounted on

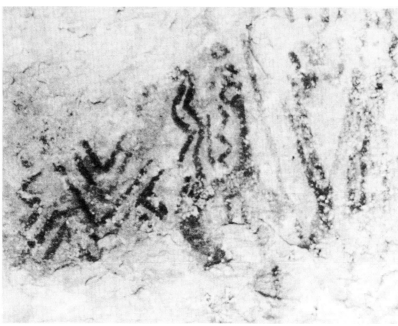

Enigmatic geometric designs of late prehistory.

*Proto-Historic dancing fig-
ures with shield symbols,
probably Plains Indian—
influenced.*

purloined horses and armed with traded and stolen weapons, took refuge in the *despoblado*, or uninhabited regions, such as the Lower Pecos and northern Mexico. Although highly mobile, these marauders of the southern Plains also left their artwork on the limestone canvas of the region. The topics they favored seem to reflect a growing familiarity with European culture. At first, they were intrigued by missions, clothing such as uniforms and dresses, and domestic animals. Sites such as Vaquero Shelter, Meyers Springs, Castle Canyon, and Caballero Shel-

ter hold extremely detailed scenes showing missions, longhorn cattle, uniformed and mounted Spanish officers, and women dressed in long gowns.

Hostility against the clergy emerges at Rattlesnake Canyon, where an unusual composite of a mission church with a priest's head and arms is impaled by a spear. The interlopers are also illustrated as stabbed, impaled, and defeated by warriors armed with their traditional weapons. The most eloquent scene is a tale of epic proportions painted under an overhang on the Devils

River, where a Comanche hero single-handedly defeats four uniformed bluecoats. Even the magic of painting could not make this vision into reality over the long term. The coming of the railroad put an end to the Native American presence in the Lower Pecos. With their extermination and final displacement came the demise of rock painting as an art form. The best that contemporary Americans have been able to muster is obscenities and signatures scrawled across the ancient artworks, perhaps as a testimonial to which is truly the superior culture. ■

THE ROCK ART OF AFRICA AND AUSTRALIA
The Imagery of Surviving Hunter-Gatherers

The Problem of Interpreting Rock Art

People began to paint long before they wrote. Indeed, graphic art had reached a high level of sophistication thousands of years before any alphabet was devised. Not only were there magnificent representations of animals and people, but abstractions as well. While materials were limited, technique was not. Scientific evidence, such as carbon-14 dating, shows that the oldest rock art known was executed about 40,000 years ago in eastern Africa (Tanzania), predating the earliest script by some 35,000 years.

Archaeologists discovering these extraordinary masterworks were delighted, for they got an insight into the mental and creative processes of our predecessors (which, however, can never be more than a glimpse). Although there is information on how these people made a living, the tools they used, what they ate, what they wore, and how they were buried, such findings shed little light on what they thought. There is, therefore, an enormous temptation to try to interpret the art work of these nonliterate groups— but consider the difficulty of interpreting the paintings of even a contemporary artist. To attempt to fathom the imagery of gifted artists living centuries ago in very dissimilar cultures is hazardous to say the least.

Cave art exists on every continent as an intriguing message from the past. Painting is the most commonly found medium, but engravings also exist, as do sculpted forms. The temptation to find a set of coded symbols is great: the figures in all of the works seem somehow to resemble the others. Handprints appear everywhere. Geometrical designs are similar in many parts of the world. Large, flat animals against a bare background, devoid of landscape, are dominant subjects across the globe. Half-human, half-animal figures as well as strange, surreal representations of apparitions and monsters are not uncommon. All this could lead one to assume that a single motive prompted all prehistoric rock art. This, however, would be a dangerous assumption. The people who produced these works were very different and evolved quite distinct cultures. There is no reason to suppose their artistry reflects a single idea.

All we can safely say is that rock art, like all art, is essentially communication, and that long before the invention of printing, rock art was one of the media people used to record and reinforce their traditions and their notions about their place in the environment. The art was one way of facing the challenge of contact between the "inside" and the "outside," and it reflects human social, psychological, and conceptual needs. Unfortunately, the people of the Lower Pecos ceased to exist centuries ago. No remnant population carries on their ancient myths or customs; therefore, we have no way of relating these to their pictorial traditions. There are, however, contemporary groups in other parts of the world, living as hunters and gatherers, who have large rock paintings as part of their heritage that demonstrate certain similarities, as well as differences, in motivation and content. Knowing something of their ways and their art may enable us to come a little closer to an understanding of the "inside-outside" relationship reflected in Lower Pecos art forms.

Elegant examples of the human figure in Bushman art, Giant's Castle, Drakensberg, South Africa.

South Africa

In Africa, one finds rock art from the shores of the Mediterranean to the Cape Peninsula. In southern Africa are the greatest number of prehistoric cave paintings, referred to as "Bushman" paintings. These cover rocks in Rhodesia, South Africa, Botswana, and Swaziland and represent a dynasty of artists that continued from at least 10,000 years ago (and possibly twice that long) to the beginning of the nineteenth century. Most of the paintings are found in the remote mountain regions that served as sanctuaries for the artists.

Modern Bushmen live in the Kalahari Desert, but in the past they had a much wider distribution. They are believed to have come from the northeast thousands of years ago to South Africa, where they occupied land from the Zambesi to the Cape of Good Hope. During the fourteenth and fifteenth centuries, the Hottentots and the Bantus migrated to southern Africa, and in 1652 the Europeans came. All these groups expelled the Bushmen from the fertile lands they once hunted. No one else wanted the Kalahari. Surviving Bushmen have made it home with a resourceful exploitation of everything it has to offer. Although no one knows precisely how many survive in the desert, educated estimates say there are about 55,000.

The Kalahari Desert is part of the great plateau of southern Africa. Temperatures are extreme: during the day, they may reach 140° F; winter nights are below freezing. Slight rainfall in the summer is adequate to sustain grass, brush, small trees, and edible plants. There are species of berries, a few fruits, green leaves, gums, tsama melons and wild cucumbers (which can replace drinking water in a drought), nuts, roots, and tubers. Life throughout the seasons is planned around the resources.

Bushmen are small people, about five feet two inches on the average, with yellow skin and short black hair worn in peppercorns. Their faces are flat and triangular, with high cheek bones and long, narrow chins. Their brown eyes are set wide apart, and their broad noses have a low bridge. Body and limbs are slender, and the small of the back has an inward curve.

According to nineteenth-century accounts, Bushmen rubbed their skin with grease and a powdered mineral called *sibilo*, which has a bluish luster, and *buchu*, a red vegetable powder. Their hair was caked with grease and clay to form a cap, into which they stuck feathers or the head of a game animal. War dress included a crown of arrows, partly for convenience and partly for frightening effect: the Bushmen's use of poison was well known.

At one time there were many separate groups of Bushmen, with a number of different languages. All of those current contain clicks (quick, implosive sounds) and a range of tones. Words are accompanied by so many graphic gestures that even one unable to speak the language can understand the communication.

Bushmen do not belong to tribes. They live in family groups that merge with other families into a loosely knit band with a titular headman who is responsible for guiding them to necessary resources. Each band owns the plants and water in its territory. No force is required to keep other Bushmen out. It is understood that one band does not encroach on another's territory.

Women do most of the gathering, which takes much of their energy and time. Some days they walk fifteen miles to a place where berries or roots are available, carrying their infants tied to them and their small children on their shoulders. Each woman owns whatever food she gathers and divides it among her relations and friends as she chooses.

Hunters pick up tortoises, grasshoppers, lizards, and snakes when they are out tracking. These are also the property of the person who finds them, to be shared or consumed as he chooses. Other small game consists of porcupines, birds, spring hares, and badgers. Larger game—various antelope of the region—requires a hunting party. These are informally organized, without a leader. Hunters sometimes have to search and track for days before finding a suitable herd.

The meat acquired by a hunting party is brought to the camp. The owner of the first arrow to hit is responsible for the initial distribution, giving a bone with all the attached meat to each member of the party. Each hunter sections off his portion to his family, beginning with his wife's parents. He then supplies meat to his own parents, his wife, and his children. If there is plenty, he will also give some to others. Everyone who gets meat gives a portion of it to someone else so that, in the end, everyone receives some.

Housing is informal. Frequently Bushmen just settle into the scrub at night. When it is necessary (during the rain, for instance), women build a grass shelter. This is accomplished in about one hour. When complete, it is a hemisphere with one open side, measuring about five feet in width and five feet in height. Each family has its own fire, which burns all night long, summer and winter.

Dancing is very popular. Several times a month a dance is organized. A number of people come together to make music and invoke spiritual power for healing and protection. A number of men and women of each group are shamans, who go into a trance that reaches frenzy and, finally, unconsciousness.

Modern Bushmen have few material possessions. Stone knives and axes have been replaced by metal ones, and the only stone implement found is that used for honing. There are also bows and arrows, assegais, bowls, spoons, mortars and pestles, and musical instruments. Clothes are scanty: men have breechclouts and women short aprons. Everyone has a *kaross* (a full cloak) and a skin bag. The implements and clothing are not decorated. The only vestige of their artistic heritage is found in the ostrich egg shell beads made by the women.

Today's Bushmen have little to say about the paintings of their ancestors. However, scientists have been able to piece together some answers. The Bushmen's aptitude for using the resources of their environment was applied to devising poisons and paints. The pigments were natural. Red came from the juice of plants or from berries. Red ochre was dug from the ground. Another plant gave them pink. Blood provided a brown of long duration and, if stirred with a twig and clotted, was useful as a fixative. Charcoal was used for sketching and as black paint. Yellow ochre came from limonite on the cave roofs and, when heated, became orange, umber, and black. Stalactites were a source of white, as was kaolin. Manganese and burnt bone provided black. Yellow shale produced yellow. Gypsum, clay, and lime yielded white, as did bird droppings.

Crayons were formed from many of these materials. These were pyramid-shaped blocks of color used by the earliest painters for entire works, but later, when technology advanced, only for roughing out compositions. Some of these chunky crayons have been found near the art sites. Pigments were ground to a fine powder on a stone slab and carried in pots made from the tips of antelope horns and earthenware, in ostrich shells, and in boxes made from tortoise shells. These items, too, have been found where they have lain all these years after being discarded by the artist.

Stone palettes were used for mixing colors, and bones for palette knives. In the earlier works, paint was applied directly onto the rocks with no preliminary sketching. Sometimes the surface was covered with a white undercoat. Many early artists used their fingers to apply paint, but some used ostrich feather brushes or hairs extracted from the tails of giraffes.

Technique can be seen to best advantage in the paintings of animals, which offer a continuous record of the maturing of the art. Color begins with the early monochromes, simple and unshaded, to reach subtle blendings in foreshortened perspective. Many species of animals were recorded, including some now extinct, such as the quagga (a zebra), a species of deer, and an extinct form of eland, as well as a number of living species. Large herds usually appear in an arranged line, as they do in nature when moving in single file behind a leader, from an open watering place to the safety of the bush. These food animals were lovingly reproduced in naturalistic style. Predators, such as lions, were more stylized, even poorly drawn.

Some animals are notable through their absence. The hyrax, for instance, is a common animal and is important in Bushman mythology, but it is missing from the art. Tortoises were an important food item, but there is no portrait of a tortoise. Only a few of the abundant insects appear, and there are no rats or hares. Among birds, only the largest are pictured.

It seems that only sizable animals were deemed worthy subjects. Most popular were elephants, elands, horses, kudus, zebras, giraffes, and snakes. There are also several paintings featuring whales and dolphins. All these extra-large animals were painted much smaller than life size, except for the snakes. These can be found vastly enlarged, wandering over wide expanses of rock in many paintings.

Elaborate and varied hunting techniques were faithfully depicted by the Bushman artists. Bows and ar-

Bushman family, Angamiland, Botswana.

rows stand out strongly, frequently larger than the people carrying them. Beaters are portrayed, driving animals toward waiting archers. One painting includes a hunter carefully dipping his arrows into poison. Hunters are shown kneeling, crouching, or lying

Women returning from gathering mongongo nuts, a high-protein staple in the Bushman diet.

flat on the ground. Trapping techniques are also depicted, as are javelin and spear throwing. Spears thrown from land or from boats and fish traps illustrate the fishing methods of the time.

One painting of an ostrich hunt shows the hunter disguised as an ostrich, with a dressed skin, complete with feathers, stretched over a framework attached to a long pole that stiffens the neck and supports the head. With this over the Bushman's shoulders and his legs rubbed with white chalk, he looks very much like an ostrich. (The method was to creep upwind to the flock, raising and lowering the bird head in an imitation of feeding and, when close enough, quickly to drop the skin and shoot. Then the disguise was replaced, and the hunter joined the entire herd in a dash to safety. When the poison took effect and the wounded bird fell, other ostriches gathered around it, and the hunter struck again.)

Women are shown in their characteristic occupation—gathering—with digging sticks and bags as tools. In most cases, the women are shown with large buttocks and the men with semierect penises, still characteristic of Bushmen today. Every form of dress is shown, from loincloths to cloaks, with many intermediate styles. In the paintings the men are fre-

quently lavishly bejeweled with strung beads used as necklaces, bracelets, anklets, and face veils. Body painting was another form of ornamentation. Colored patterns of every sort decorating these ancient people were recorded on the rocks.

Frequently, the faces in the paintings are triangular and white. One widespread technique consisted of painting a red or black outline of a head in a hook shape with white or pink filling the face. No representational portraits were done, perhaps due to a desire to keep the model from being recognized by an enemy who might do evil magic upon the image. Many subjects wore decorative horns; some also sport animal-skin caps. Sometimes men are shown with buckhead masks that, on occasion, seem to blend into a single figure. There is some evidence that these horned figures actually represent medicine men.

Dances were well recorded. One sees large numbers of people in these paintings; some participating, some admiring. No instruments are shown. People sing and clap, and dancers add to the rhythm with rattles made of antelope ears filled with seeds tied to their ankles. Some of the participants seem to be in trance states. One painting appears to depict a puberty ceremony. In other paintings one can see that musicians did exist, apart from the dances, for there are portrayals of people using a large bow, drums of various sorts, and wind instruments.

Bushman beliefs are illustrated in the paintings of "rain animals." Rain was thought of as a supernatural being and is usually shown as such, with a rainbow surrounding it. Rain animals can be elephants, giraffes, elands, or ostriches.

The early Bushmen responsible for some of the art lived primarily in caves. Middens outside cliff homes indicate long tenancy. They were hunters whose lives centered around game. Historic accounts indicate that when no cave was available, the Bushmen would find a limber tree and bend its branches to form a tent, which was then lined with soft vegetation and, within the branches, resembled a large bird's nest. From this camouflaged vantage point, the Bushmen could fire at passing game. They also ate ostrich meat and decorated the eggshells for use as water containers. When Bushmen traveled through arid country, they buried these containers along the path to ensure a supply for the return trip.

Arrow poison was made in various ways. Sometimes plant juices were combined with cobra venom. The Bushman crept up behind the snake, put his foot on its neck, hit it repeatedly with a stick to make it angry, then killed it and extracted the venom. Another form of poison was extracted from the bulb of a plant, and a third from *Amaryllis* juice mixed with spider venom. Worst of all was the poison made from a tiny grub living in the tree branches, which caused great pain accompanied by madness. Sometimes Bushmen poisoned waterholes to kill their prey, a practice that made them unpopular with neighbors who were unaware of the danger.

When the Hottentots with their grazing animals and the farming Bantus arrived in Bushman country, their coming was recorded on the rocks. Pictures of loaded oxen and detailed drawings of cow udders are abundant. The Bushmen were not well liked by the newcomers. The Bantus were fiercely aggressive and soon enslaved the Hottentots. The Bushmen could not be subjugated, so many were killed. In addition to their independent spirit, they were irksome because of their ability as cattle thieves. They rounded up whole herds of cattle and moved them through vast desert distances to their camps. What was truly infuriating was their habit of killing all the cattle. They chose only a few of the best specimens to eat, then left the other carcasses to the elements. Bantus and Hottentots banded together to hunt down the Bushmen. They rarely succeeded in catching them with the herds, since the Bushmen had their supply of water in ostrich shells hidden along the path; the pursuers, who had no water supply, had to give up and return.

Because the Bushmen had no chiefs to organize them into large fighting groups, they were always in small family bands when they were discovered by their enemies. The marauders covered themselves with large cowhide shields as a protection against the poison arrows. They then backed their small foes into their rockshelters, where the fight continued until every Bushman was killed—man, woman, and child. Such historical events are sometimes depicted in the cave paintings. When the Europeans came to southern Africa, the Bushmen made no attempt to accommodate themselves to European ways. As a result, all but those now surviving in the Kalahari were exterminated.

Many explanations of the paintings have been propounded. The frequency of animals indicates to some that they may have been rituals in sympathetic magic to ensure success in hunting. It has also been suggested that they were used in fertility magic or were illustrations of mythology. Some feel that the paint-

ings were rain magic and see rain animals everywhere. Others explain that each rockshelter was inhabited by many different bands as they made their way across the country in search of game, and the paintings were messages left behind for future inhabitants. Another suggestion is that the ancient artists may have painted for the sheer love of expressing themselves.

A modern theory is that many of the paintings were executed by medicine men while in trance during the dance celebration. As such, the paintings then became personal records of a "possessed" hunter's insights during times of altered consciousness. Modern research has also drawn attention to the special significance of the eland in Bushman art. For example, this antelope makes up more than twenty-five percent of some 4,000 animal figures counted in the Drakensberg Mountains of southern Africa. The eland must have possessed great importance for the ancient Bushmen. Today, eland fat is still closely associated with sex and fertility, and the antelope plays a central

Bushman camp at Kauri, Angamiland, Botswana.

role in current rituals associated with boys' first kills, girls' puberty, marriage, and healing.

Some scholars argue that the art is religious. They feel that each site was consecrated. The abstract forms in many paintings—dots and dashes in various configurations—lend themselves to metaphysical interpretation as a characterization of the life force. They may, in fact, have been designed to be touched by others to acquire the force of those represented. It seems probable that a combination of all these theories (and some that haven't yet been developed) would be necessary to account for the multitude of rock paintings executed over thousands of years in Africa.

Australia

The Australian Aborigines migrated from southeastern Asia about 30,000 years ago to Australia, where they continued to live as hunter-gatherers until two hundred years ago, when most were forced off their lands by European settlers. Many Aborigines today have adopted European ways. Surviving Aborigines still practicing their culture remain only in the more inhospitable central portion of the continent. Aboriginal rock paintings have been dated to 20,000 years ago. They are still being painted. According to Aboriginal beliefs, many of the old paintings were created by spiritual beings as representations of themselves.

Aborigines were traditionally nomadic people, traveling thousands of miles in family groups, living in temporary quarters—hastily built grass or stick houses or rockshelters. When food or water supplies dwindled, they moved on. In areas other than the desert, vegetation was abundant, particularly in the fertile river valleys. There were few dangerous animals to be feared by the early artists (Australia's native fauna consisted of mostly harmless marsupials) and few conflicts. Each individual lived in harmony with nature,

A hunter guts a feral cat, near Pulykara, Western Australia.

depending on the environment for survival. They ate what was available, but rarely gorged.

Aborigine religion is one of relationship with everything. All is interdependent and integrated through ancestral spirits. The Aborigines are deeply attached to the land. Their religion includes totemism, a link with ancestors, reincarnation, and supernatural spirits. They have a rich culture that includes music, dance, and storytelling as well as art.

Modern Aborigines are dark brown with dark, deep-set eyes. Their heads are long and narrow, with high cheekbones, wide mouths, and broad noses. They are slender people with narrow shoulders, slim hips, and long, thin hands and feet and legs very long in proportion to the body. An average height would be five feet six inches for men and five feet three inches for women. Usually their hair is brown and may be straight or wavy. Women frequently cut their hair short in order to make a hair-string, which has several uses. One use is to hold back the hair of men, which is worn long. The men anoint their hair with grease and ochre, so that it hangs in sausage-shaped curls, or pull it back into a chignon in which small personal treasures are placed. Men start to grow dark brown beards by the age of ten.

In the past, most Aboriginals went naked, with grease smeared over the body as a protection from the elements. In the colder areas, they wore animal skins. Aborigines were food gatherers. They did not practice any form of agriculture or animal husbandry. Cattle, sheep, and chickens are not native to Australia, but the necessary plants exist, and Aborigines were well acquainted with their seeds. They never saw any reason to sow them. They were, therefore, totally dependent on what nature produces without any assistance from them.

Hunting was a vital part of the economy, and hunting tools were diverse and precisely made, including boomerangs, spears and spear throwers, clubs, nets, traps, stone axes, and chisels, all beautifully decorated with traditional designs similar to the symbols on the cave walls. All implements were made by fully initiated men with sacred rituals that included song and chant, rendering them not only beautiful, but also magical.

Aborigines are divided into tribes of people related by actual or implied genealogy who occupy a definite territory. Boundaries are clearly defined by natural features. The size of tribal territories varies with the degree of fertility. The members of a tribe have a common language peculiar to them and have their own special laws and customs. Each tribe is composed of a number of small wandering family groups, numbering from 500 to 2,000 individuals. At certain times, they all come together. There are also intertribal gatherings between neighbors for ceremonial purposes, at which all differences are settled and large entertainments, called *corroborees*, are shared. These meetings are always organized by old men.

Family groups living together usually consist of a man and his descendants in the male line. Thus, all men in the group are brothers, fathers, father's fathers, sons, and son's sons, while the women are sisters of these men. Marriages are exogamous (outside the group), although the marriage partner belongs to the same tribe. Women usually leave the family group to join the men they marry. Each group has a headman, usually the eldest (unless he is too old to function). The headmen of the various groups of a tribe form a council that meets to discuss common problems.

Each family group has its own name, derived from some natural feature of the territory or from some totemic association. The ancestral spirits return to certain sites in the group's territory, making ties to the land very strong. Family is all-important. A man with his wife or wives and children is the fundamental unit of society. Wives are frequently exchanged; a woman may have several husbands in her lifetime. Marriage is regulated by kinship laws, preserving the children's status in the religious group of their father and the social group of their mother. Both parents take an active part in child care and are affectionate and patient.

Each family is a self-sufficient economic unit, with the marriage partners procuring all the family's requirements. If several families in a group work together, then the men band together in one group and the women in another. Aborigines regard everyone they meet as a relative and try to ascertain the exact nature of the relationship in order to establish proper mutual conduct. Thus, all people are quickly categorized as mother, father, uncle, aunt, child, grandparent, or grandchild.

Nicknames are commonly used, for personal names are taken from sacred mythological and totemic associations. They represent the real self as it relates to the spiritual, not to the mundane. There are several types of totemism, covering an individual's relationship to a natural species, sex, patrilineal and matrilineal descent, and clan, resulting in a highly complex social system. The medicine man has a special relationship

Western Desert Aborigine applying foot-pressure to straighten a spearshaft of mulati wood.

with his totem species, which acts as an assistant in curing ceremonies.

Each man has his own *churinga* (a natural or manufactured object of special significance), which is a sacred symbol of life. It represents a great hero of eternal dreamtime and is used to effect cures and to ensure hunting success. It is sometimes lent to others, as a sign of deep friendship. When an initiate is rubbed with a churinga, he is brought into conscious touch with dreamtime.

The music of Aborigines is sophisticated, with strong rhythms enriched by melody, harmony, and counterpoint. A songman is the repository of all traditional music and sometimes also "dreams up" new music and dances. Singing is accompanied by footstamping and clapping. In some areas, drums, beating sticks, and *didjeridus* (bamboo pipes) are employed. Dancing is at the core of the ceremonies. It usually involves an enactment of the adventure of some being of the dreamtime and is essentially miming.

Aborigines are accurate observers of their environment. Many are talented artists. Training begins in childhood, when they learn to copy animal tracks in the sand. Other sand drawings follow. Cave walls become churingas for special ceremonies. Adepts, accompanied by initiates, go to a secret site and assemble before the painting. They tell the traditional story while their fingers trace it on the painting. Some have become worn over the years with this treatment. They are charged with magic. Cave paintings are so sacred

Women winnowing wangunu (wild grain, Eragrostis sp.) seeds, approximately fifty miles north of Warburton Ranges, Western Australia.

Outlining was done in black. Usually charcoal and soot were used, but, where available, black manganese was preferred for its more enduring quality. White could be clay or gypsum. Ochres were not available everywhere, so a mining industry was instituted early, and trade was active. The miners quarried away the unwanted rock and pulled out the red and yellow ochre with sticks. It was frequently ground at the mine site and compressed into cakes for easy transport. Red ochre was precious because of its similarity to the color of blood. Legends of varying kinds account for its presence, and respectful ceremonies were held during its collection.

Color, restricted to black, white, red, and yellow, is less interesting than style and subject. There are geometric designs and meandering lines. There are also numerous examples of a figure resembling a *U*, which may be upright or inverted. (Modern Aborigines interpret these as spirits of children waiting to be born.) Stick figures are shown in graceful symmetry performing every sort of activity. They are spirits believed to live among the rocks, emerging at night to do mischief. *Mimi* figures are lively depictions of running women. These are very ancient and are considered to be the work of spirits.

Mythology is often illustrated on rock surfaces. One myth tells how the old ancestral beings emanated from the sea in clouds. Some stayed where they landed; others wandered from place to place, stopping to sketch pictures of themselves on rocks along the way. When they finally settled, they carefully painted a portrait on their rockshelter home.

The newer paintings are not regarded as sacred. Each has superimpositions of other paintings. Each painter used designs memorable to him in the context of his own experience of past rituals. Paintings of concentric circles linked by lines and open circles represent named localities (usually waterholes) of some dream story, with connecting lines being the tracks of ancestors.

The sites themselves are sacred, if the paintings are not. These are protected from defacement. Thus, to paint over an existing design with something irrelevant would be of no importance to the group. However, chiseling into the wall would be thought of as sacrilege, since the spiritual essence of the ancestor whose being turned to stone is thought to inhabit the rocks.

Thus, ancient rock engravings are considered sacred. The designs in these resemble those of the cave

and so secret that any unauthorized person who looks at them is condemned to death.

To judge from current practices, the ancient rock paintings were produced on special occasions—at times of ecstasy. Large groups came together for celebration: initiations, assignment of hunting grounds, and arrangement of marriages. They painted their bodies and adorned them with ornaments. Patterns were drawn in the sand and painted on rocks. There was also singing and dancing.

The tools of the artists were simple: mortar, pestle, palette, and brush. Ochres were ground into powder and mixed with water, animal fat, vegetable juice, or blood. For brushes, they used sticks with the ends chewed into fibers or sometimes a grooved stick with feathers or hair attached. They also applied paint with their fingers. Charcoal and white clay were often used in dry form, being rubbed onto the rock. Occasionally, white or red covered the entire surface before any drawing occurred. One early technique was to mix the pigment in the mouth and spray it through the lips around an object held against the rock. These objects included boomerangs, axes, lizards, and hands. Hands were also printed by being first painted with pigment then pressed onto the rock.

paintings. These are regarded as designs on the body of a novice, which were transformed into stone along with the body. The artists of various tribes tend the ancient paintings, making repairs after heavy rains, using the same pigments and techniques as in the originals.

Some people are painted as very large with no mouths and an ovoid form on the chest, symbolizing the hollow of the breastbone. The heads are surrounded by a crescent-shaped halo. The head is always painted straight forward. No profiles appear. Fish and ducks are portrayed as well as crocodiles, kangaroos, and snakes. One spectacular painting illustrates a rainbow serpent, symbolizing fertility. Groups gather before it each year to celebrate ancient rituals. There are many inverted *U*s around it.

There are some rock paintings that the modern Aborigines disdain. These are monochromes of slender, elegant, active people, shown in profile. They are tiny, with odd headdresses and skirts. The Aborigines refer to them as "trash."

Every possible interpretation has been applied to Australian Aboriginal paintings. Some think them attempts at sympathetic hunting magic or fertility rituals. One even explains the mouthless faces with their halos as depictions of extraterrestrials with space helmets. Anthropologists have been able to deduce much from living Aborigines. Many of the cave paintings relate to body designs connected with rituals performed by the cult lodge. Circles and vertical stripes set in horizontal rows, meandering lines, and lattices dominate the art. These often depict the tracks followed by ancestors or novices during their tour of other camps prior to circumcision and are linked to mythological episodes and specific songs.

Until recently, most modern Aborigines lived as nomads, frequently moving long distances in a quest for moisture. This life made heavy demands upon geographical knowledge, which was carefully passed on to succeeding nonliterate generations through initiation rites and other rituals. Much of Australian art belongs in this category and can be considered one of several methods of preserving geographical knowledge for future generations.

Conclusion

While there are great gaps in available information, what is known indicates that certain factors are common among the African, Australian, and Lower Pecos rock artists. All lived in small, nomadic groups of hunter-gatherers. The economy consisted of a home base, a division of labor between males and females, and a pattern of sharing food. There was little personal property and, therefore, a minimum of difference in wealth. Although each band was small, several came together seasonally. Marriage and residential arrangements were elaborate, since such alliances were the means of establishing reciprocal access to resources. There were no food stores, and gathering continued throughout the year. Success depended upon knowledge rather than on possession.

Most likely, the art of all hunter-forager groups is not only an aesthetic achievement, but also a mnemonic device in the service of maintaining social adaptation to the environment. Almost certainly what is recorded in the shorthand of art incorporates the belief systems of that particular society, and the pictures served to reinforce these beliefs from generation to generation. However, the exact meanings of specific figures, patterns, and shapes vary from culture to culture. Living Aborigines and Bushmen can provide clues to their respective ancestors' rock art, but when it comes to a people long extinct, such as the hunter-gatherers of the Lower Pecos, any sort of interpretation becomes strictly speculative. ■

Aborigine shelters at a *summer camp, north of the Warburton Ranges, Western Australia.*

BUSHMAN ART
A Preoccupation with Transformation

by Megan Biesele
RICE UNIVERSITY

Spread throughout the mountainous areas of southern Africa are thousands of prehistoric rock paintings attributed to San, or Bushman, hunter-gatherers. Painted by the ancestors of modern peoples who now live almost exclusively in the neighboring Kalahari Desert, these images are eloquent testimony to the tenacity and continuity of Bushman cultural traditions. Many activities depicted on the rocks, many ideas and mythological references made in the paintings, are present as part of the culture of contemporary Bushman groups. Over a hundred years of ethnographic work with living Bushmen has provided a rich source of suggestive and corroborative evidence for the interpretation of their ancestors' paintings.

At first glance, these paintings appear as a jumble of astonishingly varied images. Large broad-shouldered, half-animal and half-human figures are superimposed on naturalistic depictions of different kinds of antelope. Detailed hunting gear, skin bags of various sizes and shapes, items of vegetable food, men dancing and women clapping, abstract designs and geometric figures contend with each other for prominence. Strange relationships between animals and humans are

depicted, with one seeming to become the other. Powerful, massive rhinolike beasts or ghostly white giraffes are enclosed within wavy, rainbowlike lines or associated with circles of small dots. Red meandering lines link animals and humans with what appear to be legless, winged antelopes in flight. Carnivores ramp, and humans and herbivores flee. What can all this mean?

Quantitative studies done in recent decades have begun to reveal significant emphasis on certain key images and their relationship. New numerical data on the paintings make it evident that Bushman rock art does not consist mostly of hunting scenes. The largest group deals with social activities, a fact suggestive of the art's function. The next largest group depicts antelopes, with the imposing, muscular eland the most numerous. Other antelopes (kudu, gemsbok, springbok, etc.), though equally numerous in the area where the paintings were made, figure much less prominently and do not receive the elaborate artistic treatment lavished on the eland paintings. David Lewis-Williams, a South African archaeologist, has inquired into the reasons for the apparent preference for elands as subjects. Using the ethnography and mythology of Bushman peoples of a

century ago and of today, he presents a description of the eland symbol in its various ritual contexts that may explain its frequency in the painted record. The eland was the ritual symbol of choice for Bushmen in the initiation of young women and young men, in marriage ceremonies, in curing through altered states of consciousness, and in practices connected with the rain. Even now, for modern Bushmen, the eland holds rich connotations of fertility, plenty, life-giving moisture, and sexual and social harmony.

The eland is related to a pervasive idea in Bushman cultures of today—an idea that also seems to permeate the ancient pictographs—that a desirable supernatural potency inheres in certain natural objects. !Kung Bushmen of today call this potency *n/um*, and they believe that human beings can take possession of it through purposeful alterations of consciousness, or trance. Things like bees, rain, honey, and the ubiquitous eland itself, believed to be repositories of *n/um*, appear in the paintings as metaphors for the trance dance, as touchstones on the way to the power to be gained by the religious and social discipline of the curing ceremony.

Many paintings depict this dancing for the purposes of psychic cur-

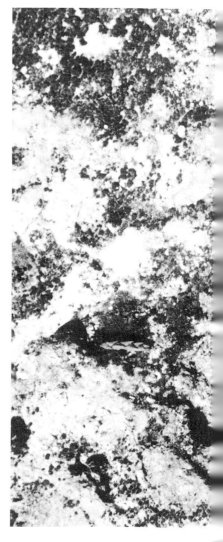

Painting of medicine man bleeding from nose during trance state while dancing, holding three antelope forelegs, Harrismith District, South Africa.

ing, which is still enthusiastically practiced among Bushman groups of the Kalahari. Painted dance scenes preserve characteristic postures of men in trance, including upper back parallel to the ground and arms swept back and upward, the use of walking sticks to add drama to the dance steps, and bleeding from the nose, associated with the altered state. It is clear that the powerful nexus of transformation represented by the trance dance, involving both the passage from human to *n/um kx"au* (owner of *n/um*) for the curers and from sick to well for their patients, is central to the interpretation of the South African painting tradition.

Lewis-Williams has proposed a hypothesis to deal not only with pictographic portrayals of the dance occasions but also with the supernatural figures appearing in the art. This "trance hypothesis" suggests that many nonnaturalistic and abstract representations may be depictions of the actual hallucinatory experiences of the trancers. W. W. Newcomb, writing on the Lower Pecos paintings of Texas, proposed a similar hypothesis in connection with the consumption of mescal beans. Whether induced by drugs or, as in the case of the Bushmen, by vigorous dancing, altered states pro-

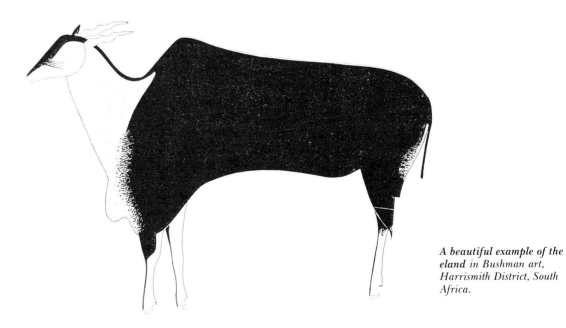

A beautiful example of the eland in Bushman art, Harrismith District, South Africa.

Various antelope, including two rear views, Giant's Castle, Drakensberg, South Africa.

vide access for individuals who have undergone shamanic initiation to reservoirs of very powerful cultural symbolism. It seems at least plausible that these kinds of images should have been chosen for preservation on the rocks.

A general and very powerful realization made possible by the combination of numerical studies with ethnographic evidence is that, if Bushman art has a single preoccupation, it is that of transformation. The transformations of trance and curing—young people becoming men and women, meat animals changed from withholders to providers of food, altering the weather from dry and death-dealing to moist and favorable, trouncing attacking carnivores by assuming spirit-forms for counterattack or flight—all are repeated over and over again as themes in the painted record and in mythology. It is evident that, if the art is *about* anything, it is about growth, change, solving problems; it is about the business of living.

This inescapable business on the South African subcontinent in prehistoric times required more than just a tool kit of physical implements. It also necessitated a "mental technology" involving the use of certain nonmaterial aids, including a complex of ritual ideas relating to the hunting of the great "red meat" animals (the antelopes) with bow and arrow. This complex, known from modern ethnography, stressed the cooperative nature of the hunting enterprise, the impartial providence of a deity—rather than human skill—in procuring game, and the necessity to share the fruits of the hunt equally among band members. Patricia Vinnicombe suggests that Bushman art developed within the evolutionary framework of the Paleolithic African environment confronted by the new technology of the bow and arrow, together with the social prescriptions that went along with its use. Every painted rock surface attests in some way to the appropriateness of this formulation. Taken together, the paintings present a graphic portrayal of the social and ritual attitudes by which life could best be lived in this environment.

Detailed numerical analysis of the various figures depicted on Lower Pecos canyon walls might provide an objective approach to the interpretation of these mysterious paintings. Of course, here we do not have the living ethnographic record (fortunately, still available from Bushman society) to use for comparison. But perhaps we could ascertain the key symbolic themes. Then, by fitting these with the archaeological evidence together with historically available ethnographic data from neighboring Indian societies, a clearer notion of how the Lower Pecos people thought and related to the environment might emerge. ■

An aardvark superimposed on a dancing group, Battle Cave, Drakensberg, South Africa.

CAVE ART OF THE AUSTRALIAN DESERT ABORIGINES
A Code to Survival

by Richard A. Gould
BROWN UNIVERSITY

Beyond the "Ooh-aah Response"

When someone first encounters an example of prehistoric cave art, the inevitable question arises: "What does it mean?" The situation is not unlike that in a fashionable gallery that is having a show of "primitive" art, where visitors are expected to react to something totally alien to their experience. Situations like these often produce what I call the "ooh-aah response." For some unexplained reason, people confronted by such examples of non-Western artistic expression feel obliged to declare their opinions about its meaning when, in fact, they haven't a clue. Of course, there is really nothing wrong with such gallery chitchat, and the same can be said for these kinds of opinions that often appear in print. These fantasies may be silly, but they are usually harmless.

One of the best-known examples is Erich von Däniken's explanation for the mouthless human faces appearing in the cave art of the Kimberley District of northwestern Australia—the famous "Wandjinas." In his widely read book *Chariots of the Gods*, he claims that these mysterious and enigmatic paintings represent extraterrestrial beings visiting the earth. The halolike designs around their heads, he argues, depict their space helmets. Even in the dizzy domain of ooh-aah archaeology, this is far out!

Given this inclination to fantasize on the subject, how can we come back down to earth and produce more convincing explanations for prehistoric cave and rock art? The case of the "Wandjinas" provides a clue, since it turns out that these paintings are less mysterious than von Däniken supposed. Historic Australian Aborigines residing in that region were renewing such paintings in connection with various rituals. Aborigine mythology and beliefs connected with these paintings are well known, and there are even some examples of this art style near the coast that depict Europeans and their boats from the earliest period of historical contact. If none of the oral traditions of the Aborigine cultures that made and preserved these paintings mentions beings from outer space, why should we?

The problem is that, like language, expressive art operates much like a code. Each cultural system has evolved its own particular set of symbolic elements and grammar for recombining these elements. We lack the functional equivalent of a Rosetta Stone to help us decode the symbols of a prehistoric system of

expressive art into terms that are familiar to us. Ancient art, like contemporary "primitive" art, is esoteric, and no amount of fantasy or wishful thinking will bring us any closer to what the ancient artist meant when he (or she) applied these designs to the rock walls where we see them today. This applies to the cave art of the Lower Pecos River region, as it does everywhere. Even when we observe present-day artists in non-Western societies, the meaning of the art we see being created is specific to the cultural tradition of that artist as we see it today. It cannot necessarily be translated into the categories of thought and expression of another culture; nor can it be assumed that it represents the prehistoric antecedents of thought and expression in that artist's own culture.

Yet, despite this apparent impasse, there are ways to build a bridge between the past and present that allow us to begin to make reliable inferences to account for the character of prehistoric cave art. By studying contemporary cave artists in a traditional hunting and gathering society, we can make comparisons that control for essential similarities with and differences from the purely archaeological cave art of the Lower Pecos. In order to do this, one must appre-

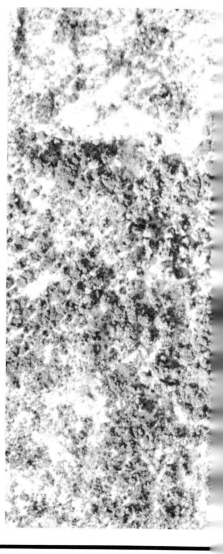

ciate the importance of the bio-geographical context in which all hunter-gatherer cave art took place and examine the possible adaptive roles that such artistic expression may have played in each case. That is, we cannot regard this simply as "art for art's sake," but must look instead for possible ways in which art of this kind may have helped people to adapt to the circumstances under which they lived.

The Western Desert Aborigines of Australia

When my wife and I studied these people from 1966 to 1970, they were actively engaged in traditional hunting and gathering and carried on their rock and cave painting—being perhaps the last hunter-gatherers in the world to do so. Some of these people had minimal contact with Europeans, providing a unique opportunity to address questions about the meaning of their expressive art. Despite many changes due to contact with Western culture, they continue to produce cave paintings along with a full repertoire of traditional oral and decorative arts.

Like most other Australian Aborigines, the Western Desert People have a concept of a timeless past, which they call *tjukurpa* (literally, "dreaming"), during which mythical beings ancestral both to humans and to natural species are believed to have traveled across vast stretches of desert landscape, having adventures and encountering other such beings. During their travels they periodically transformed themselves or the products of their activities into landmarks that remain visible today and are regarded with reverence. Thus, the concept of "dreaming" applies simultaneously to time and place. People claim descent in the male line from particular ancestral beings and combine into social groups (cult-lodges or patrilineages), based on their mutual affiliation to a common ancestor. This concept of affiliation by descent structures much of the ritual life of the Aborigines, but most of the actual rituals are performed exclusively by initiated men.

These rituals include both the initiation of young men into full membership in their respective cult-lodges and the performance by the members of a cult-lodge of maintenance ceremonies in relation to the particular ancestral species or beings involved. Thus, for example, adult men who claim common patrilinear descent from, say, the mythical bandicoot will meet whenever they can to venerate the bandicoot at those localities where— according to the

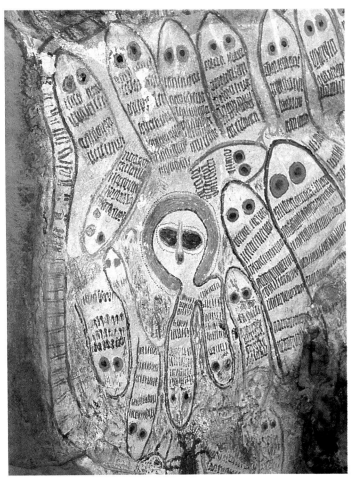

"Wandjina" paintings, Gibb River Station, Kimberley District, Western Australia. Note the mouthless faces with "halo" in center.

myths held by the cult-lodge—it transformed the landscape in some durable way. Rituals on such occasions include cleaning up or otherwise maintaining the physical appearance of the sacred site, protecting the site against trespass by uninitiated or otherwise unauthorized individuals, and performing special rituals to ensure the continuation of the natural species involved.

The vast majority of the designs I observed being painted by the Aborigines on rocks and in caves were specifically related to body designs and paraphernalia connected to initiatory or maintenance rituals of the cult-lodge to which the artists belonged. Concentric circles, often linked by parallel lines, circles, vertical stripes set in horizontal rows, meandering lines, semirepresentational motifs involving latticelike designs, and other nonnaturalistic design elements dominated the rock and cave art. Most of these were copied directly from body designs painted or scarified onto novices and ritual performers. There were also special designs depicting such things as the track followed by a particular mythical ancestor or by a novice during his "grand tour" of other distant camps prior to his circumcision. Each of these designs could be linked directly to the mythical episode it pertained to, and the song relating that myth was often sung by the painter as he worked. The atmosphere on such occasions was always relaxed and low key, and it was clear that the cave painting, while it involved depiction of sacred themes, was not a ritual activity itself.

Despite their explicitly sacred and ritual content, the paintings themselves were not regarded as intrinsically sacred. They were described as *watilu* (literally, "man-made")—that is, human depictions of sacred themes. In the Western Desert, all such cases involved superposition of new designs over old ones. No attempt was made to touch up or rejuvenate older paintings. Each individual painted designs that were memorable to him in the context of his own experience of past rituals he had seen or participated in or in relation to his images of the experiences of his dreamtime ancestor. During my interviews with Aboriginal artists in which they explained their paintings to me, I collected long lists of names of waterholes and other sacred sites along the tracks of different mythical ancestors, usually in the form of concentric circles linked by single or parallel lines.

Coming upon these paintings later, even an "insider" in this culture would be unable to identify the specific, named localities or even the particular ancestral being associated with the designs without some prior knowledge. About all he would be able to say is that the concentric circles and open circles represented named localities in some dreaming story and that the connecting lines represented the tracks of some ancestral being. In other words, particular designs tended to be esoteric not only with respect to the cultural system but even, at another level of specificity, to the individual painters.

The rocks or caves on which these designs were painted were another matter. These were regarded as intrinsically sacred— that is, pertaining directly to the particular dreaming at that site. The site itself was *tjukurpa* and was, among other things, protected from defacement by the members of the cult-lodge affiliated with the site. A good imaginary litmus test of this relationship would be to compare the kinds of alterations that would be defined as defacement by the Aborigines involved. Were one merely to paint "Kilroy Was Here" or some other irrelevant design over existing designs on the same rock face or cave wall, there would be little if any reaction by the cult-lodge But were one to *chisel* "Kilroy Was Here" into the same rock face or cave wall, the members of the cult-lodge would see this as a sacrilegious assault on their dreamtime ancestor, whose very being is believed to have turned to stone at the place and whose spiritual essence is thought to reside in the rocks, and their reaction would be immediate and violent.

With all this in mind, we may now ask: How much of the sacred content of this cave art would be directly inferable archaeologically? The answer is: *None*. The extreme esoteric and specific nature of these designs and the cosmology producing them cannot be assumed to have existed in other cultural traditions, past or present. Moreover, it would be risky even to attribute a similar specificity

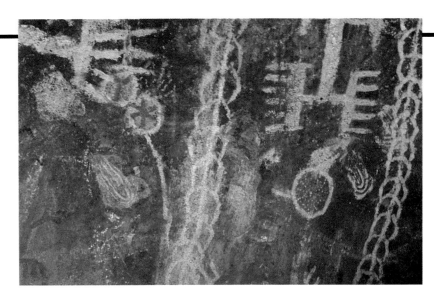

of meaning to the possible prehistoric occurrences of these designs within the same area, even when good archaeological evidence exists for culture-historical continuity there. We have absolutely no reliable basis for assuming that the internal grammar that structures the cave and rock art of the Western Desert Aborigines today operated in the same way or at all in the past. There is no universal principle of cultural uniformitarianism that we can apply comparatively to different cultures or to the prehistoric cultures of the past.

An Archaeological View of Cave Art

Because of the esoteric nature of Australian Desert cave art, no reasonable means exist for us to explain its meaning. However, we can approach the Australian Aborigine case as a problem of archaeological inference, and the same is true for extinct cultures like that of the Lower Pecos River. The question the archaeologist must ask is: When and under what circumstances can we expect certain kinds of cultural systems to operate, and what are the characteristic material remains of those cultural systems? And, of course, where does cave and rock art

fit into the ways such cultural systems operate?

The Western Desert Aborigines of Australia represent a mobile society of hunter-gatherers living in a highly stressed environment. The biogeography of the Western Desert presents extreme problems for any people living there directly off the land. Of paramount concern is the problem of drought. The Western Desert occupies a latitude that receives minimal amounts of rain, which tends to fall in a scattered, unpredictable manner. Compounding this problem is the terrain, which consists of ancient Precambrian rocks of characteristically low relief entirely lacking in permanent rivers, lakes, or springs. Thus, all surface water supplies depend upon relatively ephemeral catchments such as rockholes, small stream beds, claypans, and soakages ("native wells"). Although relatively few in number, Western Desert plant and animal species tend to be highly drought-adapted, which means that they often occur in areas remote from surface water catchments. Thus, key resources such as red kangaroos and certain staple plants may be present but inaccessible to human hunter-gatherers, who must base their foraging activities on limited and erratically distributed water supplies.

Such conditions engender a high degree of nomadism, with frequent moves over long distance. People literally "chase rain" much of the time by observing falls of rain over distances of up to fifty miles and moving to localities where those rains can be expected to have filled known surface catchments. Similarly, group size and composition fluctuate in response to local conditions. People come together into maximal groups of up to perhaps 150 individuals under conditions of heavy local rain correlated with good fodder for game. They disperse when the hunting tapers off and drought conditions ensue, with small clusters of families of around 10 to 15 individuals moving to relatively dependable water sources upon which to base their drought foraging activities. This description, of course, applies only to responses by Aborigines living off the land in a traditional manner, which was still true for some small, isolated groups until sometime between 1970 and 1972. Today all Western Desert Aborigines live on government reserves, missions, stations, or in some other regular relationship to Euro-Australians.

The case of the Western Desert Aborigines is an example of extreme opportunism of movement on a day-to-day basis, which in turn makes heavy demands upon geographical knowledge over wide areas of the desert. One of the profound ironies of traditional Aboriginal desert cultures generally is the simultaneous requirement for extreme flexibility and opportunism of movement and an equally compelling requirement for an elaborate and detailed system of geographical knowledge to be learned and passed on intact to succeeding generations in the context of a nonliterate society. In other words, the traditional Western Desert culture embodies requirements for both flexible opportunism and conservative orthodoxy, an apparent contradiction that is easy to reconcile if one accepts the proposition that these are complementary rather than opposed principles—that is, each depends upon the other.

Geographical knowledge among the Aborigines is embedded within the sacred life and consists of hundreds of specific, named localities occurring over vast areas of landscape memorized during the lifetime of each individual during initiatory rituals and visits to sacred sites for maintenance ceremonies. The

mythology provides stories, songs, and dances to go with each of these named localities, which are the sacred dreaming sites referred to earlier.

One never meets an Aborigine in the Western Desert who is lost, no matter how flat or featureless the terrain may appear. All movement across this landscape depends upon one's ability to relate these known landmarks, however small, to ephemeral water sources, food supplies, and other key resources. The entire Aboriginal sacred life, with its innumerable ritual enactments of episodes from the dreamtime myths, can be viewed as a mnemonic device for imprinting this vast body of geographical knowledge in the minds of novices and maintaining it intact in the minds of the elders. The co-occurrence of the inculcation of these myths (with their geographic locations) and various initiatory ordeals like circumcision, tooth avulsion, piercing of the nose septum, subincision, and chest scarification produces indelible and unforgettable associations in the minds of novices and elders alike.

Unlike certain parts of the world

where key resources occur in predictable patterns that can be learned in an organized, systematic way and located by reasoning through the system, Western Desert resources tend to occur randomly and unpredictably over the landscape. Western Desert Aborigine geography depends heavily upon pure memorization of long sequences of specific locations, with a strong emphasis on repetition and drill when this training occurs. This kind of geographic knowledge can be contrasted with the streets and subways of New York City, which are laid out according to an organized grid system that one can use to infer one's position almost anywhere without recourse to large inputs of memorized information.

Rock and cave art among the Western Desert Aborigines is an integral part of a cultural system that requires the ability to memorize long chains of specific information, and the art reflects this in its emphasis on the repetition of long chains of unitary and more or less equivalent symbols. Each symbol (such as a set of concentric circles) in a chain serves as a visual stimulus in the context of rituals connected with the dreaming that invokes larger and more complex images embodied in the myths and their attendant stories and songs. In the Western Desert case, these visual symbols are transferred directly from the body paintings of the novices and dancers to the rock surfaces and cave walls, where they are preserved in a more enduring and recognizably "archaeological" context.

In this case, the congruence between Western Desert biogeography and the artistic behavior of the Aborigines living there leads to the larger proposition that when mobile hunter-gatherers must adapt to heavily stressed environments, where resources occur more or less randomly in space and unpredictably in time, we should expect to find systems of

Aborigine drinking at Walaluka claypan, near Mt. Madley, Western Australia.

geographical knowledge that require long chains of memorized information imparted with the aid of whatever mnemonic devices can be used to assist in the memorization process. Rock and cave art among the Aborigines is one among many such devices within the sacred life and, as such, embodies the same degree of conservatism and orthodoxy as the rest of the sacred life. In other words, ecological stresses based upon uncertainty and risk will produce conservatism and repetition in the visual art. In cases like that of the Western Desert Aborigines, it is the very poverty of the physical environment that acts as a stimulus to the richness of the art.

Rock Art of the Lower Pecos Region

Archaeological research in this area offers evidence of a variable and generally arid climate, with no clear annual seasonality of resources, during the post-Pleistocene period, that is, during the last 10,000 years or so. The area was inhabited by mobile hunter-gatherers, termed *Archaic* by archaeologists, whose cultural assemblages, especially from about 7000 B.C. to around A.D. 1000, were stable and persisted with little change. Well-preserved plant remains suggest a strong dependence on a varied array of desert food plants, while hunting involved basically solitary game species and probably required large amounts of effort for relatively poor returns. These factors all stand as parallels to the Western Desert Aborigines, and they permit us to compare the nature of their adaptations.

As in the Western Desert case, the majority of rock and cave art designs of these Archaic Indians of the Lower Pecos are esoteric and probably had important ritual associations. We may never be able to decipher the artistic code of meaning repre-

Charlie Woods making rock paintings at Puntutjarpa Rockshelter, Western Australia.

sented by the Lower Pecos art, but we must certainly account for the essential difference between this artistic tradition and that of the Western Desert of Australia: the highly variable character of the lower canyon pictographs. While certain general themes such as the anthropomorphic figures ("shamans") are evident, they all appear in different guises, with varying colors, costumes, and paraphernalia. With these are various other themes that seem not to recur often, such as the famous panther and turtle at Panther Cave. Compared to the art of the Western Desert Aborigines, the Lower Pecos cave paintings are essentially nonrepetitive and appear to reflect a higher degree of creative expression by the individuals or groups that produced them.

Without attempting a detailed analysis here, it seems that the Lower Pecos people, while living as mobile desert hunter-gatherers, were able to obtain their basic resources in a more predictable manner than their Australian counterparts, if only because of the presence of a permanent river system within

their domain, along with numerous sheltered microhabitats in the canyons where key food species flourished on a reliable basis. We cannot yet explain why the style and content of ancient Lower Pecos cave art evolved as they did. However, by comparing it with the art of the Western Desert of Australia, we can say that it was not necessary for the Lower Pecos people to adapt to their region by memorizing geographical minutiae and by using their art to support their ability to repeat and call up this information to the same degree. The constraints imposed by uncertainty over water would have been much less severe in the Lower Pecos. Consequently, the Archaic artists there were freer to express themselves and to depict images less closely tied to the needs of memorizing geographically useful information in the form of a long chain of repeated elements. Perhaps it is this aspect of expressiveness and variability of style that projects such a strong appeal to us today, as members of a different cultural tradition that also places a high value on creativity and expressiveness. ∎

SHAMANISM, THE ECSTATIC EXPERIENCE, AND LOWER PECOS ART
Reflections on Some Transcultural Phenomena

by Peter T. Furst

STATE UNIVERSITY OF NEW YORK AT ALBANY

In view of the conspicuous yet mysterious role of the "shaman" figures in Lower Pecos rock art, the editors have asked Dr. Peter T. Furst, a world authority on shamanism, for a contribution on the subject.

It is almost inevitable that terms like *shamans* and *shamanism* should crop up in discussions of Lower Pecos rock art, if only because so much of it seems mysterious and inexplicable in anything but a mystical or supernatural framework. It is certainly not anecdotal, idle doodling, or "art for art's sake," pretty pictures meant to beautify the naked walls of one's shelter from the elements. Whatever they may mean, and whether their message is beyond recovery, we can be certain that the pictographs express deeply held beliefs and profound religious experiences for which shamanism is a convenient, if inexact, handle. What is often lacking, however, are explanations why shamans should be depicted on the walls of ancient rockshelters, or why such individuals might themselves have been the artists, as some scholars have suggested. Too often it is taken for granted that the nonspecialist reader or listener knows what is meant by shamanism, and little is said about what shamans are and do, beyond brief allusions to their greater access to the unknowable and the sacred.

"Hunting cults" also used to be a popular way to account for all kinds of rock art, from the Aurignacian cave paintings of France and Spain to California and Texas. But this is no explanation at all and, fortunately, has long since been discarded by the more thoughtful scholars as too narrow, naive, and simplistic. "Hunting cult" might be appropriate for, say, contemporary Germany or Austria, where hunters have been known to get together to toast a slain stag with a cup of its blood, but not for native societies that retain a hunting and gathering way of life or periodically supplement the fruits of agriculture with game. In any event, even if "hunting cult" were not a construct of the Western mind, it would hardly account for the enormous number of abstract symbols (abstract to us, that is, but not necessarily to their creators or the audience, if any, for whom they were painting), the relative scarcity of game animal representations, or, as Newcomb (1967:79) has noted, the presence in the Pecos River art of mountain lions, clearly not meant to be seen either as prey for human hunters or as posing a danger to human beings.

This state of affairs, in turn, raises some intriguing questions about the differences between Old World and New World rock art. Why, in contrast to Lascaux or Altamira, or the rock art of Africa, in which large game animals predominate, is there such emphasis on human or spirit figures and abstract symbols in the ancient pictographs of North America? And why have we found no representations of the large Pleistocene animals— mammoth, mastodon, giant sloth, horse, camel, giant bison— with which Paleo-Indians coexisted for at least 10,000 years? Ten millennia after they became extinct, the memory of at least the mammoth persists here and there in Indian mythology— for example, in a giant "stiff-legged bear" among the Penobscot of Maine, or Big Elk in the Pacific Northwest, who has a fifth, prehensile leg. In contrast, thus far every claim for a Paleo-Indian depiction of a mammoth or mastodon has proved spurious or extremely doubtful, at best. These are problems that should keep art historians, iconographers, and anthropologists concerned with mental, and not just material, culture guessing for years to come.

Pecos Rock Art and the "Mescal Bean"

The probability of a connection between the Pecos River pictographs and the potent psychoactive *Sophora secundiflora* seeds—misnamed "mescal beans"—that occur in virtually all levels of cultural debris covering the floors of Lower Pecos rockshelters has long been recognized and discussed in the specialized literature (cf. Campbell 1958; Troike 1962; Newcomb 1967). Newcomb, who has given us the most extensive set of possibilities for the meanings of the Pecos River paintings in his and Kirkland's classic work, *The Rock Art of Texas Indians* (unfortunately now out of print), suggests that at least some might have been painted by shamans after emerging from a mescal bean trance. Another good possibility is that some of the Pecos River Style art was the work of neophyte members of ecstatic-shamanistic *Sophora* bean medicine societies, who sought to depict what they had seen in their initiatory trances. This would imply that the so-called shamans, for example, might really be spirits or even gods, who were, in any event, typically invested with shamanic attributes by different peoples—human shamans writ large. Still, the educated layperson remains generally uninformed on the nature of the historical and sociocultural significance of the proposed relationship among the art, the shaman, and the botanical "hallucinogen," even if he or she does not share in some of the popular misconceptions, pro and con, that surround the whole subject of "mind-altering" substances.

A Transcultural Phenomenon

As a transcultural phenomenon, the use of botanical species containing nonaddictive, but temporarily intoxicating, chemicals capable of triggering and maintaining ecstatic dream states, or trances, is much too large and complex a topic to be treated adequately in the present context. More than a hundred have been identified, and there are others that have barely been investigated. Certainly each of the major ones deserves book-length treatment from the multidisciplinary points of view of ethnobotany, pharmacology, history, and culture.

The better known include the already mentioned

Sophora bean (Texas, southern Plains); peyote, *Lophophora williamsi* (Mexico and North America); the morning glories *Rivea corymbosa* and *Ipomoea violacea* (Mexico); the *Psilocybe* mushrooms (Mexico and, less certainly, Guatemala and northern South America); different species and subspecies of the solonaceous genus *Datura* (California, the Southwest, Virginia,

Mexico, South America); intoxicating snuffs prepared in South America from the seeds of two species of the leguminous genus *Anadenanthera*— *A. piptadenia* in the lowlands, *A. colubrina* in the highlands—and from the inner bark of the *Virola* tree; tobacco: *Nicotiana tabacum* (from South America to Mexico), *N. rustica* (from the Andes to Canada), *N. bigelovii*, *N. attenuata*, and *N. trigonophylla* (Great Basin of North America); *yaje* or *ayahuasca* (psychoactive drinks brewed from one or more species of *Banisteriopsis*, a genus including several closely related, hallucinogenic tropical South American vines); and the San Pedro cactus, *Trichocereus pachanoi* (Andean Peru and Ecuador)— but this is only a partial list. Some are already the subject of an extensive literature, including specialized books, but most still await more detailed and multidisciplinary consideration.

It would be nice if one could make some convenient correlation between the choice of plant and a people's economic system or level of technological complexity—for example, if it could be demonstrated that where preagricultural groups resort to "mind-altering" plants in their ritual they use species whose extraordinary qualities they could have discovered by

Recognizably shamanistic themes are more common in Colima tomb art dating between 200 B.C. and A.D. 1–200 than in any other ancient Mesoamerican art traditions. Here what appears at first sight to be a shark swallowing is on closer inspection far more complex: the apparent shark is more likely to be a killer whale—a hunter of the sea frequently associated with shamans and shamanism among coastal peoples all the way to Alaska. It also has human arms and legs, suggesting that the sculpture may depict the death-rebirth initiation of a novice shaman, who is swallowed and later regurgitated as a full-fledged shaman by an animal demon initiator—a common theme in the lore and symbolism of shamanism everywhere. Private collection.

chance in the course of food quest, without any complex preparation, and, conversely, that complex pharmacological technologies implying long observation and experimentation are reserved to populations with developed horticultural and agricultural expertise. Not so.

Accidental discovery of their intoxicating potential during the everyday food quest is certainly possible for such species as the sacred mushroom or peyote, whose effects are felt soon after ingestion, without any special preparation. But other plants require detailed knowledge and careful treatment that can result only from experimentation and observation (this, by the way, is also true for several contraceptive plants long known to different Indian populations). For example, the Yanomamo Indians of the upper Orinoco, who until recently had no agriculture, prepare their potent ritual snuff from a base of *Virola* tree bark. The bark contains tryptamine alkaloids (which are also the principal active constituents of the sacred mushrooms and other ritual plant hallucinogens of Mexico).

But tryptamines require a monoamine oxidase inhibitor to become effective in humans, a problem South American Indians have generally solved by mixing several species together. This is not always or absolutely necessary in the case of *Virola* snuff, in which investigators have recently isolated two new carbolines that help make the bark itself psychodynamically effective, even in the absence of admixtures. Nevertheless, some Yanomamo subgroups make certain that their snuff will have the desired effect by adding to the powdered *Virola* preparation an equal amount of pulverized leaves of *Justicia pectoralis*, an aromatic, acanthaceous weed containing, like *Virola*, hallucinogenic tryptamine alkaloids (Schultes 1972:43). So here we have a preagricultural hunting and gathering people engaging in what must have been considerable experimentation to arrive at the most effective chemistry for inducing a state of mystical rapture.

Indeed, the use of admixtures to assure or heighten the effects of a particular plant is widespread throughout the South American tropics, among agricultural Indians as well as hunter-gatherers. Thus, the Ecuadoran Jivaro give their *Banisteriopsis* beverage, called *natema*, extra potency with a species of *Datura* of the arborescent subgenus *Brugmansia*, and sometimes also *guayusa*, a stimulating caffeine-containing tea made from *Ilex guayusa*, a species of holly. Tukanoan Indians of Colombian Amazonia brew their ritual *yaje*

drink not from a single species of *Banisteriopsis*, but from a mixture of *B. rusbyana* with *B. caapi* or *B. inebrians*.

The reason, pharmacologists have discovered, is that *Banisteriopsis rusbyana* is a chemical oddity among its sister species: in contrast to *B. caapi* and *B. inebrians*, whose active principals are beta-carboline harmala alkaloids, its active constituents are tryptamines! The mixing of the different species causes the alkaloids of the one to function as inhibitors for the tryptamines of the other, allowing both to play their part in the ecstatic intoxication. As Schultes (1972:38) observes, here again one cannot help but wonder "how peoples in primitive societies, with no knowledge of chemistry or physiology, ever hit upon a solution to the activation of an alkaloid by a monamine oxidase inhibitor" (Furst 1976).

Also, the same plant might be employed by all sorts of societies, with widely differing social, economic, and technological systems. Thus, in western North America, both nonagricultural Indians in California and sedentary, maize-growing Pueblos in New Mexico have valued *Datura inoxia*, the former in young people's ecstatic initiation rites, the latter mainly for divination and in medicine; so have the Navajos. From the sixteenth- and seventeenth-century Spanish sources we know that in ancient Mexico the imperial, urban Aztecs as well as rural villagers all employed morning glory seeds, mushrooms, peyote, *Datura*, and a variety of other sacred plants for ritual intoxication.

In South America, ritual snuffing was practiced by hunters and gatherers, root crop and maize farmers, the agricultural Arawak Indians who inhabited the Antilles and other Caribbean islands at the time of the Conquest, and urbanized peoples in the Andes. The mescaline-containing San Pedro, a tall columnar cactus belonging, with the giant saguaro of the Southwest and the so-called Christmas cactus, to the genus *Cereus*, seems to have served as the preferred ritual hallucinogen for a great variety of Andean peoples from about 1200 B.C. to the present day. On the painted polychrome vases of the great Nazca civilization of Peru, which flourished between A.D. 100 and 600, the cactus was even anthropomorphized as a powerful supernatural being or deity, wearing a feline mouth mask and sprouting San Pedro from his forehead and shoulders. (No comparable personification of *Sophora secundiflora* has been recognized in the Lower Pecos rock art. But then, we have no idea if, or in what form, the ancient people visualized the spirit of *Sophora*, or whether he, or she, had any single, generally accepted, shape.)

Different species of tobacco also figure in this widespread, transcultural complex of ritual intoxication; thus, the shamans of the Warao, a fishing people in the Orinoco Delta of Venezuela, use only tobacco to smoke themselves into ecstatic trances (Wilbert 1972), while many other peoples employ tobacco, sometimes in liquid form, in conjunction with other psychoactive plants. Local wild species of tobacco were also used ecstatically by Indian shamans in California and the Great Basin; however, many other North American Indians employed tobacco as prayer offerings to the spirits and did not smoke or otherwise ingest it for the purpose of bringing about ecstatic visions.

Sophora secundiflora: A Special Case

Within this complex, *Sophora secundiflora* presents us with a very special situation, pharmacologically and historically. First, these seeds are not merely psychoactive but contain a physiologically dangerous, potentially deadly, chemical—cystisine, a quinolizidine alkaloid capable of causing extreme nausea, convulsions, and even death from respiratory failure (Schultes 1972; Schultes and Hofmann 1973). In fact, of all the numerous botanical hallucinogens in ritual use among Native American peoples, only the solonaceous *Daturas* pose a comparable risk to health and life. Second, in the Lower Pecos, *Sophora*—a flowering shrub with small purple blossoms that is still popular as an ornamental—has given us the oldest documented evidence for hallucinogenic plant use, not just in the Americas, but throughout the world.

Notwithstanding their toxicity, *Sophora* seeds were, on the archaeological and historical evidence, continuously employed for over 10,000 years, from the era of late Pleistocene Paleo-Indian hunters of mammoth, mastodon, giant bison, and other now long extinct animals to the end of the nineteenth century; on the ethnographic evidence, the context for their use was ecstatic-shamanistic medicine societies. The oldest dated finds in the Lower Pecos region come from Bone Bed II at Bonfire Shelter, with a carbon-14 date of 8440–8120 B.C., where the well-preserved red beans were associated with Folsom and Plainview-type projectile points and the bones of a large extinct species of Pleistocene bison, *Bison antiquus*. The Spanish explorer Alvar Núñez Cabeza de Vaca was the first European to take note, in 1539, of the importance of *Sophora* beans among Texas Indians.

Unfortunately, it was not until shortly before its demise, four and a half centuries later, that the "mescal bean cult" began to be seriously studied among what remained of the tribal peoples of the southern Plains. By the end of the nineteenth century, the red seeds of *S. secundiflora* were no longer being ingested in the initiation rituals of ecstatic-visionary medicine societies, having become increasingly replaced by peyote, none of whose thirty or more chemical constituents can cause permanent physiological harm. The "peyote cult," a new religion integrating old Indian beliefs and rituals with elements introduced by Christian missionaries that spread rapidly among the displaced, dispirited, and desperately poor reservation Indians, eventually evolved into the Native American Church, with the spineless little psychoactive cactus as its sacramental focus and a pan-Indian membership of some 225,000 from the Rio Grande to the Canadian Rockies (La Barre 1974).

La Barre's Ecstatic-Shamanistic Hypothesis

The Pecos *Sophora* material is also historically significant because it fits Weston La Barre's Paleo-Asiatic ecstatic-shamanistic hypothesis for the widespread use of botanical hallucinogens by the native peoples of the New World. He interprets interest in these plants among American Indians as a function of the survival of an essentially Paleolithic-Mesolithic Eurasiatic shamanism, which their nomadic ancestors carried with them out of northeastern Asia and which became the base religion of all Indian America. Shamanism is deeply rooted in the ecstatic visionary experience, he suggests, and the First Americans, as well as their descendants, were thus, so to speak, "culturally programmed" for a conscious exploration of the environment in search of botanical means to reach that desired state.

When considering this interesting idea, two things must be clearly understood. The first is that any attempt to reconstruct the ideological universe, the belief systems and rituals, of ancient peoples is at best educated guesswork informed by incomplete, often minimal, archaeological evidence, on the one hand, and ethnographic analogy to recent or modern cultures, on the other. The second is that the early bands of hunters and wild food collectors who slowly drifted overland from northeastern Asia into the New World were fully modern people and that subsumed under *shamanism* is a well-developed, sophisticated ideological universe encompassing a world view and an attitude toward the natural environment that is essentially ecological, specific ideas about themselves in relation to the ancestors and the natural and supernatural spheres, sacred myths, magico-religious beliefs and rituals, and the like.

The Imperative of Reciprocity

Ecological is, in fact, a proper definition of Native American religions, if we broaden the meaning of the term from its dictionary definition (i.e., recognition of the interrelationships and interdependence between organisms and their environment) to embrace what is a pretty general attitude toward the environment among Indian people to this day. First, Indians tend not to divide the natural world as Westerners do, into animate and inanimate; rather, all phenomena in the environment are alive and sentient, trees and rocks and rivers no less than human beings and animals. Second, animals and people are qualitatively equivalent, endowed with similar soul stuff; in the Native American world view, human beings are not "lords over nature" but an integral component of the natural world. Third, relations not only between people but between people and the environment are governed by the principle of reciprocity: nothing can be taken from the environment without some kind of payment, without putting something considered of equal value back into the cycle of life.

I can think of no better way to illustrate the imperative of reciprocity in the shamanistic religions of American Indians than with this example from the Vaupes region of Colombia, reported by the Colombian anthropologist Gerardo Reichel-Dolmatoff (1967), who has worked for many years with the Tukanoan-speaking Desana.

In the world view of these Indians, who practice subsistence agriculture while retaining, like the Mexican Huichols, a powerful component of hunting ideology in their religion, the environment is a closed, or finite, energy cycle, whose depletion by the unreciprocated removal of even one game animal and its soul would threaten ecological disaster and the survival of the Desana as a people. The game animals and the forest are watched over by a supernatural being, a Master of the Animal Species, known as Waimaxse to the Desana, who conceive of him as a red dwarf with a giant phallus that contains the seeds of all the useful plants. Like shamans everywhere, the Desana shaman acts as intermediary between the people and the spirit powers. He is especially close to

Waimaxse, who is thought to reside at a prominent rock outcropping covered with ancient paintings and surrounded by thick forest.

Periodically Desana men set out for the forest to supplement the agricultural staples with the meat of game. But this requires permission from Waimaxse, which only the shaman can secure by virtue of his special powers. Before the hunt, he makes a list of the game animals the people require for survival and sets out on a journey of the mind to Waimaxse's abode. Here he presents his wish list to the supernatural guardian of the animals, sometimes in the form of pictographs.

However, the shaman must guarantee some form of repayment that will restore to the environment the animal spirit power to be removed from it by the hunters. This he does by turning over to Waimaxse the souls of any people who have transgressed against the rules of life, especially through incest (i.e., the customary laws of exogamy); these are serious breaches of conduct that cannot go unpunished, because they upset the equilibrium within the community and between the community and the spirit world (significantly, in some South American origin mythologies it is precisely a primordial act of incest that caused a rupture in easy communication between humans and gods and brought vulnerability and death into the human condition). So, at the demise of the offenders, their souls will restore the energy cycle of the environment to its proper level and survival is reciprocally guaranteed on both sides, the human and the extra-human, through the medium of the shaman.

This exchange of human for animal spirit power also underscores that the Desana, like other Indian peoples, consider human beings and their animal brothers and sisters to be qualitatively equivalent, differing in their outer form, the shape of their "form soul," but not in their inner spirit essence. The same ecological principles underlie the pan-Indian emphasis in speech and ritual on respect for the Earth Mother, lest heedless, unreciprocated exploitation of her bounty bring disaster on her children.

This is pretty sophisticated stuff, but it is an integral part of the Desana hunting ethos, and its underlying assumptions about the environment and the human being's responsibilities toward it are so widespread, and so deeply embedded in Native American consciousness—including that of modern North American Indians on and off the reservations—that one must assume them to be very ancient, most likely derived from the archaic shamanistic religions their remote ancestors brought with them into the New World from northeastern Asia.

Of course, these religious systems had evolved under the specific conditions of their former homeland and surely changed over space and time, however gradually, during the hundreds, even thousands, of years it must have taken for small hunting bands to move across the Bering land bridge into Alaska and south, before the overland route was finally submerged at the close of the Wisconsin glaciation. We can only speculate on the nature of these changes and adaptations. But religion tends generally to be conservative. And even if one regards the belief system as arising from, or at least closely tied to, social and material reality, the basic lifeway of hunters and food collectors organized in small, presumably egalitarian, kin-based band societies probably did not differ markedly from that of their sub-Arctic Siberian ancestors, even in new and very different kinds of environments populated by different species of plants and animals.

Some Parallels and Survivals

Except in detail, then, the ancient systems of religious beliefs and rituals, with the ecstatic experience and the shaman at the center, presumably would not have needed to change in any substantial respect. In any case, certain vital core elements seem to have retained their basic integrity over a long span of time and through considerable geographical space, to a degree that striking cross-cultural parallels in the shamanic phenomenon can be recognized in places as far apart as the Arctic, northern Asia, India, North and South America, Southeast Asia and Oceania, Tibet, and even Hungary (Eliade 1964). That this should be so among peoples who still retain, or retained until very recently, a hunting and gathering way of life might perhaps be expected. It is more surprising that it should also apply to more complex societies that long ago turned to farming or even became urbanized. At the very least it suggests, not some mystical "collective consciousness," but that shamanism contains elements that on the level of "mental culture" have again and again answered some basic needs of the human condition.

The cross-cultural similarities and parallels in shamanic motifs are many; indeed, some are well-nigh universal. I will single out only two—the difficult, or, as Eliade (1964:482–486) calls it, "paradoxical" passage, and the shaman's ascent through the several layers of the heavens by way of a world tree as "shaman's ladder"—because they give some underlying unity to belief systems in widely separated areas that cannot possibly be accounted for by direct diffusion or borrowing.

The Symplegades Motif

The paradoxical passage or clashing gateway, a common theme in shamanic, heroic, initiatory, and funerary mythology and folk tales the world over, is also known as the *Symplegades motif*, for the clashing pair of islands at the mouth of the Euxine Sea that barred the way for Jason and the Argonauts. In the Greek myth, the heroes attempt in vain to steer the *Argo* around the perilous passage; but no matter which way they row, to the left or to the right, the Symplegades move with them. The blind soothsayer and Thracean king Phineus counsels the frightened heroes to test the dangerous passage by sending a pigeon ahead of their vessel—the rocks will slam together and when they open, the ship can follow. But if the bird is killed, they must turn back, and their quest will come to naught. Seeing the pigeon flying through, losing only some of its tail feathers as the Symplegades clash shut again with a mighty roar, Jason calls on the goddess Athene for divine assistance. She descends from her mountain and, as the rocks pull away from each other and the rowers tug desperately on their oars, gives the ship a mighty shove that sends it flying through the surging sea safely to the other side, just as the Symplegades bear down once more—like the pigeon's tail, only the *Argo*'s stern suffers minor damage.

Now listen to this Eskimo tradition: Someone has committed an offense against the rules of life and all the animals of the season on whom survival depends have mysteriously disappeared. So the shaman sets out in his kayak to search for the entrance to the undersea home of the Great Mother of the Sea Beasts, to make amends and beg her to release the seals in her care to the hunters. After paddling for many days through the ice-choked waters, he (or more correctly, his spirit, for his body lies unconscious in his house) hears a distant rhythmic crashing sound. Soon he sees before him a pair of great icebergs, with a narrow passage between them that opens and closes with a terrifying roar. Seeking to avoid the danger, the shaman paddles to the left, but the icebergs follow. Furiously he paddles to the right, but the clashing icebergs move with him. Realizing that he cannot avoid the dangerous gateway, beyond which lies the entrance to the Sea Mother's home, he sends an Arctic bird—one of his spirit helpers—ahead. The bird barely clears the clashing icebergs, losing the tips of its tail feathers, like Jason's pigeon. Paddling furiously, the shaman now slips his boat between the masses of ice just as they open up and makes it safely to the other side, although—you guessed it —not without damage to the stern of his fragile sealskin craft.

The third example, no less remarkable for the essential similarity of its message, is taken from Iroquois mythology. The story tells of a pair of young warriors who lead a band of their fellows on an expedition to find the place in the distant west where heaven and earth come together. Along the way they fight many battles, killing many men and losing many of their own. About halfway to their goal, they find their progress barred by a giant spirit, who chides them for their cruelty and orders them henceforth to proceed in peace in a quest that will eventually take them from the earth' into the celestial regions and company of the gods. By the time they reach the western end of the earth, their number has been reduced to five. They watch in awe and fear as, again and again, they see the edge of the sky lifting and falling like an opening and closing mouth. Realizing that this is their only way into the heavenly regions, they watch with great care for the right moment to make the dash from this world to the other. One after the other, four of the five young men pass safely through the perilous gateway. But when the fifth companion makes the attempt, he misjudges the distance and is crushed.

The motif recurs again and again in a great variety of forms — clashing rocks or mountains, billowing clouds, grinding millstones, floating islands, razor-sharp dancing blades of grass, snapping animal or monster jaws, jabbing spears or knives wielded by demons, fiery solar rays, rolling boulders— always in the context of a journey between two worlds by a shaman, an initiate, a dead soul, or a hero. Years ago its recurrence among so many different peoples all over the world was thought to prove historical connections. Thus, for example, to account for the striking similarity between the clashing icebergs of the Eskimos and the Symplegades of the ancient Greeks, the ghost of Alexander the Great was invoked; he was supposed to have carried the Greek tale to the Indian Ocean, from whence it somehow diffused northward all the way to the Arctic Circle, where Eskimo shamans adapted it to their own environment! This is all pretty naive, of course. There are far more sophisticated theories from students of comparative religion to account for the phenomenon, and I will return to those at the end of this essay.

World Trees and Seven Heavens

In curing rituals, the Cuna Indian shaman in Panama employs a staff in which a series of notches have been cut. This symbolizes the world tree, the *axis mundi*, that stands in the center of the four world quarters and contains some of his own spirit power; the notches represent the successive levels of the sky world in Cuna cosmology. It is also his own "shaman's ladder," on which he ascends to the highest heaven to consult with its ruling powers about his patient's illness and its cure. The patient is placed inside a miniature hut symbolizing the cosmos and the celestial vault, surrounded by wooden effigies of the shaman's spirit helpers and with head and feet sticking out.

As the shaman chants the progress of the spirit journey, he has the patient's toes touch each end of the notches, gradually moving upward to signify the difficult ascent through the levels of the cosmos. When the last notch has been touched, he raises the patient's head to the roof, where leafy branches are tied to represent the crown of the world tree. In the shaman's care, the patient has now arrived in the highest of the heavens, abode of the most powerful of the spirits enlisted in his or her behalf.

Hearing this ritual described is almost to feel oneself transported, on the one hand, to the southernmost part of South America and, on the other, across the North Pacific into Siberia, so close are the parallels. The Mapuche (also known as Araucanians) of Chile and Argentina are presumably the descendants of Paleo-Indian migrants who settled in southern South America between 10,000 and 20,000 years ago. Like the Cuna, the Mapuche conceive of the universe as multistoried, with a great world tree in the center to connect the world of the living with the several levels of the heavens above and the underworld below. The *axis mundi* is symbolized as a notched pole, called *rewe*, to which branches are tied to symbolize the crown of the world tree and into which faces and other designs representing the spirit world are carved.

Mapuche shamans, called *machi*, are commonly women; to symbolize her celestial ascent, her passage through the successive cosmic levels, and her safe arrival in the uppermost heavens, the *machi* climbs up the notched pole, and, standing on top, sings her sacred songs to the accompaniment of a rattle and a shaman's drum decorated with a cruciform design that represents the four world quarters and the sacred center (Faron 1968).

In Siberia, where the birch is preeminently the shaman's route of ascent into a sky world that is again divided into a series of superimposed levels, each with its own ruling spirits, "the Altaic shaman ritually climbs a birch tree in which a certain number of steps have been cut; the birch symbolizes the World Tree, the steps representing the various heavens through which the shaman must pass on his ecstatic journey to the highest heaven" (Eliade 1964:xiv).

These are not sporadic or isolated phenomena: the conception of a stratified cosmos, with several levels of the heavens above and one or more underworlds below the surface of the earth, and a cosmic tree as world axis in the center, is shared by many peoples. It is also commonly replicated in shamanic and priestly ritual and sacred architecture, not excluding the soaring, multilevel temple pyramids of ancient Mexico, and in folk customs and funerary mythology from Bengal and the Malay peninsula to northern Europe and Russia. For example, some Russians "bake little ladders of dough in honor of their dead, and sometimes represent the seven heavens on them by seven bars" (Eliade 1964: 487). For Moslems and cabalists, "seventh heaven" refers to the highest of the abodes of bliss, and *Webster's Third International Dictionary* defines being "in seventh heaven" as having reached "the abiding place of supreme rapture." These are obviously all very old ideas, ultimately deriving, apparently, from an ancient shamanistic cosmology.

Definitions of *Shamanism* and *Shamans*

At this point it will facilitate understanding of the whole phenomenon if we clarify what ethnologists and historians of religion mean by *shamanism* and *shamans*. First, the terminology derives from an Eastern Siberian language, Tungusic, dialects of which are spoken by many nomadic or seminomadic peoples. The Tungus word *saman*, for individuals believed to possess certain magico-religious powers who combine in themselves the functions of curer, priest, magician, mystic, poet, storyteller, and guardian of the sacred lore and traditions of their social group, was adopted into Russian in the nineteenth century by travelers and ethnologists, who described the phenomenon of the shaman as "the great master of ecstasy" over a vast region of Asiatic Russia "in which the ecstatic experi-

ence is considered the religious experience per se" (Eliade 1964:4), as it is also among American Indians. Among the latter it was not laid aside even in the state religions of such militaristic and expansionist societies as that of the Aztecs: as noted earlier, Aztec priests in their grand temples, no less than their village counterparts, the shamans and diviners, valued the ecstatic visionary trance.

Initially, shamanism was thought to be preeminently a religious phenomenon of Siberia and Central Asia. In time, essentially similar phenomena were recognized, as noted above, in many parts of the world. Likewise, the idea that "pure" shamanism required that the shaman's trance be "spontaneous" (i.e., triggered by means other than chemical) also had to be modified as the time depth and geographical distribution of the ritual use of hallucinogenic plants became known and understood.

If multiple cosmic levels and shamanic ascent of a cosmic tree have such wide distribution, what are some of the other common denominators? Here Eliade's masterful synthesis from the standpoint of the historian of religion is particularly useful, provided one also heeds his caveats, which include the following: there are many aspects to shamanism and many differences in the religious systems within which shamans function; while shamanism is above all an "archaic technique of ecstasy," at once mysticism, magic, and religion in its broadest sense, elements of shamanism may arise anywhere and at any time through history, within any religion and at any level of cultural complexity; one's perspective on shamanism shifts according to one's discipline and specific interests, and in studying shamanism as the fundamental religious experience of archaic and "tribal" societies, "we are dealing with a spiritual world which, though differing from our own, is neither less consistent nor less interesting" (Eliade 1964:xx).

The shaman is first and foremost the mediator between the people and the greater forces of the universe, preeminently the repository and guardian of the sacred traditions and of the spiritual equilibrium of the group and its individual members. The shaman is curer, philosopher, intellectual, artist, specialist in the human soul, diviner, mystic, poet, prophet of the weather and the hunt. In native or tribal societies the "pantheon" is far more numerous than it is in Western religions, permeating not only the upper- and underworlds but a natural environment in which *all* phenomena, including those Westerners classify as "inanimate," are considered alive and all species have their ruling spirits or "owner."

In order to discharge reponsibilities to the living, and by extension to their dead ancestors, the shaman must thus be on familiar terms with a myriad of extra-human forces and must also have a much more extensive vocabulary than ordinary folk, including a store of archaic words no longer in ordinary usage. In many societies, the future shaman is required to assimilate one or more secret languages with which to communicate with animals and spirits. Secret shamans' languages are especially elaborated among the Arctic Eskimos, but the same phenomenon can be found from northern Asia to Sumatra and North and South America. This alone is strong evidence against old arguments that attempt to define shamans in terms of mental illness.

Most often shamans are male, not necessarily for reasons of male dominance but perhaps more because prior to menopause women's role as childbearers and nurturers tends to preclude them from the rigorous, physically and psychically demanding, and often dangerous training and practice of the shaman, especially where this involves the ingestion of powerful plant intoxicants. Still, there are many societies with female as well as male shamans.

The Shaman as Doctor

Shamans are magicians and medicine men, but not everyone who performs magical feats or cures illness is necessarily a shaman: shamanic curing involves techniques that belong solely to shamanism. In non-Western societies, disease is commonly attributed to one of two causes: soul loss or a sickness projectile shot into the patient from afar by magical means. The shaman must determine which of these is the cause of illness through divination and consultation with the spirits, as well as his or her own familiarity with the patient's personality, history, and social relationships.

Soul loss is derived from the widespread concept of the soul being separable from the body, not just at death but at any time. The soul may stray during sleep, become disoriented and unable to find its way back to its "owner" before he or she awakens, be abducted by hostile demons and spirits after dropping out of its proper abode (often the head) through a blow, a fall, or some shock to the spiritual equilibrium (seeing a ghost, for example), or wander into the underworld in search of some beloved relative whose death has caused it unbearable suffering. In such

cases the shaman must divine, with the aid of spirit helpers, the location of the lost soul and the cause of its absence and bring it back to its proper home. Occasionally this may involve spirit combat with hostile demons, to the point where the relatives assembled around the unconscious patient can actually see blood spurting spontaneously from the shaman's nose and mouth and black and blue marks and welts appearing.

In Judeo-Christian thought, of course, the soul is supposed to leave the body only at death, but the old idea of soul loss lives on, among other places, in the expression "God bless you" when someone sneezes: people once thought the soul was momentarily expelled through the nose and invoked the name of God to forestall it being snatched away by the Devil, who, needless to say, was ever alert for any opportunity to take hold of the souls of the faithful. There is even a medieval woodcut that demonstrates how invoking God can prevent Satan from snatching the soul when someone accidentally sneezes it out of the body.

The concept of a foreign object—the sickness projectile—being shot into the patient's body from afar by a hostile shaman acting in behalf of some human enemy, or by a god or spirit in punishment for some transgression, is likewise widespread. Often it overlaps soul loss in native disease etiologies. Here again the shaman does not just treat the symptom of the illness but determines its cause, so that it may be neutralized by a payment to the offended spirit, the righting of a wrong, or even by magically turning the illness projectile back on its sender. Huichol shamans do this, and so do Australian Aborigines, Yanomamo hunters, and Eskimos.

Columbus and his companions were the first Europeans to describe the use of a potent psychoactive snuff powder—they thought it was tobacco—by Caribbean Indians. In fact, native peoples in Central and South America ingested—and some Amazonian Indian populations still ingest—a variety of vegetal snuffs in shamanistic vision-seeking rituals. This ancient whalebone snuff tablet and bird bone snuffing tube, excavated by the late Junius Bird of the American Museum of Natural History near Huaca Prieta in coastal Peru, dates to the middle of the second millennium B.C.—evidence that the South American snuffing complex dates back at least 3,500 years.

To remove the symptoms, the shaman pinpoints the location of the foreign object, brushes the illness to a central point, and applies suction to remove it from the body, usually in concrete form, such as a tiny stone, grain, twig, or spine. Whether one credits such cures—and there are many documented cases—to the well-known placebo effect or to the shaman as consummate psychologist, a shaman-curer's success rate has to be impressive in order to retain the respect and trust of the community and to avoid being accused of causing illness by sorcery or witchcraft.

If shamans function as doctors or medicine men but not all medicine men are shamans in the proper sense, the same applies to the shaman as priest. Many shamans do execute priestly functions, but not every priest is a shaman. Nor need the shaman be the only one to perform religious activity in his or her society: "In many tribes the sacrificing priest coexists with the shaman, not to mention the fact that every head of a family is also the head of the domestic cult" (Eliade 1964:4).

Mastery of Ecstasy

True shamanism implies "mastery of ecstasy," which means that in many areas the shaman is the dominant religious figure, precisely because, as already noted, for many peoples the ecstatic experience is considered *the* religious experience. Ecstatics, however, are found in many religions. What differentiates the shaman as ecstatic is that he "specializes in a trance during which his soul is believed to leave his body and ascend to the sky or descend to the underworld" (Eliade 1964:5). Also, the shaman deliberately enters a trance for that purpose. The true shaman, then, is not only technician of the sacred but *master* of ecstasy.

On occasion a shaman may travel "out of body" for the sole purpose of adding to or reinforcing his or her own sacred knowledge. But even here the objective is not self-aggrandizement but the welfare of the larger community: the very idea of a so-called sorcerer utterly divorced from a social context and seeking "power" for its own sake, like the invented "Don Juan" in Carlos Castañeda's writings, is completely foreign to the shamanism of Native Americans or any other people.

Nor may a shaman idly boast of, or exhibit, magical powers merely to enhance prestige, without being punished with illness or even death for such hubris. So, for example, the Kwakiutl of British Columbia tell the story of a young shaman named Nahanagylis, who, not for some social good but solely to impress his brothers, performed all kinds of wonderful magical tricks, such as transforming his rattle into a pair of ravens that fought with each other and flew over the village, returning to his hand in the form of a rattle. Fearful of so much magical power so boastfully and uselessly displayed, the brothers killed Nahanagylis, and, when he came back to life, returned and killed him again, "cutting him limb from limb and scattering the pieces" to make a final end of him (Curtis 1915:279–283).

Helping Spirits and Tutelaries

The shaman does not have to face the spirit forces of the upper- and underworlds alone. Rather, he or she can call on one or more helping spirits, who were recruited as the culmination of initiatory training, or who voluntarily offered themselves. Here again it is necessary to differentiate: many people claim or believe themselves to be in contact with "spirits" or to be controlled or possessed by spirits. The shaman, however, normally *controls* helping spirits, rather than being controlled by them or becoming their instrument. The majority of these helping spirits have the forms of sea and land mammals and birds. The latter are especially prominent; in fact, bird symbolism forms an important part of the shaman's costume in many parts of the world. As Eliade (1964:71) notes, the birdlike elements in their clothing may magically transform shamans into eagles and other high-soaring birds to facilitate their celestial flights, which helps explain why shamans' headdresses, from Asia through North and South America, are often adorned with bird imagery, or why, to turn again to the Yanomamo as a New World hunting and gathering people, novice shamans are adorned with white eagle down during their initiatory ecstatic trances.

Yet the animals from which spirit helpers are drawn need not be eagles or jaguars or other large or powerful creatures; worms, small lizards, swallows, ravens, or even mosquitoes will also do the job. Helping spirits may also be drawn from the souls or spirits of any other phenomena of the natural environment, such as the weather or the landscape, or a shaman's ancestor may serve as spirit helper and guardian. In addition, the shaman may have access to more powerful tutelaries, including divine or semidivine beings in the general pantheon, or some deity known only to the shaman. But these are of a different order and are not always at the shaman's disposal. There is also a widespread concept of a shaman's spirit wives, who compel him to have intercourse during his out-of-body travels, reminiscent of the seductive nature and excessive sexuality attributed to witches in medieval ecclesiastical writings.

The spirit helpers of Eskimo shamans usually appear to them in human form, and the more they have, the more effectively they can shamanize. In South America and in Mexico, the helping spirit may enter the neophyte shaman's body, a rattle, or a collection of power objects in the form of a rock or quartz crystal. Thus, in making the sacred calabash rattle, the Warao shaman in the Orinoco Delta of Venezuela "blows tobacco smoke impregnated with a fragrant resin over scores of small quartz crystals and places these one by one into the hollowed-out gourd, invoking for each a particular ancestral spirit believed by the Warao to be embodied in the stone . . . the greater the number of crystalline spirits, the more potent the instrument" (Wilbert 1973–1974: 90–91).

These rattles, frequently decorated with spirit figures with whom the shaman consorts in ecstatic dreams, are the principal instrument of communication with the spirit world. In any event, there is so striking a universality about the way rock crystals, as the embodiment of helping spirits, especially those of the celestial regions, figure in the acquisition of shamanic power and shamanic intuition that we would be well advised to treat such finds with special sensitivity.

Obtaining Shamanic Powers

Who may become a shaman and how are shamanic powers obtained or bestowed in the first place? Shamanism is above all a mystical vocation. The future shaman is divinely elected, recruited by the gods or higher powers, or even by a shaman-ancestor. Eliade (1964:13) differentiates between two main kinds of recruitment of future shamans: (1) hereditary transmission of shamanic powers from a shaman ancestor who seeks out a youth to take his or her place, and (2) spontaneous vocation through divine call. The two methods usually exist side by side. As might be ex-

Rock crystals as power objects are virtually universal in shamanic practice, from Siberia to Australia and North and South America. Shamans acquire these crystals in supernatural quests. Like other native peoples, aboriginal Americans in the Southwest conceived of them as replacing the shamans' vital organs as part of their mystical vocation and initiation. In this "yarn painting" the late Huichol artist and shaman Ramon Medina depicts a novice shaman's celestial journey to recover a rock crystal, depicted as a white star at the end of his mystical flower-lined path that leads beyond a fiery curtain of solar rays. The Huichols conceive of such crystals as the reconstituted soul stuff of a deceased shaman ancestor, who comes to live with his or her descendants as a guardian spirit. The artist here has depicted the antlered shaman in the so-called X-ray style, itself very ancient and widespread and generally related to the idea of rebirth from the bones, on the one hand, and the shaman seeing himself skeletonized during his initiatory ordeal of death and rebirth, on the other. Both concepts mark Huichol shamanic lore no less than they do that of Siberian peoples, Eskimos, and Amazonian Indians.

Huichols commonly gather only the upper half of the peyote cactus, leaving the bottom part of the tap root, conceived as its "bones," in the ground. The root regenerates new crowns, and numerous crowns growing from the same root stock— the result of human intervention—are quite common in the area regularly visited by the peyoteros. The ecologically sensible custom of leaving the root in place to assure the plant's rebirth is related to the Huichols' conception of peyote as the plant form of deer, and to a very ancient shamanistic belief, which these corn farmers share with hunting and gathering peoples the world over, that animals and human beings are reborn from their skeletal parts.

pected, hereditary shamanism is often found where the social system is one of lineages and clans, with inherited property, status, names, crests, and so forth, as among the Indian peoples of the Northwest Coast, or among some Siberians, such as the Vogul, whose shamanism is, or was, transmitted through the female line.

But shamanism may run in families even in the absence of lineages, clans, or inherited status or wealth. A son may simply expect to assume his shaman father's vocation, or a deceased shaman-ancestor may fix on a direct or collateral descendant as the proper inheritor. Among the Siberian Ostyak and Samoyed, for example, when a shaman dies his son fashions an image of his father's hand, thereby inheriting his powers (Eliade 1964:15). Even in such a case, however, the candidate must still be accepted by the spirits.

Future shamans may also be marked from birth by some sign, or they may exhibit childhood behavior that sets them apart from other youngsters, such as preferring their own company to that of others, a tendency toward solitary play and daydreaming, exceptional talent for drawing, carving, storytelling, or other artistic endeavor, and so forth. Some Siberian peoples take being born with a caul (the inner fetal membrane) as a sign of a future shaman; interestingly enough, among some Maya Indians in highland Guatemala today, for a female baby, being born with a caul is regarded as a sign that she is destined to become

a midwife, a vocation that has assumed some of the mystical attributes that formerly adhered only to shamanism, including divine election.

Sickness Vocation

Almost always and everywhere the shamanic vocation takes the form of an initiatory sickness, a profound physical and psychological crisis, in which the future shaman undergoes death-rebirth experiences, often terrifying, of the kind typical of initiation ceremonies. "The content of these first ecstatic experiences . . . almost always includes one or more of the following themes; dismemberment of the body, followed by renewal of the internal organs and viscera; ascent to the sky and dialogue with the gods or spirits; descent to the underworld and conversations with spirits and the souls of dead shamans; various revelations, both religious and shamanic (secrets of the profession)" (Eliade 1964:34). Commonly, the initiatory sickness has no immediately discernible cause and will not respond to treatment unless and until it has been properly diagnosed as a summons to shamanism and the patient has agreed to heed the call. In fact, not obeying a mystical vocation may have severe physical and psychological consequences, even death, one's own or that of some beloved relative.

Epileptic fits, psychoneurosis, and all manner of mental illness have unfortunately been invoked to account for the shaman's initiatory crisis or subsequent behavior. These suggestions are not to be taken seriously, however much the shaman's personal crisis may resemble psychopathology. As Eliade (1964:27) puts it, that real or pseudo-epilepsy and other maladies "nearly always appear in relation to the vocation of medicine men is not at all surprising. Like the sick man, the religious man is projected onto a vital plane that shows him the fundamental data of human existence, that is, solitude, danger, hostility of the surrounding world. But the primitive magician, the medicine man, or the shaman is not only a sick man; he is, above all, a sick man who has been cured, who has succeeded in curing himself."

Essential as the initiatory crisis is— with such more or less terrifying experiences as dismemberment, skeletonization, abduction and devouring by a monstrous animal or demon initiator, the dangerous or paradoxical passage, and so forth—in the teaching of the neophyte, it is not enough. He or she may have been divinely elected and been cured of sickness but will not be recognized as a full-fledged shaman until after having undergone further instruction.

As an active member of the social group, the neophyte has presumably already absorbed, from earliest childhood, considerable ritual and practical knowledge through participation in communal ritual but, as a future shaman, must now assimilate (usually from an older master shaman, but also from the spirits) an enormous amount of traditional lore to which only shamans are privy, such as techniques of divination, the diagnosis and healing of illnesses, the identity and function of spirits, secret languages, the history of the people—that is, sacred myths and other traditions and sacred geography and, as applicable, genealogies, rules of descent and exogamy, and the like.

As Eliade notes, the shaman's instruction by a human master and/or by the spirits is itself equivalent to initiation. This may be a public ritual, or it may be completely private, in the course of a dream or in an ecstatic experience, with or without the aid of some sacred plant.

Some Final Observations

La Barre's hypothesis—that the magico-religious use of psychotropic plants in the New World has its roots in an archaic Asiatic-American shamanistic substratum, with its linear ancestor presumably being an ancient form of the shamanistic Eurasiatic use of the fly-agaric mushroom (*Amanita muscaria*)—has the simple elegance that comes with real insight. Ritual fly-agaric use, a topic thoroughly investigated by the distinguished amateur ethno-mycologist R. Gordon Wasson (1968, 1972), survived in Siberia, Scandinavia, and the Baltic states well into the present century; Wasson draws on the historic, ethnological, linguistic, and folkloristic evidence to argue that in former times the mushroom was considered sacred and served as ritual intoxicant over a much wider area, and that even *Soma*, the mysterious plant deity celebrated in book 9 of the *Rig-Veda*, the Sanskrit epic dating from the mid-second millennium B.C., was none other than the sacred intoxicating fly-agaric (Wasson 1968).

Even in the absence of archaeological evidence for the great antiquity assumed by Wasson for shamanistic use of the spectacularly colored fly-agaric, we do know that as early as Neanderthal times, 50,000–100,000 years ago, there were already specialists in the healing properties of plants. The most persuasive evidence for this comes from a site called Shanindar, in Iraq. Here archaeologists excavated several Neanderthal burials, one of an old man who was interred with a whole array of flowering plants. Pollen analysis revealed most of these to be medicinal species still used in the Middle East by homeopathic healers. Also among them was *Ephedra*, source of ephedrine, an alkaloid widely used in Western medicine for asthma and hay fever.

It would be surprising if people sufficiently sophisticated even 60,000 years ago to explore their environment for the most effective species to cure physical ills—people, moreover, who on the archaeological evidence from different parts of Europe and Central Asia had well-developed concepts of the supernatural, of animal spirits, and of an afterlife—had not also discovered that some plants have extraordinary effects on the mind. We are probably not far off the mark, then, if we hypothesize the discovery of botanical hallucinogens in the Old World at least as far back as the proven beginnings of systematic homeopathy (e.g., the time of the Iraq Neanderthals).

This is not to claim, however, that the ecstatic vision is everywhere and always dependent on chemicals, now or in the past. On the contrary, there are large cultural areas where the ecstatic trance—or, to use a modern term, *altered state of consciousness*—is highly valued as *the* religious experience, yet is in no way involved with psychoactive plants, even where these are readily available in the local environment or through trade from neighbors. This has to be well understood, because of partisan claims in the literature for a cross-cultural universality of plant hallucinogens that they do not, in fact, possess, however common they were in the American subtropics and tropics.

Nonchemical techniques to bring about the desired ecstatic trance state include drumming or other rhythmic sounds, chanting, dancing, isolation, fasting, sleeplessness, exposure to the elements, self-torture, bloodletting, and other forms of pain, or a combination of several of these. The well-studied vision quest of Plains Indians, for example, in which men, and sometimes women, went to isolated places, usually a hilltop, to fast and beg the spirits for a vision and to acquire a guardian spirit, did not involve the ingestion of psychoactive substances of any kind. If shamanic ecstasy depended upon botanical hallucinogens, how would we account for shamanism in the Arctic, where any plant life is scarce and no plants with hallucinogenic properties exist at all? Or for the ecstatic shamanism of such peoples as the Crow and Cheyenne, Iroquois, Nepalese, Naskapi, Malay, Athapascan, Kwakiutl, and other Indian peoples up and down the

Northwest Coast, and hundreds of other societies where botanical hallucinogens do not now play a role and, for all we know, may never have done so? Indole alkaloids, the active principles in the psychoactive plants, then, must not be overvalued as prime movers in the ecstatic-religious experience, or mistaken for some sort of cultural universal.

However, where hallucinogenic species have been important in religious life, in divination, and in curing, they are, or were, conceived as sacred, often personified as divine beings or invested with divine power (which is why Wasson argues for *entheogen*, the god within, in place of the value-laden *hallucinogen*). Also, their primary relationship is and was always with the shaman, on the mystical level as religious specialist, technician of the sacred, and master of ecstasy, and on the pragmatic level as one who through special training and expertise was intimately familiar no less with the natural than with the supernatural component of the environment.

This leaves us with the question with which we began: how shamans and shamanism relate to these two aspects of Pecos River rock art—the apparently "naturalistic" depictions of animals and humans and objects drawn from the material culture, and a much more extensive array of images that could only have been drawn from the spirit world.

Concerned as he is with shamanism from the point of view of the history of religion, Eliade does not deal specifically with shamanic art, or with art inspired by ecstatic visions. On the other hand, Reichel-Dolmatoff (1978) has written a significant book on the art motifs of the Desana as a function of the *yajé* vision. The Desana, indeed, attribute every single design with which they decorate the walls of their circular communal dwelling, as well as everyday and ritual cooking and storage vessels or tools, to supernatural inspiration during the ecstatic trance.

So do Eskimo shamans, who, as noted, use no hallucinogens, but drum, chant, or dance themselves into ecstasy. In western Alaska, for example, shamans, or carvers working under their direction, created extraordinary composite dance masks that simultaneously contained the spirit manifestations of different creatures and natural phenomena. Appearing to the shaman in a dream, the spirits gave instructions about how they wished to be represented. For the duration of the ceremonial, the masks came alive with the spirit powers they portrayed; once it was over, the masks lost their meaning (Furst and Furst 1982:146).

Chumash rock art, Painted Cave, San Marcos Pass, near Santa Barbara, California. "Abstract" or nonnaturalistic art of this type may represent visions triggered by the ingestion of Datura inoxia, whose veneration as the supernatural Old Woman Momoy and use by the Chumash is well documented in myth and folktales.

Some of the images on the rockshelter walls of Texas might have functioned in this way. Frequently, too, in non-Western or "tribal" art, it is the act of carving or painting that does honor to the spirits and serves as prayer and invocation, while the finished object loses its power and meaning at the conclusion of the ceremony for which it was made. The great amount of overpainting and superimposition suggests something of this sort for Pecos River rock art as well.

I concur with Newcomb (1967:75) that associating the pictographs with the kind of mescal bean medicine society known from the Historic period "offers a satisfactory, reasonable and comprehensive interpretation for the Pecos River style pictographs." But Newcomb himself also saw that the situation is obviously more complex than that and that even the figures he calls "shamans" might be more than only human beings dressed up for participation in mescal bean society rites.

Another question that has not been raised is the role of women in these rituals or in the creation of the art. Were all medicine society initiates male? Was the spirit of *Sophora secundiflora* conceived as male, like the San Pedro spirits among the ancient Nazca of Peru, or as female, on the order of the *Datura* spirit of the southern California Chumash, another nonagricultural people who, like those of the Lower Pecos, created some of the greatest rock art in North America?

The Chumash personified *Datura inoxia* as a powerful, aged supernatural, Old Woman Momoy (Blackburn 1975; Applegate 1975). Momoy lived in ancient times, before the former world was drowned by a great flood. She was a great shaman who subsisted only on tobacco and who possessed all manner of esoteric knowledge that she imparted to those who drank the water in which she washed herself (i.e., the intoxicating infusion made with the pounded root of the *Datura* shrub). The Chumash were very much aware of the danger of overdosing on the potent beverage; so, for example, in one story she gives a grandson a drink of the water in which she had bathed her arms. The drink causes him to fall into a deep, six-day sleep. He had wanted more, but she tells him that, had he drunk all of her bathwater, he would have gone mad and died. One can imagine similar cautionary tales among the ancient users of *Sophora*.

When digging for *Datura* roots, the Chumash reverently addressed the plant as "Grandmother." One had to abstain from sex for a given time before and after ingesting the *Datura* drink. Just as Grandmother Momoy subsisted only on tobacco, so one who ingested *Datura* had to fast, or at the very least to abstain from meat and fat, while being allowed— indeed, required—to take tobacco. In the typical *toloache* (*Datura inoxia*) initiation rites of other southern California Indians, the neophytes were kept in a state of ecstatic trance and were instructed in esoteric knowledge by their elders. In their visions, they were expected to encounter the supernatural heroes of tribal tradition—the same heroes with whom the shamans were on intimate terms. Elaborate ground paintings played an important part in instructing the novices, but unlike the sandpaintings of the Navajos, these are not known to have been used in curing.

In contrast, among the Chumash, *Datura* played no part in instructing the young as they reached puberty. Rather, *Datura* was taken on an individual basis, usually to establish contact with supernatural helpers and guardian spirits. There was no compulsion to take *Datura*, but it was generally agreed that the plant gave one access to the spirit world, to which ordinarily only the shamans had easy entry. *Datura* was also thought to give the strength and bravery necessary to deal with all manner of hardship.

In contrast to other southern California Indians, who restricted *Datura* to men and to boys at puberty, the Chumash felt that the intoxicating beverage was especially efficacious for women, for it would give them courage to face the dangers and pains of childbearing, as well as give them protection while collecting food and other useful plants in the wilds: no bear, for example, would harm a woman gathering seeds who had taken the *Datura* drink. Here again, the emphasis was on moderation, lest an overdose drive a woman insane or even kill her.

Chumash rock art is thought to be closely connected with the taking of *Datura*, especially by shaman-artists who, upon "returning" from their out-of-body travels, would record their visions on the living rock. Like Lower Pecos art, its subject matter is essentially of two types (Grant 1965). Some of it is representational, including recognizable plant and animal forms as well as humans or spirits conceived in human form. Much is geometric or abstract, with a wide variety of "nonrepresentational" design elements, some recurring in other places, from Texas to the Old World. Any attempt to understand these leads us into the deepest levels of the human mind. In fact, as Reichel-Dolmatoff has suggested for South America, many of these abstract or geometric patterns may represent subjective inner-light experiences, luminous patterns originating in the brain and eye, the "phosphenes" that, triggered by changes in body chemistry, are a normal function of the brain, independent of any external source of light, and that are shared to a remarkable degree by all human beings (Reichel-Dolmatoff 1978; Furst and Furst 1982:78).

Obviously, however, one cannot account for more than a fraction of Lower Pecos art in these terms. I cannot escape the feeling that beyond attempts to record "inner-light" experiences and journeys of the soul and mystical encounters by enraptured shamans and initiates with the spirit world, what we may also be seeing are great mythic events of a primordial time, when the divine culture heroes and the great spirits of the sky and earth put the universe in order, established the social structure, the ceremonies and rituals, and laid down the rules of life. Shamanism is surely part of the picture, even if we cannot always pick it out, because it is through the person of the shaman—through ecstasy, ritual, and perhaps the painting placed on the rockshelter wall—that the boundaries are temporarily extinguished between the "real" present and the paradisaical past, before there was death.

As Eliade tells us, it is precisely the erasure of these divisions and contradictions that is the objective of the shaman's ecstatic quest to the other world, just as it is of the Huichol peyote pilgrimage, in which the participants assume the identities of—indeed, "become"—the divine ancestors who established the first such quest and the present merges with the mythic past. Writing of the shaman's journey through the dangerous, or "paradoxical" passage, Eliade (1964: 486) quotes from Ananda K. Coomeraswami's classic paper on the Symplegades motif: the mythic images of the clashing gateway or the narrow bridge express the need to transcend opposites, to abolish the polarities typical of the human condition, in order to attain the ultimate reality: "Whoever would transfer from this to the Otherworld, or return, must do so through the undimensioned and timeless 'interval' that divides related but contrary forces" (Coomeraswami 1946: 486). It must be done in an instant, and it can be accomplished only by one who has transcended the human condition, that is, has become "spirit."

By crossing, in ecstatic trance, the dangerous passage connecting two worlds, writes Eliade, the shaman proves that he or she has indeed become "spirit," no longer a human being, and at the same time attempts to restore the "communicability" that once existed between this world and heaven. For what the shaman can do today in ecstasy could, at the dawn of time, be done by all human beings, concretely; they went up to heaven and came down again without recourse to trance. Temporarily and for a limited number of persons —the shamans—ecstasy reestablished the primordial condition of all humankind. In this respect, the mystical experience of the "primitives" is a return to origins, a reversion to the mystical age of a lost paradise. For the shaman in ecstasy, the bridge or the tree, the vine, the cord—which, in those times, connected earth with heaven—once again, for the space of an instant becomes a present reality.

There is just one other point to be made here: unlike the dead, the shaman, after all, is spirit only temporarily, for the duration of the ecstasy, and afterward must return to the human condition. If not, he or she would never come back, dying or suffering permanent separation of psychic and physical selves—in other words, becoming psychotic. This is the message of any number of shamanic and funerary myths, in which shamans and others visiting the world of the dead in ecstatic trance are admonished to leave as quickly as possible once their business is done, lest they find themselves unable to return to the world of the living. That, surely, is also why so many versions of the Symplegades motif tell of damage to the traveler—not necessarily fatal but a sufficient reminder that the shaman, hero, or initiate is mortal and, barring death, only temporarily privy to the "ultimate reality" accessible to others only in the telling or dramatic enactment of myths.

If indeed some of the magnificent rock art of Texas is meant to convey that "ultimate reality" experienced by shamans in their ecstasy, the mythic First Times of divine creation (more accurately, transformation, inasmuch as creation out of nothing is foreign to American Indian religious ideology), what comes to mind more than anything else is the Sistine Chapel. The rock art is in a very different style, certainly, created under other conditions, in the context of quite different (though no less valid or profound religious) beliefs, emotions, and purposes, but it carries the same sublime message as Michelangelo's depiction of Genesis. ∎

LOSING A LEGACY

The art of the lower canyon country is an impressive legacy left by generations of ancient people who passed into oblivion. It is up to us to decipher their material record to learn what their thoughts and experiences taught them about life.

The record of their way of life is incredibly well preserved in the protected, dry rockshelters and overhangs. They left a detailed archive. Unfortunately, in fifty years, modern people have virtually destroyed most of this record through ignorance, greed, and even with good intentions of progress and scientific knowledge. It is disconcerting to walk into a rockshelter with deposits that span 9,000 years to see massive craters and dirt piles left by relic hunters looking for a few artifacts, or to find a faded Pecos River Style painting senselessly vandalized with a mindless "John Doe, Midland, Texas, 12-28-83" carved across the picture.

Ongoing phenomena such as water staining, fading, and spalling take their toll annually. We must find ways of preserving the legacy. Although much work has been done on the known rock art sites (some of it duplicating prior effort), very little exploration for new sites has been attempted. We cannot even estimate the number of pictographic sites in the region. Questions about geographic density, distribution of specific motifs, redundancy of panels, and frequency of variation in style remain unanswered. There is much to be learned.

The hope of gaining archaeological information about the mobile art is diminishing. More of the record is lost as each new hole is carelessly dug in a cave, disturbing the context of a painted pebble or clay figurine. The situation is discouraging and underscores the need for an all-out effort to document and study what remains.

If we stand by apathetically without attempting to preserve this rich legacy, we will be responsible for a great loss, not only in terms of the information passed on to us by our ancestors through the medium of their art, but also in depriving our descendants of the works of art themselves. Surely these are to be guarded as vigilantly as those enshrined in our museums. ∎

Losing a legacy (OPPOSITE & BELOW). *For more than a century, passersby have left their names in shelters along popular trails; more criminal are the obscenities initialed by modern lakeside vandals.*

ARCHAEOLOGISTS OF THE LOWER CANYONS
A History of Discovery

Archaeologists over the last fifty years have had the opportunity to study many aspects of the culture of the lower canyons. The unique preservation of perishable materials found in many of the rockshelters in the region has made this possible.

The native Indians of the lower canyons had disappeared long before the first Anglo-American settlers arrived in the nineteenth century. Signs of these Indians were obvious to the local ranchers. Curiosity led some of them to probe the rockshelters, where pieces of matting, sandals, pictographs, or even human burials were found. The location of many of the sites became generally known to the ranchers, who brought them to the attention of specialists in museums and universities.

Although there has been an interest in ancient cultures for a long time (Thomas Jefferson excavated an Indian mound on his Virginia plantation in 1781), archaeology was not a disciplined science until the early twentieth century.

The University of Texas Department of Anthropology initiated archaeological excavations in the state during the second decade of this century, but the pioneer period of Lower Pecos River archaeology did not begin until the 1930s. Five institutions—the Smithsonian, Gila Pueblo, Witte Museum, University of Texas, and Texas Tech— sponsored excavations in the canyons.

A. T. Jackson, working under the direction of J. E. Pearce at the University of Texas, excavated Fate Bell Shelter in 1932. The following year, George C. Martin and John Eross worked at Shumla Caves. This excavation was followed by that of Frank Setzler at Moore-head Cave and Goat Cave. A. M. Woolsey of the University of Texas was at Horseshoe Ranch Caves and Kelly Shelter in 1936, and Murrah Cave was worked by W. C. Holden of Texas Tech College in 1937. The Witte Museum sent Walter Davenport and Harding Black to excavate Eagle Cave in 1938.

Two significant studies were initiated during this period, both dealing with systematic documentation of rock art sites in the Lower Pecos River area. A. T. Jackson was the first to study the prehistoric pictograph and petroglyph sites of the region. His 1938 publication was entitled *Picture Writing of Texas Indians*. This work was followed by that of Forrest Kirkland, a commercial artist from Dallas, who used the medium of watercolor to record many of the rock art sites in the canyons. Kirkland published several short papers reporting his observations and interpretations.

The archaeological pioneers of the 1930s were attracted to the large rockshelters because of their unmistakable signs of long occupation by early humans. Classification techniques of the time were inadequate to define the key indicators of change, and excavation techniques were not sufficiently refined to provide the stratigraphic separation needed to recognize changes in certain artifacts. Collecting was selective and biased.

George C. Martin, operating through the Witte Museum, was among the first to attempt a cultural classification for the lower canyon region, using the name *Big Bend Basketmaker*. Later, Victor J. Smith of Sul Ross College revised the name to *Big Bend Culture*. E. B. Sayles of Gila Pueblo in Arizona used the name *Texas Cave Dweller* and divided the sites into three divisions: *Hueco*, *Big Bend*, and *Pecos River Cave Dwellers*.

These early pioneers provided a solid foundation for future generations of archaeologists to build upon. They collected an enormous body of data that has been useful for comparative and technological studies. Their efforts at classification were an important beginning for establishing order and control in the massive collections.

Archaeological work in the region ceased during World War II, but attention was again focused on the caves and pictographs by students of J. Charles Kelley of the University of Texas. Kelley, T. N. Campbell, and Donald J. Lehmer, using archaeological materials in association with geological deposits of different ages, were the first to show changes in artifacts through time in the Big Bend region. By assuming that artifacts of a similar style were of a similar age, H. C. Taylor, a student of Kelley's, was able to establish the first material culture sequence in the Lower Pecos River region in 1949 by cross-dating with the Big Bend sequence.

Five years later, a summary of the lower Pecos River archaeology was presented in *An Introductory Handbook of Texas Archaeology* by Dee Ann Suhm, Alex D. Krieger, and Edward B. Jelks. These authors retained and expanded the use of the Midwestern taxonomic system first applied by Kelley, Campbell, and Lehmer in 1940.

Suhm, Krieger, and Jelks divided the cultural sequence into four broad time divisions called *stages*: *Paleo-American* (or *Paleo-Indian*), when humans were associated with the extinct animals of the late Pleistocene; *Archaic*, a term used to distinguish the later hunter and gatherer cultures; *Neo-American* (or *Neo-Indian*), marked by the introduction of the bow and arrow into the region; and *Historic*, after the arrival of Europeans.

The entire Archaic of the Lower Pecos River area was grouped under the terms *Pecos River* and *Chisos Foci*, following the Midwestern system of classifying cultural units. This system of classification consisted of such taxonomic units as the *component* (a representative unit within an archaeological site or level within a site based on a list of shared cultural traits), the *focus* (groups of like components), and the *aspect* (groups of like foci).

The most intense period of archaeological activity in the Lower Pecos area was from 1958 to 1969, when

(ABOVE) *Black, Davenport, and Ritchie at Eagle Cave.* (BELOW) *George Nalle and George Martin.* (OPPOSITE, ABOVE) *W. A. Davis, left, and Jeremiah Epstein, right, at Damp Cave.* (BELOW) *Mark Parsons at Panther Cave.*

the Texas Archeological Salvage Project (now the Texas Archaeological Survey) at the University of Texas conducted a program of salvage work in the proposed Amistad Reservoir Basin. The initial efforts to document archaeological sites in the reservoir basin was conducted on both sides of the Rio Grande in 1958.

These surveys were followed by excavations at Centipede Cave and Damp Cave by Jeremiah Epstein in 1959. Epstein constructed a four-part lithic chronology for the area extending back 9,000 years. With his experience in Paleolithic cave sites in France, Epstein made a significant advance in the study of stone tool technology. His efforts had a profound influence on the direction of lithic studies.

Epstein's chronology was later refined by LeRoy Johnson, after preliminary work was completed at the Devil's Mouth Site, a deep alluvial deposit at the mouth of the Devils River. Johnson identified four major periods of occupation beginning with the Paleo-Indian period. His three subsequent periods were all placed together into the Archaic, following the system of Suhm, Krieger, and Jelks.

Other work in the area followed with the preliminary report of the excavations at rockshelters at Coontail Spin, Mosquito Cave, and Zopalote Cave and at the Doss Site, a burned-rock midden. The research design for these sites was aimed at further testing the sequence of projectile point styles established by LeRoy Johnson at the Devil's Mouth Site. Also, the first excavations at Baker Cave were conducted at this time by James H. Word, an avocational archaeologist.

Further investigations were conducted by the University of Texas at Eagle Cave and Fate Bell Shelter, sites that were first explored in the 1930s. Results from these tests provided a refined sequence of lithic and other material culture items and controlled samples of datable charcoal. Radiocarbon dating now made it possible accurately to date the long cultural sequence.

Another significant find at these excavations was the sequence of painted pebbles. Painted river pebbles were the subject of a monograph by J. Walter Davenport and Carl Chelf in the publication entitled *Painted Pebbles from the Lower Pecos and Big Bend Regions of Texas*. When the pebbles were painted and how long the tradition lasted was unknown until Mark Parsons' work on materials from shelters such as Fate Bell and Eagle Cave, excavated during the 1960s. The tradition spanned virtually the entire length of occupation in the shelters from about 9,000 to 1,000 years ago.

Excavations at Bonfire Shelter, a unique site in the Amistad region, were begun in 1963 under the direction of David S. Dibble. Bonfire Shelter was not a typical occupied rockshelter, although limited use of it was made for camping at two different times. The shelter fill contained three layers of concentrated animal bones, forming three "bone beds," two of which were the result of Indians having driven bison into a cleft.

In the late 1950s and early 1960s, Texas archaeologists were guided by the *Handbook of Texas Archaeology* and the broader implications of *Method and Theory in American Archaeology* by Gordon Willey and Philip Phillips. In both guidebooks, the emphasis was on the ordering and classification of collections. Space and time frameworks became central objectives, and the artifact was the building block for cultural constructs. Similarities and differences in cultures were based on the contrasts between collections.

Archaeologists were beginning to feel frustrated by the limitations imposed by standard taxonomy when, in the 1960s, Lewis R. Binford, the pillar of modern American archaeology, made his enlightening contribution. Archaeological research designs for the Amistad salvage program began to take a significant new direction—a change away from emphasizing artifact sequences in isolation and toward the study of the relationship between this sequence of hunters and gatherers and their environment.

The shift in orientation carried with it a change in how archaeologists defined *culture*. W. W. Newcomb provided an explicit definition in *The Rock Art of Texas Indians*: "an organized body of knowledge, beliefs, habits, customs, institutions, rituals, games, tools and other artifacts which distinguish a particular group of people." Culture was seen as a system of related parts, each functioning to maintain the whole. It was also seen as the interface between humans and the environment or that body of knowledge from which technology to cope with the environment is derived. Individuals behind this shift in research emphasis were Edward B. Jelks, Dee Ann (Suhm) Story, and Vaughn M. Bryant.

By this time, the entire sequence of Texas prehistory was found to be represented in the Lower Pecos River area. The presence of plant and animal remains provided an excellent opportunity to examine the relationship between the people and their environment, or the paleoecology. Although not all ex-

cavations were influenced by this trend, systematic sampling for pollen remains for reconstruction of ancient environments became a common practice. Story and Bryant's study greatly influenced the research at Parida Cave, Conejo Shelter, Hinds Cave, and Baker Cave, all partly excavated in the late 1960s and 1970s.

Other site recording and test excavations were carried on in the Lower Pecos River canyons in the late 1960s. The Devils Mouth Site was reexamined to secure good context charcoal samples for radiocarbon dating. Different kinds of sites were examined, such as small stratified or deeply buried sites, burned-rock middens, and small rockshelters with limited amounts of cultural deposits. In 1965, excavations were begun at a large, deeply stratified alluvial site, Arenosa Shelter, under the direction of David Dibble. Three seasons of work were carried out at this terrace site, and analysis of the material is still being conducted.

Some testing was done to provide information on human ecology. The excavations at Parida Cave and Conejo Shelter by Robert Alexander were oriented specifically to that purpose. The analysis of perishable remains included a small sample of prehistoric human coprolites by David Riskind. This constituted the first controlled study of prehistoric diet and subsistence economy for the later part of the Archaic continuum in the Lower Pecos area. Alexander continued his human ecology study at Conejo Shelter, where he began to study the phenomenon of cultural stability that had been recognized by LeRoy Johnson, W. W. Taylor, and others.

By the end of the 1960s, archaeologists had knowledge of a long cultural chronology provided by excavations at Devil's Mouth, Fate Bell Shelter, Arenosa Shelter, Bonfire Shelter, Baker Cave, and Devil's Rockshelter. The shift in thinking brought about an application of different excavation and collecting procedures for the new emphasis on paleontology.

The publication of Forrest Kirkland's watercolor reproductions of Lower Pecos River rock art accompanied by W. W. Newcomb's narrative in *The Rock Art of Texas Indians* brought rock art studies closer to the mainstream of research. Since the publication of this book, attempts have been made to integrate all forms of rock art in the Lower Pecos region with the activities of the people who produced them.

Archaeological fieldwork diminished in the 1970s, but the significance of the finished projects is great. Site recording and testing outside the Amistad basin, such as at San Felipe Creek near Del Rio, Sanderson Canyon in Terrell County, Musk Hog Canyon in Crockett County, and along the path of Interstate Highway 10, has added to the understanding. Archaeological and botanical studies at Conejo Shelter by Robert Alexander and associates, at Hinds Cave by the author and Vaughn M. Bryant, and at Baker Cave by T. R. Hester and R. F. Heizer have provided the most detailed sampling and analysis of material related to the paleoecology of the prehistoric groups.

Analysis of human fecal remains from several periods at Hinds Cave by Glenna Williams-Dean and Janet Stock along with systematic studies of the plant and animal remains by Phil Dering, Vaughn Bryant, and Kenneth Lord have resulted in a better understanding of ancient diets. Further information on how people used the plant, animal, and mineral resources comes from the stone technology studies of Michael Collins and Phil Bandy. Newly completed excavations at Baker Cave directed by T. R. Hester and sponsored by the Witte Museum will provide an important testing ground for some of the trends and patterns noted at single site studies such as Conejo Shelter and Hinds Cave.

There are major gaps in the information we have. Jan Diamond, in an honors thesis at the University of Texas, provided a healthy critique of the region's archaeology. The emphasis has been placed on large rockshelter sites, particularly those located along the major canyons. No single area has been systematically inspected to record all kinds of sites. A recent study by Joe Saunders of the uplands between Lewis and Still canyons has helped to fill in the gaps.

The data acquired from fifty years of intense archaeological activity in the Lower Pecos River region is probably unmatched by that from any other area in North America. ∎

David Dibble at Bonfire Shelter.

BIBLIOGRAPHY

Abie, A. A.
  1969 *The Original Australians*. New York: American Elsevier Publishing.

Adkins, W. S.
  1932 The Mesozoic Systems in Texas. In The Geology of Texas, *University of Texas Bureau of Economic Geology Bulletin* 3232: 239–517.

Alexander, Robert K.
  1970 *Archaeological Excavations at Parida Cave, Val Verde County, Texas*. Austin: University of Texas, Texas Archeological Survey Project Papers, 19.
  1974 The Archaeology of Conejo Shelter: A Study of Cultural Stability at an Archaic Rockshelter Site in Southwestern Texas. Ph.D. dissertation, University of Texas.

Anati, Emmanuel
  1984 The State of Research in Rock Art, A World Report Presented to UNESCO. *Bollettino del Centro Comune di Studi Preistorici* 21: 13–56.

Andrews, R. L. and J. M. Adovasio
  1980 *Perishable Industries from Hinds Cave, Val Verde County, Texas*. Pittsburgh: University of Pittsburgh, Department of Anthropology, Ethnology Monographs, no. 5.

Antevs, Ernest
  1962 Late Quaternary Climates in Arizona. *American Antiquity* 28(2): 193–198.

Applegate, Richard B.
  1975 The Datura Cult among the Chumash. *Journal of California Anthropology* 2(1): 7–17.

Bandy, Philip A., S. A. Skinner, T. Turner
  1980 *Archaeological Investigations at Sanderson Canyon Watershed, Terrell, Pecos and Brewster Counties*. Dallas: Texas Environmental Consultants.

Biesele, Megan
  1983 Interpretations in Rock Art and Folklore: Communication Systems in Evolutionary Perspective. *African Archaeological Society* 4: 54–60.

Binford, Lewis R.
  1983 *In Pursuit of the Past*. New York and London: Thames and Hudson.

Blackburn, Thomas C.
  1975 *December's Child: A Book of Chumash Oral Narratives*. Berkeley and Los Angeles: University of California Press.

Blair, W. Frank
  1950 The Biotic Provinces of Texas. *Texas Journal of Science* 2(1): 93–117.
  1958 Distribution Patterns of Vertebrates in the Southern United States in Relation to Past and Present Environments. In *Zoogeography*, edited by C. L. Hobbs, pp. 433–568. American Association of Science Publication, 51.

Brooks, R. R. and V. S. Wakankar
  1976 *Stone Age Painting in India*. New Haven: Yale University Press.

Brown, K. M., Elton R. Prewitt, and David S. Dibble
  1976 *Additional Archaeological Resource Assessments in the Sanderson Canyon Watershed Project Area, Terrell County, Texas*. Austin: Texas Archaeological Society Research Report, 62.

Bryant, Vaughn M., Jr.
1974 Prehistoric Diet in Southwest Texas: The Coprolite Evidence. *American Antiquity* 39(3): 407–420.
1977 A 16,000 Year Pollen Record of Vegetational Change in Central Texas. *Palynology* 1: 143–156.

Bryant, Vaughn M., Jr., and Harry J. Shafer
1977 The Late Quaternary Paleoenvironment of Texas: A Model for the Archaeologist. *Bulletin of the Texas Archaeological Society* 48: 1–25.

Campbell, T. N.
1958 Origins of the Mescal Bean Cult. *American Anthropologist* 60: 156–160.

Chadderdon, Mary F.
1983 *Baker Cave, Val Verde County, Texas: The 1976 Excavations.* San Antonio: University of Texas, Center for Archaeological Research, Special Report, 13.

Clark, John W., Jr.
1967 Three Pictograph Sites in the Central Pecos Valley of Texas. *Texas Journal of Science* 19(3): 245–257.

Collins, Michael B.
1969 *Test Excavations at Amistad International Reservoir, Fall 1967.* Austin: University of Texas, Texas Archeological Survey Project Papers, 16.

Collins, Michael B. and Thomas R. Hester
1968 A Wooden Mortar and Pestle from Val Verde County, Texas. *Bulletin of the Texas Archaeological Society* 39: 1–8.

Coomeraswami, Ananda K.
1946 Symplegades. In *Studies and Essays in the History of Science and Learning Offered in Homage to George Sarton on the Occasion of His Sixtieth Birthday, 31 August 1944,* edited by Ashley M. F. Montague, pp. 463–488. New York: Schuman.

Crabtree, Don E.
1966 A Stoneworker's Approach to Analyzing and Replicating the Lindenmeier Folsom. *Tebiwa* 9(1): 3–39.

Curtis, Edward S.
1915 *The North American Indian*, vol. 10. Norwood, Mass.: Plimpton Press.

Davenport, J. Walker
1938 *Archaeological Exploration of Eagle Cave, Langtry, Texas.* San Antonio: Witte Memorial Museum Bulletin, 4.

Davenport, J. Walker and Carl Chelf
1941 *Painted Pebbles of the Lower Pecos and Big Bend Regions of Texas.* San Antonio: Witte Memorial Museum Bulletin, 5.

Dering, J. Phillip
1979 Pollen and Plant Macrofossil Vegetation Record Recovered from Hinds Cave, Val Verde County, Texas. M.A. thesis, Texas A & M University.

Diamond, Jan
1976 The Paradox of the Lower Pecos. Honors thesis, Department of Anthropology, University of Texas at Austin.

Dibble, David S.
1967 *Excavations at Arenosa Shelter 1965–66.* Austin: University of Texas, Texas Archeological Salvage Project.

Dibble, David S. and Dessamae Lorrain
1968 *Bonfire Shelter: A Stratified Bison Kill Site, Val Verde County, Texas.* Austin: Texas Memorial Museum, Miscellaneous Papers, 1.

Dibble, David S. and Elton R. Prewitt
1967 *Survey and Test Excavations at Amistad Reservoir, 1964–65.* Austin: University of Texas, Texas Archeological Salvage Project, Survey Report, 3.

Dillehay, Tom D.
1974 Late Quaternary Bison Population Changes on the Southern Plains. *Plains Anthropologist* 19(65): 180–196.

Eliade, Mircea
1964 *Shamanism: Archaic Techniques of Ecstasy.* New York: Bollingen.

Elkin, A. P.
1964 *The Australian Aborigines.* New York: Doubleday.

Epstein, Jeremiah F.
1962 Centipede and Damp Caves: Excavations in Val Verde County, Texas, 1958. *Bulletin of the Texas Archaeological Society* 33: 1–330.

Fagan, Brian
1985 *In the Beginning.* Boston: Little, Brown.

Faron, Louis C.
1968 *The Mapuche Indians of Chile.* New York: Holt, Rinehart and Winston.

Frison, George C. and Bruce A. Bradley
    1980   *Folsom Tools and Technology at the Hanson Site, Wyoming*. Albuquerque: University of New Mexico Press.

Frye, J. C. and A. B. Leonard
    1957   *Ecological Interpretations of Pliocene and Pleistocene Stratigraphy in the Great Plains Region*. Austin: University of Texas Bureau of Economic Geology Report of Investigations, no. 29.

Furst, Peter T.
    1972   *Flesh of the Gods: The Ritual Use of Hallucinogens*. New York: Praeger.
    1974   Hallucinogens in Precolumbian Art. In *Art and Environment in Native North America*, edited by M. E. King and I. R. Traylor, Jr., pp. 55–102. Lubbock: Special Publications, The Museum, Texas Tech University.
    1976   *Hallucinogens and Culture*. San Francisco: Chandler and Sharp.

Furst, Peter T. and Jill L. Furst
    1982   *North American Indian Art*. New York: Rizzoli.

Gebhard, David
    1960   The Diablo Cave Paintings. *Art Journal* 20(2): 79–82.

Gould, Richard A.
    1980   *Living Archaeology*. New York: Cambridge University Press.

Graham, John A. and William Davis
    1958   *Appraisal of the Archeological Resources of Diablo Reservoir, Val Verde County, Texas*. Report to the National Park Service. Austin: Archeological Salvage Program Field Office.

Grant, Campbell
    1965   *The Rock Paintings of the Chumash*. Berkeley and Los Angeles: University of California Press.

Greer, John W.
    1967   Midden Circles versus Mescal Pits. *American Antiquity* 32: 108–109.

Greer, John W. and R. A. Benfer
    1962   Langtry Creek Burial Cave, Val Verde County, Texas. *Bulletin of the Texas Archaeological Society* 33: 229–253.

Grieder, Terence
    1965   *Report on a Study of the Pictographs in Satan Canyon, Val Verde County, Texas*. Austin: University of Texas,

Texas Archeological Salvage Project, Miscellaneous Papers, 2.
    1966   Periods in Pecos Style Pictographs. *American Antiquity* 31(5): 710–720.

Griffen, William B.
    1969   *Culture Change and Shifting Populations in Central Northern Mexico*. Tucson: Anthropological Papers of the University of Arizona, 13.
    1979   *Indian Assimilation in the Franciscan Area of Nueva Viscaya*. Tucson: Anthropological Papers of the University of Arizona, 33.

Hafsten, Ulf
    1961   Pleistocene Development of Vegetation and Climate in the Southern High Plains as Evidenced by Pollen Analysis. In *Paleoecology of the Llano Estacado*, pp. 59–91. Albuquerque: University of New Mexico Press.

Halifax, Joan
    1979   *Shamanic Voices*. New York: E. P. Dutton.

Hall, Robert L.
    1977   An Anthropocentric Perspective for Eastern United States Prehistory. *American Antiquity* 42(4): 499–518.

Harris, Arthur H.
    1977   Biotic Environments of the Paleo-Indian. In *Paleoindian Lifeways*, edited by Eileen Johnson, pp. 1–12. Lubbock: *Museum Journal* 17, West Texas Museum Association.

Harrison, B. R. and Kay Killen
    1978   *Lake Theo: A Stratified Early Man Butchering and Camp Site, Briscoe County, Texas*. Canyon: Panhandle-Plains Historical Museum, Special Archeological Report, 1.

Haury, Emil W., Edwin B. Sayles, and William W. Wasley
    1959   The Lehner Mammoth Site, Southeastern Arizona. *American Antiquity* 25(1): 2–30.

Haynes, C. Vance
    1969   The Earliest Americans. *Science* 166: 709–715.
    1980   The Clovis Culture. *Canadian Journal of Anthropology* 1(1): 115–121.

Hester, J. J. (ed.)
    1972   *Blackwater Locality No. 1: A Stratified Early Man Site in Eastern New Mexico*. Dallas: Fort Burgwin Research Center, Southern Methodist University.

Hester, Thomas R.
1981   *Digging in South Texas Prehistory*. San Antonio: Corona Publishing.
1983   Late Paleo-Indian Occupations at Baker Cave, Southwestern Texas. *Bulletin of the Texas Archaeological Society* 53: 101–119.

Holliday, Vance T., Eileen Johnson, Herbert Hass, and Robert Stuckenrath
1983   Radiocarbon Ages at the Lubbock Lake Site, 1950–1980: Framework for Cultural and Ecological Changes in the Southern High Plains. *Plains Anthropologist* 28(101): 165–182.

Jackson, A. T.
1938   *Picture Writing of Texas Indians*. Austin: University of Texas Publication 3809.

Johnson, Eileen and Vance T. Holliday
1980   A Plainview Kill-Butchering Local on the Llano Estacado—The Lubbock Lake Site. *Plains Anthropologist* 25(88), pt. 1: 89–111.
1981   Late Paleoindian Activity at the Lubbock Lake Site. *Plains Anthropologist* 26(93): 173–193.

Johnson, LeRoy
1964   *The Devil's Mouth Site: A Stratified Campsite at Amistad Reservoir, Val Verde County, Texas*. Austin: University of Texas Archaeological Series, 6.

Johnston, M. C.
1963   Past and Present Grasslands of Southern Texas and Northeastern Mexico. *Ecology* 44(3): 456–466.

Jopling, Carol F. (ed.)
1971   *Art and Aesthetics in Primitive Societies*. New York: E. P. Dutton.

Kelley, J. Charles
1974   Pictoral and Ceramic Art in the Mexican Cultural Littoral of the Chichimec Sea. In *Art and Environment in Native America*, edited by M. E. King and I. R. Traylor, Jr., pp. 23–54. Lubbock: Special Publications, The Museum, Texas Tech University.

Kelley, John Charles, Thomas N. Campbell, and Donald J. Lehmer
1940   *The Association of Archaeological Materials with Geological Deposits in the Big Bend Region of Texas*. Sul Ross State Teacher College Bulletin, 8.

Kirkland, Forrest and W. W. Newcomb, Jr.
1967   *The Rock Art of Texas Indians*. Austin: University of Texas Press.

Kurten, Bjorn and Elaine Anderson
1980   *Pleistocene Mammals of North America*. New York: Columbia University Press.

La Barre, Weston
1974   *The Peyote Cult*. Hamden, Conn.: Shoestring Press.

Langston, Wann, Jr.
1974   Nonmammalian Comanchean Tetrapods. *Geoscience and Man* 8: 77–102.

Lee, D. N. and H. C. Woodhouse
1970   *Art on the Rocks of Southern Africa*. New York: Charles Scribner's.

Lee, Richard B. and Irven DeVore (eds.)
1968   *Man the Hunter*. Chicago: Aldine.

Lee, Thomas A., Jr.
1969   *The Artifacts of Chiapa de Corzo, Chiapas, Mexico*. Provo, Utah: Papers of the New World Archaeological Foundation, 26.

Levine, Morton H.
1957   Prehistoric Art and Ideology. *American Anthropologist* 59: 949–964.

Lewis-Williams, J. D. and Megan Biesele
1978   Eland Hunting Rituals among Northern and Southern San Groups: Striking Similarities. *Africa* 48(2): 117–133.

Lorraine, Dessamae
1968   *Archaeological Investigations in Northwestern Crockett County, Texas, 1966–1967*. Austin: State Building Commission Archaeological Program Report, 12.

Lundelius, Ernest L., Jr.
1967   Late-Pleistocene and Holocene Faunal History of Central Texas. In *Pleistocene Extinctions: The Search for a Cause*, edited by P. S. Martin and H. E. Wright, Jr., pp. 287–319. New Haven: Yale University Press.
1974   The Last Fifteen Thousand Years of Faunal Change in North America. *Museum Journal* 15: 141–160.

Marshall, Lorna
1965   The !Kung Bushman of the Kalahari. In *Peoples of Africa*, edited by J. L. Gibbs. New York: Holt, Rinehart and Winston.
1976   *The !Kung of Nyae Nyae*. Cambridge, Mass.: Harvard University Press.

Martin, George C.
  1933 The Big Bend Basket Maker. In *Southwest Texas Archaeological Society, Big Bend Basket Maker Papers*, 1. San Antonio: Witte Memorial Museum.

Martin, P. S.
  1963 *The Last 10,000 Years: A Fossil Pollen Record of the American Southwest*. Tucson: University of Arizona Press.

Martin, P. S. and Richard G. Klein (eds.)
  1984 *Quaternary Extinctions: A Prehistoric Revolution*. Tucson: University of Arizona Press.

Maxwell, R. A., J. T. Lonsdale, R. T. Hazzard, and J. A. Wilson
  1967 *Geology of the Big Bend National Park, Brewster County, Texas*. Austin: University of Texas Publication, no. 6711.

Moore, W. E.
  1983 Archeological Investigations at Musk Hog Canyon, Crockett County, Texas. *Bulletin of the Texas Archaeological Society* 53 (for 1982): 13–82.

Morse, Noel
  1954 Clay Figurines of the American Southwest. *Peabody Museum of American Archaeology and Ethnology, Harvard University, Papers* 49: 1.

Newcomb, W. W., Jr.
  1961 *The Indians of Texas from Prehistoric to Modern Times*. Austin: University of Texas Press.

Nunley, John P., L. F. Duffield, and E. B. Jelks
  1965 *Excavations at Amistad Reservoir, 1962 Season*. Austin: University of Texas, Texas Archeological Salvage Project, Miscellaneous Papers, 3.

Otten, Charlotte M. (ed.)
  1971 *Anthropology and Art*. Austin: University of Texas Press.

Parsons, Mark L.
  1965a *1963 Test Excavation at Fate Bell Shelter, Amistad Reservoir, Val Verde County, Texas*. Austin: University of Texas, Texas Archeological Salvage Project, Miscellaneous Papers, 4.
  1965b Painted and Engraved Pebbles. Appendix in *The Archaeology of Eagle Cave*, by Richard E. Ross. Austin: University of Texas, Texas Archeological Salvage Project, Miscellaneous Papers, 7.

Patton, P. C.
  1977 Geomorphic Criteria for Estimating the Magnitude and Frequency of Flooding in Central Texas. Ph.D. dissertation, University of Texas at Austin.

Pearce, James E. and A. T. Jackson
  1933 *A Prehistoric Rock Shelter in Val Verde County, Texas*. Austin: University of Texas, Anthropology Papers, 1(3).

Pfeiffer, John E.
  1982 *The Creative Explosion*. New York: Harper and Row.

Reichel-Dolmatoff, Gerardo
  1964 Anthropomorphic Figurines from Colombia, Their Magic and Art. In *Essays in Pre-Columbian Art and Archaeology*, edited by S. K. Lothrop and others, pp. 229–241. Cambridge, Mass.: Harvard University Press.
  1967 Rock Paintings of the Vaupés: An Essay in Interpretation. *Folklore Americas* 27(2): 107–112.
  1978 *Beyond the Milky Way: Hallucinatory Imagery of the Tukano Indians*. Los Angeles: UCLA Latin American Center Publications.

Ridington, Robin
  1982 Technology, World View, and Adaptive Strategy in a Northern Hunting Society. *Canadian Review, Sociology and Anthropology* 19(4): 469–479.

Riskind, David H.
  1970 Pollen Analysis of Human Coprolites of Parida Cave. Appendix A in *Archaeological Investigations at Parida Cave, Val Verde County, Texas*, pp. 89–101. Austin: R. K. Alexander Papers of the Archeological Salvage Project, no. 19.

Ritchie, Carson I. A.
  1979 *Rock Art of Africa*. Cranbury: A. S. Barnes.

Ross, Richard E.
  1965 *The Archaeology of Eagle Cave*. Austin: University of Texas, Texas Archeological Salvage Project, Miscellaneous Papers, 7.

Rudner, J. and I. Rudner
  1970 *The Hunter and His Art*. Cape Town: C. Struick.

Rutter, N. W. and C. E. Schweger (eds.)
  1980 The Ice-Free Corridor and Peopling of the New World. Proceedings of the Fifth Biennial Conference of the American Quaternary Association, Edmonton, 1978. *Canadian Journal of Anthropology* 1(1): 1–139.

Saunders, Jeffery J.
1972 Lehner Ranch Revisited. In *Paleoindian Lifeways*, edited by Eileen Johnson, pp. 65–77. Lubbock: *Museum Journal* 17, West Texas Museum Association.

Saunders, Joe W.
1986 The Economy of Hinds Cave. Ph.D. dissertation, Southern Methodist University.

Sayles, Edward B.
1935 *An Archaeological Survey of Texas*. Gila Pueblo, Medallion Papers, 17.

Schmidly, David J.
1977 *The Mammals of Trans-Pecos Texas*. College Station: Texas A & M University Press.

Schultes, Richard Evans
1972 An Overview of Hallucinogens in the Western Hemisphere. In *Flesh of the Gods: The Ritual Use of Hallucinogens*, edited by Peter T. Furst, pp. 1–54. New York: Praeger.

Schultes, Richard Evans and Albert Hofmann
1973 *The Botany and Chemistry of Hallucinogens*. Springfield, Ill.: Charles C. Thomas.

Sellards, E. H.
1952 *Early Man in America: A Study in Prehistory*. Austin: University of Texas Press.

Shafer, Harry J.
1970 *An Archeological Reconnaissance of the Sanderson Canyon Watershed, Texas*. Austin: University of Texas, Texas Archeological Salvage Project, Survey Report, 7.
1975 Clay Figurines from the Lower Pecos Region, Texas. *American Antiquity* 40(2): 148–157.

Shafer, Harry J. and Vaughn M. Bryant, Jr.
1977 *Archaeological and Botanical Studies at Hinds Cave, Val Verde County, Texas*. College Station: Texas A & M University Anthropology Laboratory, Special Series, 1.

Shafer, Harry J. and Fred Speck, Jr.
1974 A Clay Figurine Cache from the Lower Pecos Region, Texas. *Plains Anthropologist* 19: 228–230.

Schapera, Isaac
1930 *The Khoisan Peoples of South Africa*. London: Routledge and Kegan Paul.

Sorrow, William M.
1968a *The Devil's Mouth Site: The Third Season, 1967*. Austin: University of Texas, Texas Archeological Salvage Project Papers, 15.
1968b *Text Excavations at the Nopal Terrace Site, Val Verde County, Texas, Spring 1967*. Austin: University of Texas, Texas Archeological Salvage Project Papers, 15.

Stock, Janet A.
1983 The Prehistoric Diet of Hinds Cave (41 VV 456), Val Verde County, Texas: The Coprolite Evidence. M.A. thesis, Texas A & M University.

Story, Dee Ann and Vaughn M. Bryant, Jr.
1966 *A Preliminary Study of the Paleoecology of the Amistad Reservoir Area*. National Science Foundation Research Report G2667. Austin: University of Texas, Archaeological Research Laboratory.

Stubbs, D.
1974 *Prehistoric Art of Australia*. New York: Charles Scribner's Sons.

Suhm, Dee Ann, Alex D. Krieger, and Edward B. Jelks
1954 *An Introductory Handbook of Texas Archaeology*. Bulletin of the Texas Archaeological Society.

Taylor, Herbert C., Jr.
1948 An Archaeological Reconnaissance in Northern Coahuila. *Bulletin of the Texas Archaeological Society* 19: 74–87.
1949a The Archaeology of the Area about the Mouth of the Pecos. M.A. thesis, University of Texas at Austin.
1949b A Tentative Cultural Sequence for the Area about the Mouth of the Pecos. *Bulletin of the Texas Archaeological Society* 20: 73–88.

Taylor, Walter W.
1972 The Hunter-Gatherer Nomads of Northern Mexico: A Comparison of the Archival and Archaeological Records. *World Archaeology* 4(2): 167–178.

Troike, Rudolph C.
1962 The Origins of Plains Mescalism. *American Anthropologist* 64: 946–963.

Turpin, Solveig A.
1982 *Seminole Canyon: The Art and the Archeology, Val Verde County, Texas*. Austin: University of Texas, Texas Archeological Survey Research Report, 83.
1984 The Red Linear Style Pictographs of the Lower Pecos River Region, Texas. *Plains Anthropologist* 29(105): 181–198.

Twiss, P. C.
1972 Cenozoic History of Rim Rock Country, Trans-Pecos Texas. In *The Geologic Framework of the Chihuahua Tectonic Belt*, pp. 139–155. R. K. DeFord Symposium, West Texas Geological Society.

Ucko, P. J. and A. Rosenfeld
1967 *Paleolithic Cave Art*. New York: McGraw-Hill.

Van der Post, Laurens
1958 *The Lost World of the Kalahari*. New York: William Morrow.

van Devender, T. R.
1977 Holocene Woodlands in the Southwestern Deserts. *Science* 198: 189–192.
1979 Development of Vegetation and Climate in the Southwestern United States. *Science* 204: 701–710.

Vinnicombe, Patricia
1972 Motivation in African Rock Art. *Antiquity* 46: 124–133.

Wasson, R. Gordon
1968 *Soma, Divine Mushroom of Immortality*. New York: Harcourt, Brace and World.
1972 What Was the Soma of the Aryans? In *Flesh of the Gods: The Ritual Use of Hallucinogens*, edited by Peter T. Furst, pp. 201–213. New York: Praeger.

Wasson, R. Gordon and Valentina P. Wasson
1957 *Mushrooms, Russia and History*. New York: Pantheon Books.

Wells, Phillip V.
1966 Late Pleistocene Vegetation and Degree of Pluvial Climatic Change in the Chihuahuan Desert. *Science* 153: 970–975.
1970 Postglacial Vegetation History of the Great Plains. *Science* 167: 1574–1581.

Wheat, Joe B.
1972 The Olsen-Chubbock Site: A Paleo-Indian Bison Kill. *American Antiquity Memoir* 25: 1–180.

Wilbert, Johannes
1972 Tobacco and Shamanic Ecstasy among the Warao Indians of Venezuela. In *Flesh of the Gods: The Ritual Use of Hallucinogens*, edited by Peter T. Furst, pp. 55–83. New York: Praeger.

Willey, Gordon R. and Philip Phillips
1958 *Method and Theory in American Archaeology*. Chicago: University of Chicago Press.

Williams-Dean, Glenna
1978 Ethnobotany and Cultural Ecology of Prehistoric Man in Southwest Texas. Ph.D. dissertation, Texas A & M University.

Wilmsen, E. N. and F. H. H. Roberts, Jr.
1978 *Lindenmeier, 1934–1974*. Smithsonian Contributions to Anthropology, no. 24.

Wilson, John A.
1977 Stratigraphic Occurrence and Correlation of Early Tertiary Vertebrate Faunas, Trans-Pecos Texas. *Texas Memorial Museum Bulletin* 25: 1–42.

Word, James H. and C. L. Douglas
1970 *Excavations at Baker Cave, Val Verde County, Texas*. Austin: Texas Memorial Museum Bulletin, 16.

Yellen, John
1977 *Archaeological Approaches to the Present: Models for Reconstructing the Past*. New York: Academic Press. ■

P H O T O C R E D I T S

All photographs in this volume were produced by Jim Zintgraff, with the exception of those appearing on the following pages:

51, 53, 55, 133, 134, 135; Vaughn M. Bryant, Jr., *Texas A&M University*

67, 89, 90, 91, 105, 136, 137, 139, 178, 187, 188, 189, 229, 231 (above); Solveig A. Turpin, *TARL*

68 (above); Al Redder
68 (below); Frank Weir, *Texas Dept. Highways*

71, 80, 98; Harry J. Shafer, *Texas A&M*

85, 86, 87; Thomas R. Hester, *UT San Antonio*

177, 179; Terence Grieder, *UT Austin*

191, 202, 203; J. D. Lewis-Williams, *Witwatersrand Univ.*

193, 195; Megan Biesele

194; Jean MacGregor

196, 197, 198, 199, 205, 207, 208, 209; Richard A. Gould, *Brown Univ.*

211, 218, 220, 221, 223; Peter T. Furst, *State Univ. of N.Y. Albany*

I L L U S T R A T I O N
C R E D I T S

All illustrations in this volume were produced by George Strickland, with the exception of those appearing on the following pages:

35, 36, 37, 38, 59, 64, 97, 118, 172–175; Witte Museum
181–185; Mark L. Parsons
201; J. D. Lewis-Williams, Witwatersrand Univ.